INSTRUCTOR'S MANUAL

VIRTUAL CHEMLAB
GENERAL CHEMISTRY LABORATORIES
v.2.5

BRIAN F. WOODFIELD
MATTHEW C. ASPLUND
Brigham Young University

STEVEN HADERLIE
Springville High School

PEARSON

Prentice
Hall

Upper Saddle River, NJ 07458

Project Manager: Kristen Kaiser
Editor-in-Chief: Dan Kaveney
Executive Managing Editor: Kathleen Schiaparelli
Assistant Managing Editor: Karen Bosch
Production Editor: Amanda Phillips
Supplement Cover Manager: Paul Gourhan
Supplement Cover Designer: Christopher Kossa
Manufacturing Buyer: Ilene Kahn
Manufacturing Manager: Alexis Heydt-Long

© 2006 Pearson Education, Inc.
Pearson Prentice Hall
Pearson Education, Inc.
Upper Saddle River, NJ 07458

The author and publisher of this book have used their best efforts in preparing this book. These efforts include the development, research, and testing of the theories and programs to determine their effectiveness. The author and publisher make no warranty of any kind, expressed or implied, with regard to these programs or the documentation contained in this book. The author and publisher shall not be liable in any event for incidental or consequential damages in connection with, or arising out of, the furnishing, performance, or use of these programs.

Printed in the United States of America

10 9 8 7 6 5 4 3 2

ISBN 0-13-173468-7

Pearson Education Ltd., *London*
Pearson Education Australia Pty. Ltd., *Sydney*
Pearson Education Singapore, Pte. Ltd.
Pearson Education North Asia Ltd., *Hong Kong*
Pearson Education Canada, Inc., *Toronto*
Pearson Educación de Mexico, S.A. de C.V.
Pearson Education—Japan, *Tokyo*
Pearson Education Malaysia, Pte. Ltd.

Table of Contents

Colligative Properties

Gas Properties

Acid-Base Chemistry

Electrochemistry

Descriptive Chemistry

Additional Assignments

Titrations

Gas Properties

Atomic Theory and Quantum Mechanics

Inorganic Qualitative Analysis

Overview

Introduction

Welcome to *Virtual ChemLab*, a set of realistic and sophisticated simulations covering general and organic chemistry laboratories. In these laboratories, students are put into a virtual environment where they are free to make the choices and decisions that they would confront in an actual laboratory setting and, in turn, experience the resulting consequences. These laboratories include simulations of inorganic qualitative analysis, fundamental experiments in quantum chemistry, gas properties, titration experiments, calorimetry, organic synthesis, and organic qualitative analysis. This Instructor's Manual contains an overview of the full capabilities of the site license version of *Virtual ChemLab v2.5*, installation instructions, and the answers for the laboratory assignments provided in the student laboratory workbook.

Virtual ChemLab is sold as a site license version and as a single user or student version. The site license version is intended for institutions and the student version is intended for individual student use on a single computer, although they can be used together as will be described later. The site license version, in addition to allowing multiple installations of the software at an institution, is the only version that includes the stockroom or *Instructor Utilities* which is the management side of *Virtual ChemLab*. *Instructor Utilities* allows an instructor to establish classes, make assignments, and view the results, grades, and lab books of the students. The site license version also includes an option to install the software in an electronic workbook mode that is designed to be used in conjunction with an accompanying student laboratory workbook. Details on the various software configurations are given in the next section. Given below is a brief description of each of the five general chemistry laboratories.

The features of the inorganic simulation include 26 cations that can be added to test tubes in any combination, 11 reagents that can be added to the test tubes in any sequence and any number of times, necessary laboratory manipulations, a lab book for recording results and observations, and a stockroom for creating test tubes with known mixtures, generating practice unknowns, or retrieving instructor assigned unknowns. The simulation uses over 2500 actual pictures to show the results of reactions and over 220 videos to show the different flame tests. With 26 cations that can be combined in any order or combination and 11 reagents that can be added in any order, there are in excess of 10^{16} possible outcomes in the simulation.

The purpose of the quantum laboratory is to allow students to explore and better understand the foundational experiments that led to the development of quantum mechanics. Because of the very sophisticated nature of most of these experiments, the quantum laboratory is the most "virtual" of the *Virtual ChemLab* laboratory simulations. In general, the laboratory consists of an optics table where a source, sample, modifier, and detector combination can be placed to perform different experiments. These devices are located in the stockroom and can be taken out of the stockroom and placed in various locations on the optics table. The emphasis here is to teach students to probe a sample (e.g., a gas, metal foil, two-slit screen, etc.) with a source (e.g., a laser, electron gun, alpha-particle source, etc.) and detect the outcome with a specific detector (e.g., a phosphor screen, spectrometer, etc.). Heat, electric fields, or magnetic fields can also be applied to modify an aspect of the experiment. As in all *Virtual ChemLab* laboratories, the focus is to allow students the ability to explore and discover, in a safe and level-appropriate setting, the concepts that are important in the various areas of chemistry.

The gas experiments included in the *Virtual ChemLab* simulated laboratory allow students to explore and better understand the behavior of ideal gases, real gases, and van der Waals gases (a model real gas). The gases laboratory contains four experiments each of which includes the four variables used to describe a gas: pressure (P), temperature (T), volume (V), and the number of moles (n). The four experiments differ by allowing one of these variables to be the dependent variable while the others are independent. The four experiments include (1) V as a function of P, T, and n using a balloon to reflect the volume changes; (2) P as a function of V, T, and n using a motor driven piston; (3) T as a function of P, V, and n again using a motor driven piston; and (4) V as a function of P, T, and n but this time using a frictionless, massless piston to reflect volume changes and using weights to apply pressure. The gases that can be used in these experiments include an ideal gas; a van der Waals gas whose parameters can be changed to represent any real gas; real gases including N_2, CO_2, CH_4, H_2O, NH_3, and He; and eight ideal gases with different molecular weights that can be added to the experiments to form gas mixtures.

The virtual titration laboratory allows students to perform precise, quantitative titrations involving acid-base and electrochemical reactions. The available laboratory equipment consists of a 50 mL buret, 5, 10, and 25 mL pipets, graduated cylinders, beakers, a stir plate, a set of 8 acid-base indicators, a pH meter/voltmeter, a conductivity meter, and an analytical balance for weighing out solids. Acid-base titrations can be performed on any combination of mono-, di-, and tri-protic acids and mono-, di-, and tri-basic bases. The pH of these titrations can be monitored using a pH meter, an indicator, and a conductivity meter as a function of volume, and this data can be saved to an electronic lab book for later analysis. A smaller set of potentiometric titrations can also be performed. Systematic and random errors in the mass and volume measurements have been included in the simulation by introducing buoyancy errors in the mass weighings, volumetric errors in the glassware, and characteristic systematic and random errors in the pH/voltmeter and conductivity meter output. These errors can be ignored, which will produce results and errors typically found in high school or freshman-level laboratory work, or the buoyancy and volumetric errors can be measured and included in the calculations to produce results better than 0.1% in accuracy and reproducibility.

The calorimetry laboratory provides students with three different calorimeters that allow them to measure various thermodynamic processes including heats of combustion, heats of solution, heats of reaction, the heat capacity, and the heat of fusion of ice. The calorimeters provided in the simulations are a classic "coffee cup" calorimeter, a dewar flask (a better version of a coffee cup), and a bomb calorimeter. The calorimetric method used in each calorimeter is based on measuring the temperature change associated with the different thermodynamic processes. Students can choose from a wide selection of organic materials to measure the heats of combustion; salts to measure the heats of solution; acids, bases, oxidants, and reductants for heats of reaction; metals and alloys for heat capacity measurements; and ice for a melting process. Temperature versus time data can be graphed during the measurements and saved to the electronic lab book for later analysis. Systematic and random errors in the mass and volume measurements have been included in the simulation by introducing buoyancy errors in the mass weighings, volumetric errors in the glassware, and characteristic systematic and random errors in the thermometer measurements.

Software Configurations

Although the *Virtual ChemLab* simulations can be used as an exploratory activity or tool for students, the true power of the simulations is realized when students enter the virtual laboratory and perform assignments or experiments given to them by the instructor just as they would do in an actual laboratory setting. Because these laboratories are virtual, a wide variety of experiences can be provided ranging from very basic and guided to very complex and open-ended. It is up to the instructor to decide the best use of the laboratories whether it be as a pre-lab, a lab replacement, a homework or quiz assignment, a lab supplement, or a lecture discussion activity. Because each instructor will have a different comfort level using software in the classroom or laboratory and will have different levels of technical support available, several different methods of implementing the simulations at an institution have been provided. Brief descriptions of these are listed below. Details on actually installing the software are given in the installation instructions.

Individual Student Versions. Individual copies of *Virtual ChemLab* can be purchased by students and installed on personal computers and/or installed on institution computers using a site license version. In the student version, an electronic workbook is provided at the beginning of the simulation that allows students to select experiments that correspond to laboratory assignments in an accompanying student workbook that can be purchased separately. Students can also enter the laboratory, bypassing the preset experiments, to explore in the laboratory on their own or to perform custom experiments designed by the instructors. This version of the software, when initially installed, is configured to have the full functionality of the various simulations, but it cannot receive nor submit electronic assignments. This version is the most simple to install and use and requires almost no oversight by the instructor. Since this version cannot receive nor submit electronic assignments, assignments are expected to be given using worksheets. This version, however, can be enabled to use the Web Connectivity Option for transferring electronic assignments. (See the Electronic Assignments and Web Connectivity Option section below.)

Direct Access Computer Lab (A Network Version). In this implementation, a centralized database is installed on a network drive accessible to all client computers in the local area network, and the *Virtual ChemLab* software is installed on any client computers needing access to the simulations. This installation is called a direct access installation since the client software accesses the database containing the class lists, assignments, lab books, and scores directly using a mapped or named network drive. This version allows instructors to give assignments and receive results electronically. This is a simple installation for computer labs and allows multiple instructors to use the software, but there are some network security issues associated with this type of installation. The electronic workbook is not available in this installation.

Web Access Computer Lab (A Network Version). This implementation is very similar to the direct access installation described above except in this instance, the assignment and lab book data is passed indirectly to the database using a servlet engine running on a TomCat web server. This installation does not require a local area network but, instead, only requires a simple connection to the internet. This installation also corrects several security issues associated with a direct access connection. Details on setting up and using the web connectivity feature is given in the *Instructor Utilities* user guide from the management perspective and in the various simulation user guides from the student perspective. It is strongly suggested the user guides be reviewed before trying to implement this version. Most questions and problems can be avoided if the user guides are studied carefully.

Web Access Student Version. The student version of *Virtual ChemLab* described above can be activated to a full web version when students are provided with a user name, password, and the URL address for the servlet engine. After the web functionality is activated, the software is no longer configured with the electronic workbook and access to the laboratories is gained solely through the General Chemistry door or card reader. This option allows students to install individual copies of the simulations on their personal computers and then perform their assignments and submit their results electronically over the web. This option has all the advantages of the Web Access Computer Lab installation but relieves the instructor from having to maintain the software on institution computers. In all respects, this installation is identical to the workbook version, except the workbook will not be available.

Electronic Assignments and the Web Connectivity Option

As was described previously, one of the key features of the *Virtual ChemLab* simulations is the ability to give assignments to students using either worksheets out of an accompanying workbook or electronically. Although worksheets are a convenient method to give assignments to students, electronic assignments offer the largest variety of activities and the most control over them. The purpose of the *Instructor Utilities* component of *Virtual ChemLab* is to allow instructors to create electronic assignments, submit them to students, retrieve the student lab books, and assign scores. The ability to give assignments and retrieve results is only available when students running the software have access to the *Virtual ChemLab* database (see the *Database* section below). Installing a direct access version in a local area network is one way of doing this; however, this generally limits students to working in a computer lab.

A more flexible approach has been developed where the necessary information for assignments from the instructor and the results from students can be passed indirectly through a servlet engine running on a TomCat server. (Details on installing and setting up the servlet engine can be found in the installation instructions below.) This method of passing data is called the Web Connectivity Option or Web Database Access. The advantages of this method include (a) it allows an institution to still setup the software in a computer lab without requiring read/write privileges on a network drive (a moderate security hole) and (b) students can install their own copies of the software and still have access to electronic assignments wherever they are as long as they have access to the internet. The general principles upon which the Web Connectivity Option is based are described next.

1. The database containing the class lists, assignments, lab books, and scores must still be maintained but it can now be stored on a local computer if only one instructor will be using it or it can be stored on a network drive if multiple instructors will be using the same servlet engine to pass data to and from the students. See the *Database* section below for more details.

2. The Web Connectivity Option works by using the servlet engine as a vehicle to receive data from both the instructor and students and save it temporarily on the server. The instructor will send (update) data for each class (from the main database), which the student can, in turn, retrieve and download to their own computer and incorporate it into their own local database. In a like manner, a student submits (updates) their results for an assignment to the server and the instructor, in turn, will retrieve those results and incorporate them into the main database. This synchronization of the instructor and student databases is the responsibility of the individual users. If regular synchronization is not performed by both the students and instructor then unpredictable results can occur.

3. For *Instructor Utilities*, the Update and Retrieve functions can be performed at two locations. First, the *Class Roll* folder for each class has an *Update Web* button and *Retrieve Web* button. Clicking these buttons performs the indicated action for the selected class. Secondly, the *Utilities* drawer contains a *Web Tools* folder where multiple classes can be selected and the Update and Retrieve functions performed for the selected classes.

4. When a student version is first installed, the software is *not* initially configured to receive electronic assignments. The Web Connectivity Option is activated by going to the *Web Options* button in the lab book, enabling the *Web Connection*, and adding the user. The information a student must have to add a user is their user name, password, and the URL address for the servlet engine. The user name and password are assigned when a student is added to a class. Once a local user has been added, entry into the laboratories is only allowed by providing a password at the card reader as is the case for a direct access installation. After the first user has been added, other users can be added by using the *Add New User* button on the card reader. It is useful to note that the student side has the ability to enable automatic updates and retrieves. This option is mandatory for computer lab installations and highly recommended for students with continuous internet connections. Details on using the student side of the Web Connectivity Option is given in the individual laboratory user guides.

5. Before the Web Connectivity Option can be used, the Web Connectivity Option must be enabled and the URL address for the servlet engine specified in the Web Tools folder. Details on configuring the Web Connectivity Option and other important web functions are found in the Web Tools section.

Database

The database that contains the classes, students, assignments, scores, and lab books is kept in the *Data* directory inside the main installed *Virtual ChemLab* directory. The database is stored as encrypted text files and cannot be accessed or modified without the encryption key. All login information is stored in a separate file, and student lists, assignments, and scores are stored in files for each individual class. A separate subdirectory is created for each student inside the *Data* directory and contains the data for each student's lab book. In a direct access network installation, the database (and other common files and directories) must be kept on a mapped (PC) or named (Mac) network drive that all *Virtual ChemLab* client computers can access with read/write privileges. In a web access network installation, the database can be stored on a network drive if several instructors will need access to the database or it can be kept on a local drive, even on a portable computer, as long as there is an internet connection to allow for the update and retrieval of the web data.

System Requirements

Minimum system requirements are as follows:

PC
Pentium 500 MHz (Pentium II or better recommended)
128 Mb RAM (256+ Mb Recommended)
CD-ROM drive (for installation only)
600 Mb of free disk space
Display capable of **and** set to millions of colors (24 bit color)
Minimum resolution 800 x 600 (1024 x 768 or higher strongly recommended)
Windows 2000 Professional or Windows XP
QuickTime 5.x/6.x/7.x

Macintosh
PowerPC (G3 or better recommended)
128 Mb RAM (256+ Mb recommended)
CD-ROM drive (for installation only)
600 Mb of free disk space
Display capable of **and** set to millions of colors (24-bit color)
Recommended minimum resolution 832 x 624 (1024 x 768 or higher strongly recommended)
OS X (any version)
QuickTime 5.x/6.x/7.x

Server (For network installations)
For a Direct Database Access network installation or common database sharing amongst instructors, a file server running an operating system capable of mapped or named drives accessible to all clients in the local area network is required. The clients must be running an operating system compatible with the *Virtual ChemLab* software (see above). Linux, OS X, Windows, and Novell file servers have all been successfully implemented to host the *Virtual ChemLab* database.

Note: The above requirements are the recommended minimum hardware and system software requirements for reasonable execution speeds and reliability. However, it should be noted that the software has been successfully installed and used on computers with significantly lower capabilities than the recommendations given above with corresponding reductions in execution speed and media access time.

Access option. The Web Connectivity Option servlet engine must first be installed before this installation will function properly. The user must provide the web address for the web servlet engine during the installation.

- **Install Instructor Utilities with Client.** This option will install *Instructor Utilities* along with the client installation for a Direct Database Access option. *Instructor Utilities* is required for assigning and retrieving electronic assignments either through Direct Access or Web Access.

All users who will be running *Virtual ChemLab* where they will be accessing a centralized database on a network drive must have read/write privileges to that database directory (including subdirectories). This does not imply that users must be given access to these files and directories but only that they have read/write privileges to enable the software to run correctly. Multiple users access the same database in a direct access installation and when multiple instructors manage classes with the Web Connectivity Option but using a common database. Further installation instructions can be found in the Installation and Overview Guide found on the CD.

Getting Started with the Student Version

After the student version of *Virtual ChemLab* has been successfully installed, the *VCL* icon used to launch the program will be located on the desktop, in a Program Group on PC machines, and on the Dock for Macintosh machines. Clicking on the *VCL* icon will start the simulation where you will be brought to a hallway containing three doors and a workbook sitting on a table (see Figure 1). Clicking on the electronic workbook opens and zooms into the workbook pages (see Figure 2) where you can select preset assignments that correspond to the assignments in the laboratory workbook. The *Previous* and *Next* buttons are used to page through the set of assignments, and the different assignments can also be accessed by clicking on the section titles located on the left page of the workbook. Clicking on the *Enter Laboratory* button will allow you to enter the general chemistry laboratory (see below), and the *Exit* button is used to leave *Virtual ChemLab*.

From the hallway, students can also enter the general chemistry laboratory by clicking on the General Chemistry door. Once in the laboratory (shown in Figure 3), students will find five laboratory benches that represent the five different general chemistry laboratories. By mousing over each of these

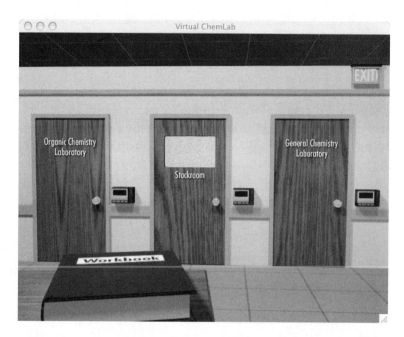

Figure 1. The "hallway" leading into the different virtual rooms in *Virtual ChemLab*. The general chemistry laboratory can be accessed by clicking on the General Chemistry door and the electronic workbook is accessed by clicking on the workbook.

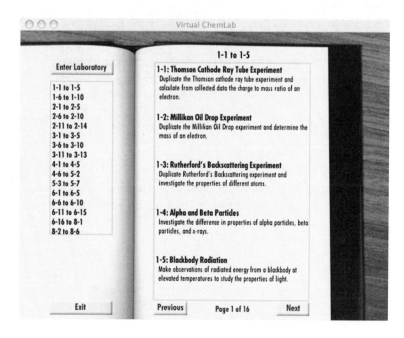

Figure 2. The electronic workbook. Preset laboratories corresponding to assignments in the workbook are accessed by clicking on the assignment.

11

laboratory benches, students can display the name of the selected laboratory. To access a specific laboratory, click on the appropriate laboratory bench. While in the general chemistry laboratory, the full functionality of the simulation is available, and students are free to explore and perform experiments as directed by their instructors or by their own curiosity. The Exit signs in the general chemistry laboratory are used to return to the hallway.

Detailed instructions on how to use each of the five laboratory simulations can be found in the User Guides Folder located on the *Virtual ChemLab* CD. These same user guides can also be accessed inside each laboratory by clicking on the Pull-Down TV and clicking on the *Help* button. For those students who will be given electronic assignments from their instructor through the web, the laboratory can be changed from the workbook configuration to the Web Connectivity Option by clicking on the *Web Options* button in the electronic lab book located in each of the laboratories. Details on using the Web Connectivity Option can be found by clicking on the *Help* button in the electronic lab book.

Figure 3. The general chemistry laboratory. The general chemistry laboratory contains five different laboratories, each of which is accessed by clicking on the appropriate lab bench. The exit signs are used to return to the hallway.

Important Installation Notes and Issues

1. The graphics used in the simulations require the monitor to be set to 24-bit true color (millions of colors). Lower color resolutions can be used, but the graphics will not be as sharp.

2. When installing *Virtual ChemLab*, you must be logged in as an Administrative User in order for all files and folders to be installed correctly and to have correctly configured file permissions; otherwise, unpredictable results such as hard crashes and other errors can occur during installation and running *Virtual ChemLab*.

3. Occasionally when installing on the OS X operating system, the system fails to copy over the VCL icon for aliases created on the desktop. There is no known cause for this. Aliases with the correct icon can be created manually inside the installation directory or by copying a VCL icon on to an already existing alias.

4. When installing on the OS X operating system v10.4 (or Tiger), selecting the option to place an alias on the dock causes the dock to be reset to its initial installed state and any dock customization is lost.

5. In the directory where *Virtual ChemLab* is installed, the user must always have read/write privileges to that directory and all directories underneath. This is the default state for all Administrative Users (both Mac and PC), and this condition has been set by the installer for Standard Users in OS X as well. However, if users will be logged in as Restricted Users in Windows (such as in a computer lab), then the privileges for the *Virtual ChemLab* directory must be set manually to "Full Access" for Everyone. The installer attempts to set these permissions for Windows installations, but for unknown reasons it is not always successful. In addition, if the system crashes hard while running *Virtual ChemLab* (either on Windows or OS X), these permissions may have to be reset to read/write for everyone.

6. The installer does not allow installation and other directory paths to be typed in directly, but all installation paths must be identified or select by browsing to the desired location. When installing on the OS X operating system, browsing to a folder using aliases occasionally causes the installer to spontaneously shutdown. Consequently, it is recommended that aliases be avoided when browsing. There is no known cause for this.

7. All users running *Virtual ChemLab* where they will be accessing a centralized database on a network drive (Direct Database Access) must have read/write privileges to that database directory (including subdirectories). This does not imply that users must be given access to these files and directories but only that they have read/write privileges to enable the software to run correctly.

8. When installing *Virtual ChemLab* on to the OS X operating system, the user must have read/write permission for the folder into which *Virtual ChemLab* will be installed. In the vast majority of cases, *Virtual ChemLab* will be installed into the Applications folder, but

in order for this to be successful the user must be an Administrative User. In some cases, however, the permissions for the Applications folder have been modified by other software installed on the machine, which will prevent *Virtual ChemLab* from being installed in the Applications folder. These permissions can be reset back to their default state using the *Repair Disk Permissions* function in the Disk Utility program located in the Applications folder.

9. QuickTime 5.0 or later is required for the software to run properly. The most recent version of QuickTime can be obtained at http://www.apple.com/quicktime/

10. When the simulation software has been installed on a Windows 2000 Professional operating system, there is better performance and better system stability when the Windows 2000 Support Pack 2 has been installed.

11. For unknown reasons, on some machines the QuickTime videos will not play properly if the system QuickTime settings are in their default state. This can be corrected by changing the Video Settings in QuickTime to Normal Mode.

Workbook Assignments

The following laboratory assignments cover most of the topics taught in the general chemistry curriculum. The purpose of these assignments is to allow you to put into practice the concepts and problem solving skills you have been learning in the classroom. Some of these assignments merely allow you to measure and collect the data that would normally be provided for you in a homework problem. Other assignments allow you to perform sophisticated and foundational experiments to which you would not normally have access, while other assignments allow you to perform experiments typically available in the undergraduate laboratory but much more quickly and cleanly. In all, you will find that these laboratory assignments using the virtual laboratory will provide a bridge in understanding between the abstract concepts of the classroom and their application in the actual laboratory.

For each laboratory assignment provided in this workbook, there is a corresponding assignment listed in the electronic workbook. You will find the electronic workbook on the table in the virtual hallway at the beginning of *Virtual ChemLab*. Clicking on an assignment in the electronic workbook will bring the user to the appropriate laboratory bench in the general chemistry laboratory and setup the lab bench for the selected experiment. Most assignments should take no longer than 15 to 20 minutes, especially once you have learned how to use *Virtual ChemLab*. Remember, the purpose of these experiments is to give you practice in thinking, problem solving, and applying concepts. Feel free to setup experiments and explore in the virtual laboratory. There are, essentially, an unlimited number of things you can discover.

1-1: Thomson Cathode Ray Tube Experiment

As scientists began to examine atoms, their first discovery was that they could extract negatively charged particles from atoms. They called these particles electrons. In order to understand the nature of these particles, scientists wanted to know how much charge they carried and how much they weighed. John Joseph (J.J.) Thomson was a physics professor at the famous Cavendish Laboratory at Cambridge University. In 1897, Thomson showed that if you could measure how far a beam of electrons was bent in an electric field and in a magnetic field, you could determine the charge-to-mass ratio (q/m_e) for the particles (electrons). Knowing the charge-to-mass ratio (q/m_e) and either the charge on the electron or the mass of the electron would allow you to calculate the other. Thomson could not obtain either in his cathode ray tube experiments and had to be satisfied with just the charge-to-mass ratio.

1. Start *Virtual ChemLab* and select *Thomson Cathode Ray Tube Experiment* from the list of assignments. The lab will open in the Quantum laboratory.

2. *What source is used in this experiment?* Drag your cursor over to the source to identify it._____

    electron gun

    What type of charge do electrons have? **negative**

    What detector is used in this experiment? **a phosphor screen**

3. Turn on the *Phosphor Screen* by clicking on the red/green light switch.

    What do you observe? **a spot in the center of the phosphor screen**

    The phosphor screen detects charged particles (such as electrons) and it glows momentarily at the positions where the particles impact the screen.

4. It may be helpful to drag the lab window down and left and the phosphor screen window up and right in order to minimize overlap. Push the **Grid** button on the phosphor screen, and set the *Magnetic Field* to 30 µT. (Click buttons above and below the digits in the meter to raise and lower the value. Clicking between digits moves the decimal point.)

    What happens to the spot from the electron gun on the phosphor screen? **The spot moves to the**

    right.

5. Set the *Magnetic Field* back to zero and set the *Electric Field* to 10 V.

    What happens to the spot on the phosphor screen? **The spot moves to the left.**

    Where should the signal on the phosphor screen be if the electric and magnetic forces are balanced?

    in the center of the phosphor screen

6. Increase the voltage of the *Electric Field* so the spot is 5 cm left of center.

    What voltage is required? **13 V**

7. Increase the magnetic field strength until the spot reaches the center of the screen.

   What magnetic field creates a magnetic force that balances the electric force? **44 μT**

   Summarize your data.

deflected distance (d)	electric field (V)	magnetic field (B)
5 cm	13 V	44 μT

8. In a simplified and reduced form, the charge-to-mass ratio (q/m_e) can be calculated as follows:

   $$q/m_e = \left(5.0826 \times 10^{12}\right) \cdot V \cdot d/B^2$$

   where V = the electric field in volts, d = the deflected distance from center in cm after applying just the voltage, and B = magnetic field in μT.

   *What is your calculated value for the charge-to-mass ratio for an electron (q/m_e)?*_____

   1.706×10^{11}

   The modern accepted value is 1.76×10^{11}.

   Calculate your percent error as follows:

   $$\% \ Error = \frac{|your \ value - accepted \ value|}{accepted \ value} \times 100$$

   $\% \ Error = $ _____**3.07%**_____

9. You may want to repeat the experiment several times using different size deflections.

1-2: Millikan Oil Drop Experiment

In the Thomson Cathode Ray Tube Experiment, it was discovered that you can use the deflection of an electron beam in an electric and magnetic field to measure the charge-to-mass ratio (q/m_e) of an electron. If you then want to know either the charge or the mass of an electron, you need to have a way of measuring one or the other independently. In 1909, Robert Millikan and his graduate student Harvey Fletcher showed that they could make very small oil drops and deposit electrons on these drops (1 to 10 electrons per drop). They would then measure the total charge on the oil drops by deflecting the drops with an electric field. You will get a chance to repeat their experiments and, using the results from the Thomson assignment, be able to experimentally calculate the mass of an electron.

1. Start *Virtual ChemLab* and select *Millikan Oil Drop Experiment* from the list of assignments. The lab will open in the Quantum laboratory.

2. *What is the purpose of the electron gun in this experiment?* **to produce electrons for the**

   experiment

   How does this source affect the oil droplets in the oil mist chamber? **Some of the electrons adhere**

   to the oil drops.

3. The detector in this experiment is a video camera with a microscopic eyepiece attached to view the oil droplets. Click the *On/Off* switch (red/green light) to turn the video camera on.

   What do you observe on the video camera screen? **There are large and small oil drops falling**

   from top to bottom.

   Do all the oil drops fall at the same speed? **No, some are falling fast and some slow.**

   What force causes the drops to fall? **gravity**

   The oil drops fall at their terminal velocity, which is the maximum velocity possible due to frictional forces such as air resistance. The terminal velocity is a function of the radius of the drop. By measuring the terminal velocity (v_t) of a droplet, the radius (r) can be calculated. Then the mass (m) of the drop can be calculated from its radius and the density of the oil. Knowing the mass of the oil droplet will allow you to calculate the charge (q) on the droplet.

   IMPORTANT: Read instructions 4 and 5 before beginning the procedure for 5.

4. *Measure the terminal velocity of a drop.* Identify a small drop near the top of the window that is falling near the center scale and click the *Slow Motion* button on the video camera. Wait until the drop is at a tick mark and start the timer. Let the drop fall for at least two or more tick marks and stop the timer. Do not let the drop fall off the end of the viewing scope. Each tick mark is 0.125 mm. Record the distance and the time in the data table on the following page.

5. *Measure the voltage required to stop the fall of the drop.* Having measured the terminal velocity, you now need to stop the fall of the drop by applying an electric field between the two voltage plates. This

is done by clicking on the buttons on the top or bottom of the *Electric Field* until the voltage is adjusted such that the drop stops falling. This should be done while in slow motion. When the drop appears to stop, turn the slow motion off and do some final adjustments until the drop has not moved for at least one minute. Record the voltage, *V*, indicated on the voltage controller.

Complete the experiment for three drops and record your measurements in the data table.

Data Table

Drop	Voltage (*V*, in volts)	Time (*t*, in seconds)	Distance (*d*, in meters)
1		(sample student data)	
2	52	11.45	3.75×10^{-4}
3			

The *Millikan Oil Drop Experiment* is a classic due to the simplicity of the experimental apparatus and the completeness of the data analysis. The following calculations have reduced very complex equations into simpler ones with several parameters combined into a single constant. Millikan and Fletcher accounted for the force of gravity, the force of the electric field, the density of the oil, the viscosity of the air, the viscosity of the oil, and the air pressure.

6. *Calculate the terminal velocity and record the value.* Calculate the terminal velocity, v_t, in units of $m \cdot s^{-1}$ using this equation:

    $v_t = \dfrac{d}{t}$, where *d* is the distance the drop fell in meters and *t* is the elapsed time in seconds. Do not forget that the scale on the viewing scope is in mm (1000 mm = 1 m). **Answers will vary, but a**

    typical answer might be 3.28×10^{-5} m·s^{-1}.

    Each of the equations in instructions 7-10 is shown with and without units. You will find it easier to use the equation without units for your calculations.

7. *Calculate the radius (r) of the drop and record the value.* With the terminal velocity, you can calculate the radius, in m, of the drop using this equation:

    $$r = \left(9.0407 \times 10^{-5}\, m^{1/2} \cdot s^{1/2}\right) \cdot \sqrt{v_t} \quad = (9.0407 \times 10^{-5}\sqrt{v_t} \text{ , without units})$$

    Answers will vary, but a typical answer might be 5.17×10^{-7} m.

8. *Calculate the mass of the drop and record the value.* You can use the answer from #7 for the radius (*r*) to calculate the mass of the drop given the density of the oil. The final equation to calculate the mass, in kg, is

    $$m = V_{oil} \cdot \rho_{oil} = 4\pi/3 \cdot r^3 \cdot 821 kg \cdot m^{-3}$$
    $$= \left(3439.0 kg \cdot m^{-3}\right) \cdot r^3 \qquad = (3439.0 \cdot r^3 \text{ , without units})$$

    Answers will vary, but a typical answer might be 4.76×10^{-18} kg.

9. Since you applied a voltage across the *Electric Field* to stop the fall of the oil drop, the forces being exerted on the drop must be balanced; that is, the force due to gravity must be the same as the force due to the electric field acting on the electrons stuck to the drop: $qE = mg$.

    Calculate the total charge (Q_{tot}) on the oil drop due to the electrons using the equation:

    $$Q_{tot} = Q(n) \cdot e = \left(9.810 \times 10^{-2}\,C \cdot kg^{-1} \cdot J^{-1}\right) \cdot m/V = (9.81 \times 10^{-2}\,m/V,\text{ without units})$$

    where $Q(n)$ is the number of electrons on the drop, e is the fundamental electric charge of an electron, m is the mass calculated in #8, and V is the voltage.

    This answer will provide the total charge on the drop (Q_{tot}). The fundamental electric charge of an electron (e) is 1.6×10^{-19} C (coulombs). Divide your total charge (Q_{tot}) by e and round your answer to the nearest whole number. This is the number of electrons ($Q(n)$) that adhered to your drop. Now divide your total charge (Q_{tot}) by $Q(n)$ and you will obtain your experimental value for the charge on one electron.

10. Complete the experiment and calculations for at <u>least</u> three drops and summarize your results in the results table.

Results Table

Drop #	Terminal Velocity (v_t, in m/s)	Radius (r, in meters)	Mass (m, in kg)	Total charge on drop (Q_{tot}, in Coulombs)	Charge on one electron (C)
1	**(sample results)**				
2	3.28×10^{-5}	5.18×10^{-7}	4.78×10^{-16}	8.49×10^{-19}	1.69×10^{-19}
3					

11. Average your results for the charge on one electron. Calculate the percent error by:

    $$\% \, Error = \frac{\left| your\ answer - 1.6 \times 10^{-19} \right|}{1.6 \times 10^{-19}} \times 100\%$$

    What is your average charge for an electron? <u>**Answers will vary but should range between 1.4 ×**</u>

    <u>**10^{-19} C and 1.8 × 10^{-19} C.**</u>

    What is your percent error? <u>**Answers will vary but should range between 0% and 10%.**</u>

12. You will recall that in the Thomson experiment you were able to calculate the charge-to-mass ratio (q/m_e) as 1.7×10^{11}. Using this value for q/m_e and your average charge on an electron, calculate the mass of an electron in kg.

What is your calculated value for the mass of an electron in kg? <u>**Answers will vary but should**</u>

<u>**range between 9.41 × 10^{-31} kg and 1.02 × 10^{-30} kg.**</u>

The actual equations used to derive the simplified versions in this lab are in Appendix D Quantum Equations, Millikan Experiment of the Instructor Utilities Guide.

1-3: Rutherford's Backscattering Experiment

A key experiment in understanding the nature of atomic structure was completed by Ernest Rutherford in 1911. He set up an experiment that directed a beam of alpha particles (helium nuclei) through a gold foil and then onto a detector screen. According to the "plum-pudding" atomic model, electrons float around inside a cloud of positive charge. Based on this model, Rutherford expected that almost all of the alpha particles should pass through the gold foil and not be deflected. A few of the alpha particles would experience a slight deflection due to the attraction to the negative electrons (alpha particles have a charge of +2). Imagine his surprise when a few alpha particles deflected at all angles, even nearly straight backwards.

According to the "plum-pudding" model there was nothing in the atom massive enough to deflect the alpha particles. Rutherford's reaction was that this was ". .almost as incredible as if you fired a 15-inch shell at a piece of tissue paper and it came back and hit you." He suggested that the experimental data could only be explained if the majority of the mass of an atom was concentrated in a small, positively charged central nucleus. This experiment provided the evidence needed to prove the nuclear model of the atom. In this experiment, you will make observations similar to those of Professor Rutherford.

1. Start *Virtual ChemLab* and select *Rutherford's Backscattering Experiment* from the list of assignments. The lab will open in the Quantum laboratory.

2. The experiment will be set up on the lab table. The gray box on the left side of the table contains a sample of ^{241}Am.

   What particles are emitted from this source? **alpha particles**

   What are alpha particles? **helium nuclei, which each have two protons, two neutrons and a**

   charge of +2

3. Mouse over the metal foil stand in the middle of the table.

   What metal foil is used? If you want to see the metal foil, click and hold on the metal stand. **gold**

4. Point the cursor to the detector (on the right).

   What detector is used in this experiment? **phosphor screen**

5. Turn on the detector by clicking on the red/green light switch.

   What does the signal in the middle of the screen represent? **the alpha particles coming straight**

   through the gold foil undeflected or only slightly deflected

   The phosphor screen detects charged particles (such as alpha particles) and it glows momentarily at the positions where the particles impact the screen.

   What other signals do you see on the phosphor detection screen? **There are other momentary spots**

   of light.

What do these signals represent? __hits from alpha particles being deflected at small angles__

Click the *Persist* button (the dotted arrow) on the phosphor detector screen.

According to the plum pudding model, what is causing the deflection of the alpha particles?

__As the positively charged alpha particles pass through the gold atoms they are attracted to the__

__negative electrons and their path is bent slightly.__

Make a general observation about the number of alpha particles that hit the phosphor detection screen in a minute's worth of time.

__The alpha particle hits fill the screen rapidly.__

6. Now, you will make observations at different angles of deflection. Click on the main laboratory window to bring it to the front. Grab the phosphor detection screen by its base and move it to the spotlight in the top right corner. The *Persist* button should still be on.

Observe the number of hits in this position as compared with the first detector position. __The hits are__

__not quite as frequent and the forward scattering spot is no longer visible.__

7. Move the detector to the top center spotlight position at a 90° angle to the foil stand.

Observe the number of hits in this spotlight position as compared with the first detector position. __The__

__hits show up every few seconds.__

8. Move the detector to the top left spotlight position and observe the number of hits on the phosphor screen in one minute.

Observe the number of hits in this spotlight position as compared with the first detector position. __It__

__takes nearly a minute for even a single hit to appear.__

What causes the alpha particles to deflect backwards? __a large mass in the center of the atom__

How do these results disprove the plum pudding model? Keep in mind that there are 1,000,000 alpha particles passing through the gold foil per second.

__The mass of the gold atom is not spread over the full atomic volume but concentrated in a__

__central atomic nucleus.__

Are the gold atoms composed mostly of matter or empty space? __mostly empty space__

How does the Gold Foil Experiment show that almost all of the mass of an atom is concentrated in a small positively charged central atom?

__Most of the alpha particles came straight through with little or no deflections, but there was the__ occasional large deflection. If the mass of an atom were not concentrated, the number of

deflections would be smaller and there would be no large deflections.

Students often ask, "Why did Rutherford use gold foil?" The most common response is that gold is soft and malleable and can be made into very thin sheets of foil. There is another reason, which you can discover for yourself.

9. Turn off the phosphor detection screen. Double-click the base of the metal foil holder to move it to the stockroom window. (You can also click and drag it to the counter.) Click on the *Stockroom* to enter. Click on the metal sample box on the top shelf. Click on *Mg* to select magnesium. Click on the *Return to Lab* arrow.

10. Move the metal foil sample holder from the stockroom window back to the center of the table. Move the phosphor screen back to its original location on the right side of the table and turn it on. Click *Persist*. Observe the number of hits with magnesium compared with the number of hits with a gold sample.

Why would Rutherford choose gold foil instead of magnesium foil? Explain. **The magnesium atom**

is much smaller than the gold atom and the same is true for the nuclei. The magnesium nucleus

is so small that you have a very small chance of hitting it directly and having any alpha particles

bounce back. Gold atoms have a much larger cross-section.

1-4: Investigating the Properties of Alpha and Beta Particles

As scientists began investigating the properties of atoms, their first discovery was that they could extract negatively charged particles. They called these particles electrons, but they are also known as beta particles in the context of nuclear decay. Robert Millikan used beta particles in his famous Oil Drop Experiment. Another particle ejected during nuclear decay is the alpha particle. An alpha particle is a helium nucleus, or a helium atom without its two electrons. Consequently, an alpha particle is positively charged. Ernest Rutherford used alpha particles in his Gold Foil Experiment.

1. Start *Virtual ChemLab* and select *Alpha and Beta Particles* from the list of assignments. The lab will open in the Quantum laboratory.

2. *What source is used in this experiment?* Drag your cursor over the source to identify it. **electron gun**

    What type of charge do electrons have? **negative**

    What detector is used in this experiment? **a phosphor screen**

3. Turn on the *Phosphor Screen*. (Click on the green/red button.)

    What do you observe? **a spot in the center of the phosphor screen**

    The phosphor screen detects charged particles (such as electrons) and it glows momentarily at the positions where the particles impact the screen.

4. Drag the lab window down and left and the phosphor screen window up and right in order to minimize the overlap. Push the **Grid** button on the phosphor screen, and set the *Magnetic Field* to 30 µT. (Click the button above the tens place three times. If you mistakenly click between digits, it will move the decimal point. Click it to place it where it was originally and then click above the tens place.)

    What happens to the spot from the electron gun on the phosphor screen? **The spot moves right.**

5. Click once above the tens place on the *Electric Field* meter. Observe the spot. Click a second time above the tens place on the *Electric Field*.

    What happens to the spot from the electron gun on the phosphor screen? **The spot moves left.**

6. Zero out the *Magnetic Field* and *Electric Field* meters by clicking on the appropriate digit buttons until the spot on the phosphor screen is centered again.

7. Double-click or click and drag the electron gun to move it to the *Stockroom* counter. Enter the *Stockroom* by clicking inside the *Stockroom*. Double-click the electron gun to move it back to the shelf. Double-click on the alpha source to select it and move it to the *Stockroom* counter. Click on the green *Return to Lab* arrow to return to the lab. Drag the alpha source from the *Stockroom* counter and place it on the table where the electron gun was originally placed (the middle spot light). Click on the front of the alpha source to open the shutter.

    What appears on the phosphor screen? **another spot**

8. Change the unit for the *Magnetic Field* from μT to mT by clicking once above the unit. Click above the hundreds place three times to set the *Magnetic Field* to 300 mT (millitesla). This magnetic field is one million times stronger than what we used for the electron gun.

   Which direction is the spot deflected when the magnetic field is increased this time? **left**

   How does this compare with the direction of movement when the magnetic field was turned on for the electrons?

   It is opposite. Electrons move right when applying a magnetic field and alpha particles move

   left.

9. Change the unit for the *Electric Field* from V to kV by clicking once above the unit. Observe the spot as you increase the *Electric Field* strength from 0 kV to 5 kV. The movement is slight so pay careful attention.

   Which direction is the spot moved when you increase the Electric Field? **The spot moves right.**

   How does this compare with the direction of movement for the electron beam in the Electric Field?

   Again, it is opposite. Electrons move left in the electric field and alpha particles move right.

   Why does it take significantly stronger magnetic and electric field strengths to move the beam of alpha particles compared with the beam of electrons (beta particles)?

   The alpha particle is massive compared with the electron. It is more than 7000 times heavier!

10. Return the values on the two meters to zero. Double-click (or click and drag) the alpha source and the phosphor screen to return them to the *Stockroom* counter. Enter the *Stockroom*. Double-click on the alpha source and the phosphor screen to place them on the shelf. Select the laser and the video camera by double-clicking on them, and then click on the green *Return to Lab* arrow to return to the lab. Place the laser in the center spotlight on the left and turn the laser on (click on the red/green light). Place the video camera on the center spotlight on the right and click the video camera to turn it on. Set the laser intensity to 1 nW and the wavelength to 20 nm. This wavelength is in the x-ray region of the electromagnetic spectrum. The purple dot is a representation of the x-rays hitting the video camera. Change the *Electric Field* and *Magnetic Field* to determine the effect on the x-rays.

    Did the electric or magnetic fields affect the x-rays? Why or why not? **There is no affect. The**

    x-rays do not have a charge and are unaffected by magnetic or electric fields.

    Summarize what you have learned about electrons (beta particles), alpha particles, and x-rays.

    Electrons are the smallest particles and have a charge which is opposite than that of alpha

    particles. Alpha particles are significantly more massive than beta particles. X-rays do not

    have a charge and are unaffected by magnetic or electric fields.

1-5: Blackbody Radiation

In the early 1900s several experimental results appeared to be in conflict with classical physics. One of these experiments was the study of blackbody radiation. A blackbody is a solid (such as a piece of iron) that does not emit light at low temperatures, but, when heated, the "blackbody" begins to emit first red and then orange light and at higher temperatures eventually becomes white hot. The intensity of the emitted light is also a function of temperature. In this problem you will make observations similar to those of Max Planck (1858-1947) who, through his study of blackbody radiation, found an explanation that revolutionized how scientists think about radiated energy.

1. Start *Virtual ChemLab* and select *Blackbody Radiation* from the list of assignments. The lab will open in the Quantum laboratory. A metal sample holder with tungsten metal will be on the lab bench with an electric heater set at a temperature of 3000 K. A spectrometer is on the right and is switched on (the spectrometer window is open). Locate the switch that changes the display from wavelength to frequency and the switch that displays either the full electromagnetic spectrum or just the visible spectrum. These will be used later.

2. The spectrometer detects the intensity of the emitted light as a function of the wavelength (or frequency). In the grid below draw the spectrum detected by the spectrometer with wavelength (in nm) on the *x*-axis and intensity on the *y*-axis. If you drag your cursor over a peak, it will identify the wavelength (in nm) in the *x*-coordinate field in the bottom right corner of the detector window. Record the wavelength of the peak in the data table on the following page. (Round to whole numbers.)

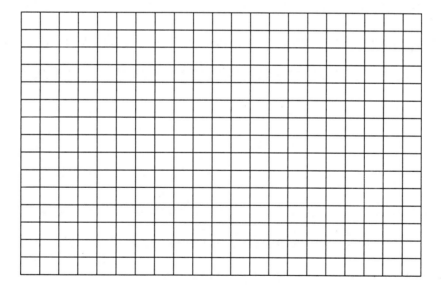

3. Change the temperature on the heater to 3100 K by clicking on the button above the hundreds place on the heater LCD controller. Record the shape of the curve on the same graph (label each line with a temperature) and the wavelength of the peak intensity in the data table. Continue with temperatures of 3200 K, 3300 K, 3400 K, 3500 K, and 3600 K. If you raise the temperature to 3700 K you will have to start over by clicking on the *Reset Lab* button just under the Danger sign, entering the *Stockroom*, clicking on the clipboard and selecting Preset Experiment #3 Blackbody Radiation.

Data Table

Temperature (K)	Wavelength (nm)
3000	950
3100	922
3200	880
3300	853
3400	839
3500	826
3600	798

4. *What observations can you make about the shape of the curve as temperature changes?*

   The intensity increases as the temperature increases. The maximum shifts left as the temperature increases.

5. The visible portion of the electromagnetic spectrum occurs between 400 nm and 700 nm. Mark the visible spectrum on your graph.

   Does the peak intensity ever occur in the visible region? Does this mean that there is no visible light radiated over this temperature range? Explain. **The peak intensity does not move far enough to occur in the visible region and is always in the infrared region. The fact that the peak intensity does not occur in the visible range does not mean that there is no visible light radiated. The curve does show significant intensity of light in the visible region, just not the peak intensity.**

6. Classical physics predicted that as the wavelength decreases the intensity should increase.

   Does your graph of wavelength and intensity confirm this result? Explain. **The intensity increases as the wavelength decreases to a point, but then the intensity decreases as the wavelength decreases. Classical physics did not predict a maximum in the curve, which is clearly evident.**

7. In the spectrometer window, change the display from wavelength to frequency.

   What observations can you make about the magnitude of the intensity as the temperature is lowered from 3600 K to 3000 K by increments of 100 K? **The intensity decreases as the temperature decreases.**

8. Change the temperature to 3700 K while observing the tungsten foil.

   What occurs at 3700 K? **The tungsten metal melts.**

9. This disparity between classical theory and experimental results was known as the "ultraviolet catastrophe." Classical physics predicted that the curve should continue to infinity as the wavelength is decreased. The conflicting experimental data required an innovative explanation. This explanation was provided by Max Planck who stated that the energy given off by the vibrating heated atoms was *quantized* and only vibrations of specific energy could occur. The quantized energy must be a multiple of $h\nu$ where h is known as Planck's constant (6.626×10^{-34} J·s) and ν is the frequency of the light in 1/s or s^{-1}. Calculate the energy of the peak intensity at 3400 K.

Use the wavelength from the data table for 3400 K to determine first the frequency ($\nu = c/\lambda$, where c = speed of light = 2.998×10^8 m·s^{-1} and λ is the wavelength in meters) and then find the energy using $E = h\nu$.

$$\text{wavelength at 3400 K} = 839 \text{ nm}\left(\frac{1\text{ m}}{1\times 10^9 \text{nm}}\right) = 8.39 \times 10^{-7} \text{ m}$$

$$\nu = \frac{c}{\lambda} = \frac{3\times 10^8 \text{ m} \cdot \text{s}^{-1}}{8.39\times 10^{-7} \text{ m}} = 3.58 \times 10^{14} \text{ s}^{-1}$$

$$E = h\nu = (6.626\times 10^{-34} \text{ J}\cdot\text{s})(3.58\times 10^{14} \text{ s}^{-1}) = 2.37\times 10^{-19} \text{ J}$$

1-6: Photoelectric Effect

Although Albert Einstein is most famous for $E = mc^2$ and for his work describing relativity in mechanics, his Nobel Prize was for understanding a very simple experiment. It was long understood that if you directed light of a certain wavelength at a piece of metal, it would emit electrons. In classical theory, the energy of the light was thought to be based on its intensity and not its frequency. However, the results of the photoelectric effect contradicted classical theory. Inconsistencies led Einstein to suggest that we need to think of light as being composed of particles (photons) and not just as waves. In this experiment, you will reproduce a photoelectric experiment and show that the energy (E) of a photon of light is related to its frequency and not its intensity.

1. Start *Virtual ChemLab* and select *Photoelectric Effect* from the list of assignments. The lab will open in the Quantum laboratory.

2. *What source is used in this experiment and what does it do?* **The laser emits coherent light at a single wavelength that is in phase.**

   At what intensity is the laser set? **1 nW**

   At what wavelength is the laser set? **400 nm**

   Record the wavelength (in nm) in the data table on the following page. Calculate the frequency (in Hz) and the energy (in J) using $c = \lambda v$ and $E = h v$ where $c = 2.998 \times 10^8$ m·s^{-1} and $h = 6.626 \times 10^{-34}$ J·s. Also record the color of the light by clicking on the *Spectrum Chart* (just behind the laser); the marker indicates what color is represented by the wavelength selected.

   Which metal foil is used in this experiment? **Na, sodium metal**

   What detector is used in this experiment and what does it measure? **The phosphor screen detects electrons and glows momentarily at the positions where the electrons impact the screen.**

   Turn on the detector by clicking on the red/green light switch.

   What does the signal on the phosphor screen indicate about the laser light shining on the sodium foil? **The laser light is causing the electrons to be ejected from the surface of the sodium metal.**

3. *Decrease the Intensity to 1 photon/second, how does the signal change?* **The signal is not as intense and flickers as each electron impacts the phosphor screen.**

   Increase the Intensity to 1kW, how does the signal change? **The signal is more intense than at 1 photon/second, but the same as at 1 nW.**

   Change the *Intensity* back to 1 nW and increase the *Wavelength* to 600 nm.

   What do you observe? Record the wavelength in the data table. **The signal disappears.**

Determine the maximum wavelength at which emission of electrons occurs in the metal. **450 nm**

What is the difference between intensity and wavelength? **Wavelength corresponds to the energy of light emitted but intensity corresponds to the amount of light.**

Which matters in the formation of photoelectrons: intensity or wavelength? **wavelength or frequency**

Data Table

wavelength (nm)	frequency (1/s)	energy (J)	light color
400	7.50×10^{14}	4.97×10^{-19}	violet
600	5×10^{14}	3.32×10^{-19}	orange
450	6.66×10^{14}	4.42×10^{-19}	blue

4. Click inside the *Stockroom* to enter the stockroom. Click on the clipboard and select the preset experiment *Photoelectric Effect (2)*. Click on the green *Return to Lab* arrow to return to the laboratory. The intensity of the laser will be set at 1 nW and the wavelength at 400 nm. The detector used in this experiment is a bolometer and will be automatically turned on. This instrument measures the kinetic energy of electrons. You should see a green peak on the bolometer detection screen. The intensity or height of the signal corresponds to the number of electrons being emitted from the metal, and the *x*-axis is the kinetic energy of the electrons. Zoom in on the peak by clicking and dragging from the left of the peak to the right. –

5. *Increase and decrease the Intensity, what do you observe?* **The height of the peak changes according to the intensity, but the energy of the electrons remain the same.**

Increase and decrease the Wavelength, what do you observe? **As wavelength decreases the kinetic energy of the emitted electrons increases and when wavelength increases the kinetic energy of the emitted electrons decreases.**

What is the maximum wavelength that ejects electrons from the sodium metal? **450 nm**

Based on this experiment, explain why violet light causes photoemission of electrons but orange light does not. **Violet light has a shorter wavelength, but more energy (4.97×10^{-19} J) than orange light (3.32×10^{-19} J). Violet light has enough energy to eject electrons but orange light does not.**

1-7: The Rydberg Equation

When a sample of gas is excited by applying a large alternating electric field, the gas emits light at certain discrete wavelengths. In the late 1800s two scientists, Johann Balmer and Johannes Rydberg, developed an emperical equation that correlated the wavelength of the emitted light for certain gases such as H_2. Later, Niels Bohr's concept of quantized "jumps" by electrons between orbits was shown to be consistent with the Rydberg equation. In this assignment, you will measure the wavelengths of the lines in the hydrogen emission spectra and then graphically determine the value of the Rydberg constant, R_H.

1. Start *Virtual ChemLab* and select *The Rydberg Equation* from the list of assignments. The lab will open in the Quantum laboratory. The *Spectrometer* will be on the right of the lab table. The hydrogen emission spectra will be in the detector window in the upper right corner as a graph of intensity vs. wavelength (λ).

2. *How many distinct lines do you see and what are their colors?* **four: violet, blue, aqua (blue-green), red**

3. Click on the *Visible/Full* switch to magnify only the visible spectrum. You will see four peaks in the spectrum. If you drag your cursor over a peak, it will identify the wavelength (in nm) in the *x*-coordinate field in the bottom right corner of the detector window. Record the wavelengths of the four peaks in the visible hydrogen spectrum in the data table. (Round to whole numbers.)

4. The Rydberg equation has the form $\dfrac{1}{\lambda} = R_H \left(\dfrac{1}{n_f^2} - \dfrac{1}{n_i^2} \right)$ where λ is the wavelength in meters, R_H is the Rydberg constant, n_f is the final principal quantum (for the Balmer series, which is in the visible spectrum, $n_f = 2$), and n_i is the initial principal quantum number ($n = 3, 4, 5, 6, . .$). Calculate from your experimental data the wavelength in meters and $1/\lambda$ in m^{-1}. Record your answers in the data table.

Data Table

	λ (nm)	λ (m)	$1/\lambda$ (m^{-1})
Line #1 (left)	411	4.11×10^{-7}	2.43×10^6
Line #2	435	4.35×10^{-7}	2.30×10^6
Line #3	487	4.87×10^{-7}	2.05×10^6
Line #4 (right)	657	6.57×10^{-7}	1.52×10^6

5. The formula for the determination of energy is $E = h\nu = hc/\lambda$ where h is Planck's constant and c is the speed of light. *What is the relationship between wavelength and energy?*

Energy and wavelength are inversely proportional.

6. *Of the four measured hydrogen spectrum lines recorded on the previous page, which line corresponds to the transition n = 3 to n = 2, and from n = 4 to n = 2, and so on from n = 6 to n = 2?*

   Since energy and wavelength are inversely proportional the *smallest* energy transition from 3 to

   2 would correspond to the *longest* wavelength and the *largest* energy transition from 6 to 2

   would correspond to the *shortest* wavelength.

7. Calculate the value of $\left(\dfrac{1}{n_f^2} - \dfrac{1}{n_i^2}\right)$ for the transitions $n = 6$ to $n = 2$, $n = 5$ to $n = 2$, $n = 4$ to $n = 2$ and $n = 3$ to $n = 2$. Match the values for these transitions and record them with the appropriate reciprocal wavelength in the results table.

   ### Results Table

Transition n_i to n_f	$\left(\dfrac{1}{n_f^2} - \dfrac{1}{n_i^2}\right)$	$1/\lambda \ (\text{m}^{-1})$
6 to 2	0.2222	2.43×10^6
5 to 2	0.2100	2.30×10^6
4 to 2	0.1875	2.05×10^6
3 to 2	0.1388	1.52×10^6

8. The Rydberg equation, $\dfrac{1}{\lambda} = R_H\left(\dfrac{1}{n_f^2} - \dfrac{1}{n_i^2}\right)$, is in the form of $y = mx + b$ where $1/\lambda$ corresponds to y,

   $\left(\dfrac{1}{n_f^2} - \dfrac{1}{n_i^2}\right)$ corresponds to x, and $b = 0$. If you plot $1/\lambda$ on the y-axis and $\left(\dfrac{1}{n_f^2} - \dfrac{1}{n_i^2}\right)$ on the x-axis, the resulting slope will be the Rydberg constant, R_H.

   Using a spreadsheet program or a piece of graph paper, plot your experimental data and determine

   the value of the Rydberg constant. **Experimental value for Rydberg constant is $1.09 \times 10^7 \ \text{m}^{-1}$.**

9. The accepted value for R_H is $1.0974 \times 10^7 \ \text{m}^{-1}$.

   Determine the % error using the formula:

   $$\% \ Error = \frac{\left|your \ answer - accepted \ answer\right|}{accepted \ answer} \times 100$$

   % Error = **0.67%.**

1-8: Atomic Emission Spectra

When a sample of gas is excited by applying a large alternating electric field, the gas emits light at certain discrete wavelengths. The intensity and wavelength of the light that is emitted is called the atomic emission spectrum and is unique for each gas. In this assignment, you will measure the emission spectra for several gases and then make some observations about the differences in their spectra.

1. Start *Virtual ChemLab* and select *Atomic Emission Spectra* from the list of assignments. The lab will open in the Quantum laboratory. The *Spectrometer* will be on the right of the lab table. The hydrogen emission spectra will be in the detector window in the upper right corner as a graph of Intensity vs. wavelength (λ).

2. *How many distinct lines do you see and what are their colors?* **four: violet, blue, aqua (blue-**

   green), red

3. Click on the *Visible/Full* switch to magnify only the visible spectrum. You will see four peaks in the spectrum. If you drag your cursor over a peak, it will identify the wavelength (in nm) in the *x*-coordinate field in the bottom right corner of the detector window. Record the wavelengths of the four peaks in the visible hydrogen spectrum in the data table. (Round to whole numbers.)

4. The wavelength of each line can also be described in terms of its frequency. Use the wavelength of each line to calculate its frequency given that $v = c/\lambda$ where $c = 2.998 \times 10^{17}$ nm·s^{-1} (2.998×10^{8} m·s^{-1}). The energy (E) of a single quantum of light emitted by an atom is related to its frequency (v) by the equation $E = hv$ where $h = 6.626 \times 10^{-34}$ J·s. Calculate the frequency of each line and the corresponding energy and record your results in the data Table.

Data Table

	λ (nm)	v (1/s)	Energy (J)
Line #1 (left)	410	7.32×10^{14}	4.85×10^{-19}
Line #2	434	6.91×10^{14}	4.58×10^{-19}
Line #3	487	6.16×10^{14}	4.08×10^{-19}
Line #4 (right)	656	4.57×10^{14}	3.03×10^{-19}

5. Now, investigate the emission spectra for a different element, helium. Helium is the next element after hydrogen on the periodic table and has two electrons.

   Do you think the emission spectra for an atom with two electrons instead of one will be much

   different than hydrogen? **With only one additional electron the spectrum should be similar.**

6. To exchange gas samples, double-click or click and drag the *Electric Field* and place it on the stockroom counter, and double-click or click and drag the *Gas (H₂)* sample tube and place it on the stockroom counter as well. You may have to first click on the main laboratory window in order to move the items.

7. Enter the stockroom by clicking in the *Stockroom*. Click on the *Gases* samples on the top shelf. Click on the cylinder labeled *He* to replace the H_2 in the sample tube with helium gas. If you point to the gas sample tube with the cursor it should read *He*.

8. Return to the laboratory and drag the gas sample tube off the stockroom counter and place it in the middle of the table as indicated by the spotlight. Drag the *Electric Field* and place it on the gas sample tube. Carefully click the button just above the left zero on the *Electric Field* controller and change the voltage to 300 V. Turn on the *Spectrometer* by clicking on the red/green button and click the ***Visible/Full*** switch to view only the visible spectrum.

9. *Is this spectrum different than hydrogen? How many lines are present and what are their*

   colors? **Yes, it has six lines: there are two more blue lines, an orange-yellow line and green line.**

10. *Determine the wavelength (in nm), the frequency (in 1/s) and the energy (in J) for the peak on the far right.*

	λ (nm)	v (1/s)	Energy (J)
Line (far right)	668	4.49×10^{14}	2.98×10^{-19}

1-9: Heisenberg Uncertainty Principle

It has long been known that if you shine light through narrow slits that are spaced at small intervals, the light will form a diffraction pattern. A diffraction pattern is a series of light and dark patterns caused by wave interference. The wave interference can be either constructive (light) or destructive (dark). In this experiment, you will shine a laser through a device with two slits where the spacing can be adjusted and then you will investigate the patterns that will be made at a distance from the slits.

1. Start *Virtual ChemLab* and select *Heisenberg Uncertainty Principle* from the list of assignments. The lab will open in the Quantum laboratory.

2. *What source is used in this experiment and for what reason?* **The laser is used because it provides light at a single wavelength.**

    At what wavelength is the laser set? **500 nm**

    What is the spacing of the two slits on the two-slit device? **3.0 μm**

    Sketch a small picture of the pattern displayed on the video screen.

3. Change the *Intensity* of the laser from 1 nW to 1W.

    Does the intensity of the light affect the diffraction pattern? **no**

    Change the *Slit Spacing* to 1μm. Observe the pattern displayed on the video screen as you change the slit spacing from 1 μm to 7 μm in increments of 1μm.

    What can you state about the relationship between slit spacing and diffraction pattern?

    As the slit spacing increases, the number of lines in the diffraction pattern increases.

4. Increase the *Wavelength* of the laser to 700 nm.

    What effect does an increase in the wavelength have on the diffraction pattern? **The color changes from green to red. The number of lines also changes.**

5. Decrease the *Intensity* on the laser to 1000 photons/second. Click on the ***Persist*** button on the video camera to look at individual photons coming through the slits. Observe for one minute.

    What observation can you make about this pattern compared with the pattern from the continuous beam of photons? **The pattern is the same after allowing enough photons to pass through the slits.**

    Decrease the *Intensity* to 100 photons/second. Observe for another minute after clicking ***Persist***. At these lower intensities (1000 and 100 photons/second), there is never a time when two photons pass through the slits at the same time.

    How can a single photon diffract?

    It cannot diffract. What you see as the diffraction pattern builds up over time and is really the statistic of where each individual photon will hit the screen. It is uncertain what each individual photon will do, but the properties of a large collection of photons can be easily predicted.

    Based on this experiment, what conclusions can you make about the nature of light?

    Light behaves like a particle, and the wave-nature of light is really a representation of the statistics, or uncertainty, exhibited in an experiment.

6. Click inside the *Stockroom* to enter the stockroom. Click on the clipboard and select the preset experiment *Two-Slit Diffraction – Electrons*. Click on the green *Return to Lab* arrow to return to the laboratory.

    What source is used in this experiment? **an electron gun**

    Sketch a small picture of the diffraction pattern shown on the Phosphor Screen.

    How does this diffraction pattern compare with the diffraction pattern for light? **The patterns look similar.**

Louis de Broglie was the first person to suggest that particles could be considered to have wave properties.

7. Decrease the *Intensity* to 10 electrons/second. The pattern now builds one electron at a time. Click on the ***Persist*** button and observe for one minute.

    Has the diffraction pattern changed? Why or why not? **No, even though the pattern builds up one electron at a time, collectively they still form the same diffraction pattern.**

    How can a single electron diffract? **It cannot diffract. What you see as the diffraction pattern builds up over time and is once again really the statistic of where each individual electron will hit the screen. It is uncertain what each individual electron will do, but the properties of a large collection of electrons can be predicted. Thus, electrons also appear to have wave properties.**

When you look at the complete diffraction pattern of a stream of particles, you are seeing all the places you expect particles to scatter. If you start the source over multiple times, you will see that the first particle is never detected in the same place twice. This is an application of the Heisenberg Uncertainty Principle, which is directly connected with measurement. It takes into account the minimum uncertainty of the position (Δx) and the uncertainty of the momentum (Δp) using the equation $(\Delta x)(\Delta p) \geq h/4\pi$. Because you know the energy at which the particle is traveling, you can precisely know the momentum, but you cannot know the position. Consequently, you cannot predict where each particle will hit.

1-10: Emission Spectra for Sodium and Mercury

In the 1800s, scientists found that when a sample of gas was excited by an alternating electric field, light with only certain discrete wavelengths was emitted. This property allowed for the development of spectroscopic techniques that can be used in the identification and analysis of elements and compounds. Even though scientists found spectroscopy very useful, they could not explain why the spectrum was not continuous. The explanation of this was left to Niels Bohr, a Danish physicist, who first proposed that energy levels of electrons are quantized and that excited electrons can only fall to discrete energy levels. This assignment illustrates the measurements that helped Bohr develop his original quantum model, as well as some practical uses for this science by measuring the emission spectra for mercury and sodium. Mercury vapor is used in fluorescent lights and sodium vapor is used in street lighting.

1. Start *Virtual ChemLab* and select *Emission Spectra for Sodium and Mercury* from the list of assignments. The lab will open in the Quantum laboratory. A sample of gaseous sodium is on the lab bench in a sample tube and an alternating electric field of 300 V has been applied to cause the sodium gas to emit light. A spectrometer is on the right side of the lab bench and has been turned on. You can separate the light in an emission spectrum by using an optical prism or a diffraction grating. A spectrometer is an instrument designed to separate the emitted light into its component wavelengths. The detector window shows the output from the spectrometer.

2. Click on the *Visible/Full* switch in the detector window to change the output from the spectrometer to the visible spectrum. One spectral line is much more intense than all the others.

   What is the color and wavelength (in nm) of this line? (To determine the wavelength, move the cursor over the line and read the wavelength in the *x* field at the bottom of the detector window.)

   <u>**orange: 590 nm**</u>

   Astronomers are excited about cities changing from normal incandescent streetlights to sodium vapor streetlights because astronomers can easily filter out the peak at 589 nm and minimize light pollution. Incandescent lights emit light at all wavelengths and make filtering impractical.

3. To exchange gas samples, double-click or click and drag the *Electric Field* and place it on the stockroom counter, and double-click or click and drag the *Gas (Na)* sample tube and place it on the stockroom counter as well. You may have to click on the main laboratory window in order to move the items.

4. Enter the stockroom by clicking in the *Stockroom*. Click on the *Gases* samples on the top shelf. Click on the cylinder labeled *Hg* to replace the Na in the sample tube with mercury vapor. If you point to the gas sample tube with the cursor it should read *Hg*.

5. Return to the laboratory and drag the gas sample tube off the stockroom counter and place it in the middle of the table as indicated by the spotlight. Drag the *Electric Field* and place it on the gas sample tube. Carefully click the button just above the left zero on the *Electric Field* controller and change the voltage to 300 V. Turn on the *Spectrometer* by clicking on the red/green button.

6. *How does the spectrum for mercury look different from sodium?* <u>**There are numerous spectral lines**</u>

   <u>**in the ultraviolet region and an intense blue line.**</u>

Mercury vapor is used in the fluorescent light tubes that you see at school and home. The emitted light is not very bright for just the mercury vapor, but when scientists examined the full spectrum for mercury they saw what you just observed. There is an enormous emission in the ultraviolet region (UV). This light is sometimes called black light. You may have seen it with glow-in-the-dark displays.

Scientists coat the inside of the glass tube of fluorescent light tubes with a compound that will absorb UV and emit the energy as visible light with all the colors of the visible spectrum. All colors together create white light, which is why fluorescent light tubes emit very white light.

Laundry detergents contain compounds that absorb UV light and emit visible light. These compounds allow advertisers to claim *whiter and brighter whites and colors*. If you attend an event using black light, you may have seen your white socks or white shirt "glow."

2-1: Names and Formulas of Ionic Compounds

In this problem, you will go into the virtual laboratory and make a series of ionic compounds containing the cations Ag^+, Pb^+, Ca^{2+}, Fe^{3+}, and Cu^{2+}; observe the reactions and identify the color of the compound formed; write the chemical formulas; and write the chemical name.

1. Start *Virtual ChemLab* and select *Names and Formulas of Ionic Compounds* from the list of assignments. The lab will open in the Inorganic laboratory.

2. Enter the stockroom by clicking inside the *Stockroom* window. Once inside the stockroom, drag a test tube from the box and place it on the metal test tube stand. You can then click on the bottle of Ag^+ ion solution on the shelf to add it to the test tube. Click **Done** to send the test tube back to the lab. Click on the *Return to Lab* arrow.

3. Place the test tube containing the Ag^+ solution in the metal test tube stand. Click on the **Divide** button on the bottom (with the large red arrow) four times to make four additional test tubes containing Ag^+. With one test tube in the metal stand and four others in the blue rack, click on the Na_2S bottle located on the lab bench. You will be able to observe what happens in the window at the bottom left. Record your observation in the table on the following page and write a correct chemical formula and name for the product of the reaction. If the solution remains clear, record NR, for no reaction. Drag this test tube to the red disposal bucket on the right.

4. Place a second tube from the blue rack (containing Ag^+) on the metal stand. Add Na_2SO_4. Record your observations and discard the tube. Use the next tube but add $NaCl$, and record your observations. Use the next tube but add $NaOH$, and record your observations. With the last tube add Na_2CO_3 and record your observations. When you are completely finished, click on the red disposal bucket to clear the lab.

5. Return to the stockroom and repeat steps 2-4 for Pb^{2+}, Ca^{2+}, Fe^{3+}, and Cu^{2+}. Complete the table on the following page.

    Each cell should include a description of what you observed when the reagents were mixed and a correct chemical formula and name for all solutions that turned cloudy and NR for all solutions that did not react or remained clear. Remember to include roman numerals where appropriate.

	Ag^+	Pb^{2+}	Ca^{2+}	Fe^{3+}	Cu^{2+}
Na_2S (S^{2-})	black Ag_2S silver sulfide	black PbS lead (II) sulfide	NR	black Fe_2S_3 Iron (III) sulfide	black CuS copper (II) sulfide
Na_2SO_4 (SO_4^{2-})	NR	white $PbSO_4$ lead (II) sulfate	NR	NR	NR
NaCl (Cl^-)	white AgCl silver chloride	white $PbCl_2$ lead (II) chloride	NR	NR	NR
NaOH (OH^-)	pinkish brown AgOH silver hydroxide	NR	white $Ca(OH)_2$ calcium hydroxide	red $Fe(OH)_3$ iron (III) hydroxide	blue $Cu(OH)_2$ copper (II) hydroxide
Na_2CO_3 (CO_3^{2-})	pink Ag_2CO_3 silver carbonate	white $PbCO_3$ lead (II) carbonate	white $CaCO_3$ calcium carbonate	red $Fe_2(CO_3)_3$ iron (III) carbonate	blue/white $CuCO_3$ copper (II) carbonate

2-2: Writing Balanced Precipitation Reactions

In this problem, you will go into the virtual laboratory and perform a series of precipitation reactions using Ag^+, Pb^{2+}, and Sb^{3+}. After observing the reactions, you will write the net ionic equations representing these reactions and then balance them.

1. Start *Virtual ChemLab* and select *Writing Balanced Precipitation Reactions* from the list of assignments. The lab will open in the Inorganic laboratory.

2. Enter the stockroom by clicking inside the *Stockroom* window. Once inside the stockroom, drag a test tube from the box and place it on the metal test tube stand. You can then click on the bottle of Ag^+ ion solution (it is $AgNO_3$) on the shelf to add it to the test tube. Click ***Done*** to send the test tube back to the lab. Repeat for Pb^{2+} ($Pb(NO_3)_2$ and Sb^{3+} ($Sb(OH)_3$). Click on the *Return to Lab* arrow.

3. Click on the handle at the bottom of the TV monitor. Moving your mouse over each test tube in the test-tube rack will allow you to identify it on the TV monitor. You can also click on the label at the top of each test tube in order to label the test tubes. Place the test tube containing the Ag^+ solution in the metal test tube stand. You will be able to observe what happens in the window at the bottom left. Click on the Na_2CO_3 reagent bottle to add it to the test tube in the stand.

   What color is the precipitate? Write a correct balanced net ionic equation for the reaction.

   pink: $2Ag^+$ (aq) $+$ CO_3^{2-} (aq) $=$ Ag_2CO_3 (s)

   When you have finished writing the equation and making your observations, place the test tube containing the precipitate in the red disposal bucket.

4. Place the test tube containing the Pb^{2+} solution in the metal test tube stand. Click on the $NaCl$ reagent bottle to add it to the test tube in the stand.

   What color is the precipitate? Write a correct balanced net ionic equation for this reaction.

   white: Pb^{2+} (aq) $+$ $2Cl^-$ $=$ $PbCl_2$ (s)

   When you have finished writing the equation and making your observations, place the test tube containing the precipitate in the red disposal bucket.

5. Place the test tube containing the Sb^{3+} solution in the metal test tube stand. Note that the antimony is not soluble and you will have a double displacement reaction. Click on the Na_2S reagent bottle to add it to the test tube in the stand.

   What color is the precipitate? Write a correct balanced net ionic equation for the reaction.

   orange: $2Sb(OH)_3$ (aq) $+$ $3Na_2S$ (aq) $=$ Sb_2S_3 (s) $+$ Na^+ (aq) $+$ OH^- (aq)

2-3: Strong and Weak Electrolytes

1. Start *Virtual ChemLab* and select *Strong and Weak Electrolytes* from the list of assignments. The lab will open in the Titration laboratory.

2. Enter the stockroom by clicking inside the *Stockroom* window. Once inside the stockroom, double-click or click and drag on the three reagents, *NaCl*, *Na₂CO₃* (100%), and *NaHCO₃* (100%) to move them to the stockroom counter. Click on the green *Return To Lab* arrow to return to the laboratory.

3. For each salt that was selected in the stockroom, complete the following procedure: double-click or click and drag the bottle on the stockroom counter to move it to the spotlight next to the balance. Click on the *Beakers* drawer and place a beaker in the spotlight next to the salt bottle in the balance area. Click on the *Balance* area to zoom in and open the bottle by clicking on the lid (*Remove Lid*). Drag a piece of weighing paper and drop it on the balance and then *Tare* the balance. Pick up the *Scoop* and scoop out some sample by first dragging the scoop to the mouth of the bottle and then pulling the scoop down the face of the bottle. As the scoop is dragged down the face of the bottle it will pick up different quantities of solid. Select the largest sample possible and drag the scoop to the balance and drop it on the weighing paper. This will put approximately 1 g of sample on the balance. Now drag the weighing paper with the sample and drop it in the beaker. Click on the green *Zoom Out* arrow to return to the laboratory.

   Move the beaker to the stir plate. Pick up the 25 mL graduated cylinder near the sink and hold it under the water tap until it fills. Pour the water into the beaker by dragging and dropping the cylinder on the beaker. Turn on the conductivity meter located on the lower right of the table and place the conductivity probe in the beaker and record the conductivity of the solution in the data table below. Double-click on the salt bottle to place it back on the stockroom counter. Place the beaker in the red disposal bucket. Repeat for the other two reagents.

4. When you have completed the three reagents, return to the *Stockroom*. Double-click on each bottle to return it to the shelf. Obtain three more samples (two salts and one solution): KNO₃, NH₄Cl, and NH₃ and return to the laboratory. Follow procedure #3 for NH₄Cl, and KNO₃.

   For the NH₃ solution, complete the following procedure: Place a beaker on the stir plate. Pick up the NH₃ solution from the stockroom shelf, drag it to the 25 mL graduated cylinder, and let go to fill the cylinder. The solution bottle will automatically go back to the stockroom shelf. Drag the 25 mL graduated cylinder to the beaker on the stir plate and drop it to transfer the solution into the beaker. Place the conductivity meter probe in the beaker and record the conductivity in the data table.

5. When you have completed the three reagents, return to the *Stockroom*. Double-click on each bottle to return it to the shelf. Obtain two more samples: *HCl* and *HCN*. Measure the conductivity of each solution following procedure #4 and record the conductivity in the data table.

Data Table

NaCl	Na₂CO₃	NaHCO₃	KNO₃
42.60	69.00	33.44	37.23
NH₄Cl	NH₃	HCl	HCN
57.70	0.84	39.29	0.01

6. Electrolytes are compounds that conduct electricity in aqueous solutions. *Which compounds in your table are electrolytes? Which are not electrolytes?* **electrolytes: NaCl, Na$_2$CO$_3$, NaHCO$_3$, KNO$_3$, NH$_4$Cl, HCl; non-electrolytes: NH$_3$, HCN**

7. *Would any of these electrolytes conduct electricity in the solid form? Explain.* **No, in order to conduct electricity there must be *mobile* charges. Charges cannot be mobile in the solid form.**

8. *Are these ionic or covalent compounds? Classify each compound in the grid as ionic or covalent. For a compound to be an electrolyte, what must happen when it dissolves in water?* **ionic: NaCl, Na$_2$CO$_3$, NaHCO$_3$, KNO$_3$, NH$_4$Cl, HCl; covalent: NH$_3$, HCN; When dissolved in water the compound must ionize and have positive and negative ions.**

9. When an ionic solid dissolves in water, water molecules attract the ions causing them to dissociate or come apart. The resulting dissolved ions are electrically charged particles that allow the solution to conduct electricity. The following chemical equations represent this phenomenon:

$$NaCl\,(s)\ =\ Na^+\,(aq)\ +\ Cl^-\,(aq)$$
$$Na_2CO_3\,(s)\ =\ 2Na^+\,(aq)\ +\ CO_3^{2-}\,(aq)$$

Write a similar balanced chemical equation for each electrolyte in the data table.

$$NaHCO_3\,(s)\ =\ Na^+\,(aq)\ +\ HCO_3^-\,(aq)$$
$$KNO_3\,(s)\ =\ K^+\,(aq)\ +\ NO_3^-\,(aq)$$
$$NH_4Cl\,(aq)\ =\ NH_4^+\,(aq)\ +\ Cl^-\,(aq)$$
$$HCl\,(aq)\ =\ H^+\,(aq)\ +\ Cl^-\,(aq)$$

10. *After examining the chemical reactions for the electrolytes, why does Na$_2$CO$_3$ have a higher conductivity than all of the other electrolytes?* **All of the electrolytes except Na$_2$CO$_3$ ionize into two ions while Na$_2$CO$_3$ ionizes into three. Since there are more ions, there is higher conductivity.**

2-4: Precipitation Reactions

1. Start *Virtual ChemLab* and select *Precipitation Reactions* from the list of assignments. The lab will open in the Inorganic laboratory.

2. React each of the cations (across the top) with each of the anions (down the left) according to the data table using the following procedures:

Data Table

	AgNO$_3$ (Ag$^+$)	Pb(NO)$_3$ (Pb^{2+})	Ca(NO$_3$)$_2$ (Ca^{2+})
Na$_2$CO$_3$ (CO$_3^{2-}$)	*a* pink	*f* white	*k* white
Na$_2$S (S^{2-})	*b* black	*g* black	*l* NR
NaOH (OH$^-$)	*c* dark pink/brown	*h* NR	*m* white
Na$_2$SO$_4$ (SO$_4^{2-}$)	*d* NR	*i* white	*n* NR
NaCl (Cl$^-$)	*e* white	*j* white	*o* NR

a. Enter the stockroom by clicking inside the *Stockroom* window. Once inside the stockroom, drag a test tube from the box and place it on the metal test tube stand. You can then click on the bottle of *Ag$^+$* ion solution on the shelf to add it to the test tube. Click **Done** to send the test tube back to the lab. Click on the *Return to Lab* arrow.

b. Place the test tube containing the *Ag$^+$* solution in the metal test tube stand. Click on the **Divide** button on the bottom (with the large red arrow) four times to make four additional test tubes containing *Ag$^+$*. With one test tube in the metal stand and four others in the blue rack, click on the Na$_2$CO$_3$ bottle on the reagent shelf and observe what happens in the window at the bottom left. Record your observation in the table above. If the solution remains clear, record NR for no reaction. Drag this test tube to the red disposal bucket on the right.

c. Drag a second tube from the blue rack to the metal stand. Add Na$_2$S, record your observations and discard the tube. Continue with the third, fourth and fifth tube, but add NaOH, Na$_2$SO$_4$, and NaCl respectively. Record your observations and discard the tubes. When you are finished, click on the red disposal bucket to clear the lab.

d. Return to the stockroom and repeat steps a-c for five test tubes of Pb^{2+} and Ca^{2+}. Record your observations in the data table. If no precipitate forms write NR for no reaction.

3. *What happens in grid space d? What other reactions give similar results? Is it necessary to write an equation when no reaction occurs? Explain.* **There is no reaction (NR), as is the same for *h, l, n,* and *o*. It is not necessary to write an equation because there is no precipitate since all ions are soluble.**

4. *Write balanced equations for all precipitation reactions you observed.*

    a. **AgNO$_3$ + Na$_2$CO$_3$ = NaNO$_3$ + AgCO$_3$**

b. $AgNO_3 + Na_2S = NaNO_3 + Ag_2S$

c. $AgNO_3 + NaOH = NaNO_3 + AgOH$

e. $AgNO_3 + NaCl = NaNO_3 + AgCl$

f. $Pb(NO_3)_2 + Na_2CO_3 = NaNO_3 + PbCO_3$

g. $Pb(NO_3)_2 + Na_2S = NaNO_3 + PbS$

i. $Pb(NO_3)_2 + Na_2SO_4 = NaNO_3 + PbSO_4$

j. $Pb(NO_3)_2 + NaCl = NaNO_3 + PbCl_2$

k. $Ca(NO_3)_2 + Na_2CO_3 = NaNO_3 + CaCO_3$

m. $Ca(NO_3)_2 + NaOH = NaNO_3 + Ca(OH)_2$

5. *Write balanced net ionic equations for all precipitation reactions you observed.*

a. $Ag^+ (aq) + CO_3^{2-} (aq) = AgCO_3 (s)$

b. $Ag^+ (aq) + S^{2-} (aq) = Ag_2S (s)$

c. $Ag^+ (aq) + OH^- (aq) = AgOH (s)$

e. $Ag^+ (aq) + Cl^- (aq) = AgCl (s)$

f. $Pb^{2+} (aq) + CO_3^{2-} (aq) = PbCO_3 (s)$

g. $Pb^{2+} (aq) + S^{2-} (aq) = PbS (s)$

i. $Pb^{2+} (aq) + SO_4^{2-} (aq) = PbSO_4 (s)$

j. $Pb^{2+} (aq) + Cl^- (aq) = PbCl_2 (s)$

k. $Ca^{2+} (aq) + CO_3^{2-} (aq) = CaCO_3 (s)$

m. $Ca^{2+} (aq) + OH^- (aq) = Ca(OH)_2 (s)$

2-5: Counting Atoms

1. Start *Virtual ChemLab* and select *Counting Atoms and Molecules* from the list of assignments. The lab will open in the Calorimetry laboratory.

2. Enter the stockroom by clicking inside the *Stockroom* window. Once inside the stockroom, click on the *Metals* cabinet and then open the top drawer by clicking on it. When you open the drawer, a Petri dish will appear on the counter next to the cabinet. Place the sample of gold (Au) found in the drawer into the sample dish by double-clicking on the sample or by clicking and dragging it to the dish. Return to the stockroom view by clicking on the green *Zoom Out* arrow. Place the Petri dish on the stockroom counter by double-clicking on it or by clicking and dragging it to the counter. Click on the *Return to Lab* arrow to return to the laboratory.

3. Drag the Petri dish to the spotlight near the balance. Click on the *Balance* area to zoom in. Drag a piece of weighing paper to the balance pan, *Tare* the balance, and then drag the gold sample to the balance pan and record the mass.

    Mass = 59.9341 g Au (*Answers will vary slightly.*)

4. *Calculate the moles of Au contained in the sample.*

$$59.9341 \text{ g Au} \cdot \frac{1 \text{ mol Au}}{196.97 \text{ g Au}} = 0.30428 \text{ mol Au}$$

5. *Calculate the atoms of Au contained in the sample.*

$$0.30428 \text{ mol Au} \cdot \frac{6.022 \times 10^{22} \text{ atoms Au}}{1 \text{ mol Au}} = 1.83 \times 10^{23} \text{ atoms Au}$$

2-6: Counting Atoms

1. Start *Virtual ChemLab* and select *Counting Atoms and Molecules* from the list of assignments. The lab will open in the Calorimetry laboratory.

2. Enter the stockroom by clicking inside the *Stockroom* window. Once inside the stockroom, click on the *Metals* cabinet and then open the third drawer by clicking on it. When you open the drawer, a Petri dish will appear on the counter next to the cabinet. Place the sample of lead (Pb) found in the drawer into the sample dish by double-clicking on the sample or by clicking and dragging it to the dish. Return to the stockroom view by clicking on the green *Zoom Out* arrow. Place the Petri dish on the stockroom counter by double-clicking on it or by clicking and dragging it to the counter. Click on the *Return to Lab* arrow to return to the laboratory.

3. Drag the Petri dish to the spotlight near the balance. Click on the *Balance* area to zoom in. Drag a piece of weighing paper to the balance pan, **Tare** the balance, and then drag the lead sample to the balance pan and record the mass.

    Mass = 31.9812 g Pb (Answers will vary slightly)

4. *Calculate the moles of Pb contained in the sample.*

$$31.9812 \text{ g Pb} \cdot \frac{1 \text{ mol Pb}}{207.20 \text{ g Pb}} = 0.1543 \text{ mol Pb}$$

5. *Calculate the atoms of Pb contained in the sample.*

$$0.1543 \text{ mol Pb} \cdot \frac{6.022 \times 10^{23} \text{ atoms Pb}}{1 \text{ mol Pb}} = 9.29 \times 10^{22} \text{ atoms Pb}$$

6. Repeat steps 2-5 for uranium. Record the mass, the moles, and the atoms of uranium.

    Mass of uranium = **51.9042 g** *(Answers will vary slightly)*
    Moles of uranium = **0.2181 mol**
    Atoms of uranium = **1.31×10^{23} atoms**

2-7: Counting Atoms

1. Start *Virtual ChemLab* and select *Counting Atoms and Molecules* from the list of assignments. The lab will open in the Calorimetry laboratory.

2. Enter the stockroom by clicking inside the *Stockroom* window. Once inside the stockroom, click on the *Metals* cabinet and then open the first drawer by clicking on it. When you open the drawer, a Petri dish will appear on the counter next to the cabinet. Place the sample of erbium (Er) found in the drawer into the sample dish by double-clicking on the sample or by clicking and dragging it to the dish. Return to the stockroom view by clicking on the green *Zoom Out* arrow. Place the Petri dish on the stockroom counter by double-clicking on it or by clicking and dragging it to the counter. Click on the *Return to Lab* arrow to return to the laboratory.

3. Drag the Petri dish to the spotlight near the balance. Click on the *Balance* area to zoom in. Drag a piece of weighing paper to the balance pan, *Tare* the balance, and then drag the erbium sample to the balance pan and record the mass in the data and results table.

4. *Calculate the moles and the atoms of erbium and enter the results in the data and results table below.*

5. Repeat steps 2-4 for sodium, tungsten, and a metal of your choice.

Data and Results Table

	erbium (Er)	sodium (Na)	tungsten (W)	your choice
Mass (grams)	25.8016	2.7779	52.8043	
Molar Mass (g/mol)	167.26	22.99	183.84	
Moles of each element	0.1543	0.1208	0.28723	
Atoms of each element	9.29×10^{22}	7.27×10^{22}	1.73×10^{23}	

2-8: Counting Molecules

1. Start *Virtual ChemLab* and select *Counting Atoms and Molecules* from the list of assignments. The lab will open in the Calorimetry laboratory.

2. Enter the stockroom by clicking inside the *Stockroom* window. Once inside the stockroom, click on the sodium chloride (NaCl) bottle located on the Salts shelf and drag it to the stockroom counter. You can also double click on the bottle to move it to the counter, while the left and right blue arrow keys can be used to see additional bottles. Click on the *Return to Lab* arrow to return to the laboratory.

3. Drag the bottle to the spotlight near the balance, and click on the *Balance* area to zoom in. Drag a piece of weighing paper to the balance pan and then **Tare** the balance so the balance reads 0.0000 g. Click on the bottle lid (*Remove Lid*) to remove the lid.

4. Pick up the *Scoop* and scoop out some sample by first dragging the scoop to the mouth of the bottle and then pulling the scoop down the face of the bottle. As the scoop is dragged down the face of the bottle it will pickup different quantities of solid. Select the largest sample possible and drag the scoop to the weighing paper on the balance until it snaps in place and then let go. This will put approximately 1 g of sample on the balance.

   Record the mass of the sample.   **_Mass_ = 0.9992 g NaCl**

5. *Calculate the moles of NaCl contained in the sample.*

$$0.9992 \text{ g NaCl} \cdot \frac{1 \text{ mol NaCl}}{58.442 \text{ g NaCl}} = 0.0342 \text{ mol NaCl}$$

6. *Calculate the moles of each element in NaCl.* **0.0342 mol Na, 0.0342 mol Cl**

7. *Calculate the number of atoms for each element in NaCl.* **2.06×10^{22} atoms Na;**

   2.06×10^{22} atoms Cl

2-9: Counting Molecules

1. Start *Virtual ChemLab* and select *Counting Atoms and Molecules* from the list of assignments. The lab will open in the Calorimetry laboratory.

2. Enter the stockroom by clicking inside the *Stockroom* window. Once inside the stockroom, click on the bottle containing table sugar (sucrose, $C_{12}H_{22}O_{11}$) located on the Organics shelf and drag it to the stockroom counter. You can also double click on the bottle to move it to the counter, while the left and right blue arrow keys can be used to see additional bottles. Click on the *Return to Lab* arrow to return to the laboratory.

3. Drag the bottle to the spotlight near the balance, and click on the *Balance* area to zoom in. Drag a piece of weighing paper to the balance pan and then **Tare** the balance so the balance reads 0.0000 g. Click on the bottle lid (*Remove Lid*) to remove the lid.

4. Pick up the *Scoop* and scoop out some sample by first dragging the scoop to the mouth of the bottle and then pulling the scoop down the face of the bottle. As the scoop is dragged down the face of the bottle it will pickup different quantities of solid. Select the largest sample possible and drag the scoop to the weighing paper on the balance until it snaps in place and then let go. This will put approximately 1 g of sample on the balance. Record the mass of the sample in the data and results table on the following page.

5. Repeat steps 2-4 for NH_4Cl (ammonium chloride) located on the Salts shelf and record the mass in the Data and Results Table.

6. *Calculate the moles of $C_{12}H_{22}O_{11}$ contained in the first sample and record your results in the data and results table.*

$$0.9992 \text{ g } C_{12}H_{22}O_{11} \cdot \frac{1 \text{ mol } C_{12}H_{22}O_{11}}{342.3 \text{ g } C_{12}H_{22}O_{11}} = 0.002919 \text{ mol } C_{12}H_{22}O_{11}$$

7. *Calculate the moles of each element in $C_{12}H_{22}O_{11}$ and record your results in the data and results table.*

$$0.002912 \text{ mol } C_{12}H_{22}O_{11} \cdot \frac{12 \text{ mol C}}{1 \text{ mol } C_{12}H_{22}O_{11}} = 0.03494 \text{ mol C}$$

$$0.002912 \text{ mol } C_{12}H_{22}O_{11} \cdot \frac{22 \text{ mol H}}{1 \text{ mol } C_{12}H_{22}O_{11}} = 0.06406 \text{ mol H}$$

$$0.002912 \text{ mol } C_{12}H_{22}O_{11} \cdot \frac{11 \text{ mol O}}{1 \text{ mol } C_{12}H_{22}O_{11}} = 0.03203 \text{ mol O}$$

8. *Calculate the number of atoms of each element in $C_{12}H_{22}O_{11}$ and record your results in the data and results table.*

$$0.03494 \text{ mol C} \cdot \frac{6.022 \times 10^{23} \text{atoms C}}{1 \text{ mol C}} = 2.104 \times 10^{22} \text{atoms C}$$

$$0.06406 \text{ mol H} \cdot \frac{6.022 \times 10^{23} \text{atoms H}}{1 \text{ mol H}} = 3.858 \times 10^{22} \text{atoms H}$$

$$0.03203 \text{ mol O} \cdot \frac{6.022 \times 10^{23} \text{atoms O}}{1 \text{ mol O}} = 1.929 \times 10^{22} \text{atoms O}$$

9. Repeat steps 6-8 for NH_4Cl and record your results in the data and results table.

10. *Which of the compounds contains the most total number of atoms?* __$C_{12}H_{22}O_{11}$__

Data and Results Table

	$C_{12}H_{22}O_{11}$	NH_4Cl
Mass (grams)	0.9992	1.1676
Molar Mass (g/mol)	342.3	53.5
Moles of compound	0.002919	0.0218
Moles of each element	C: 0.03494 H: 0.06406 O: 0.03203	N: 0.0218 H: 0.0873 Cl: 0.0218
Atoms of each element	C: 2.10×10^{22} H: 3.86×10^{22} O: 1.93×10^{22}	N: 1.31×10^{22} H: 5.26×10^{22} Cl: 1.31×10^{22}

2-10: Counting Protons, Neutrons, and Electrons

1. Start *Virtual ChemLab* and select *Counting Protons, Neutrons, and Electrons* from the list of assignments. The lab will open in the Calorimetry laboratory.

2. Enter the stockroom by clicking inside the *Stockroom* window. Once inside the stockroom, click on the *Metals* cabinet and then open the third drawer by clicking on it. When you open the drawer, a Petri dish will appear on the counter next to the cabinet. Place the sample of scandium (Sc) found in the drawer into the sample dish by double-clicking on the sample or by clicking and dragging it to the dish. Return to the stockroom view by clicking on the green *Zoom Out* arrow. Place the Petri dish on the stockroom counter by double-clicking on it or by clicking and dragging it to the counter. Click on the *Return to Lab* arrow to return to the laboratory.

3. Drag the Petri dish to the spotlight near the balance. Click on the *Balance* area to zoom in. Drag a piece of weighing paper to the balance pan, *Tare* the balance and drag the scandium sample to the balance pan.

   Record the mass of the sample. <u>**Mass = 8.0377 g Sc (Answers will vary slightly)**</u>

4. *Calculate the moles of Sc contained in the sample.*

$$8.0377 \text{ g Sc} \cdot \frac{1 \text{ mol Sc}}{44.9559 \text{ g Sc}} = 0.17879 \text{ mol Sc}$$

5. *Calculate the atoms of Sc contained in the sample.*

$$0.17879 \text{ mol Sc} \cdot \frac{6.022 \times 10^{23} \text{ atoms Sc}}{1 \text{ mol Sc}} = 1.08 \times 10^{23} \text{ atoms Sc}$$

6. ^{45}Sc is the only naturally occurring isotope of scandium.

   How many protons, neutrons and electrons are there in one atom of ^{45}Sc? <u>**There are 21 protons, 24**</u>

   <u>**neutrons, and 21 electrons.**</u>

7. *Calculate the number of protons, neutrons, and electrons in the sample of scandium that you weighed if it is 100% ^{45}Sc.*

$$1.08 \times 10^{23} \text{ atoms Sc} \left(\frac{21 \text{ protons}}{1 \text{ atom Sc}} \right) = 2.27 \times 10^{24} \text{ protons}$$

$$1.08 \times 10^{23} \text{ atoms } Sc \left(\frac{24 \text{ neutrons}}{1 \text{ atom } Sc} \right) = 2.59 \times 10^{24} \text{ neutrons}$$

$$1.08 \times 10^{23} \text{ atoms } Sc \left(\frac{21 \text{ electrons}}{1 \text{ atom } Sc} \right) = 2.27 \times 10^{24} \text{ electrons}$$

2-11: Counting Protons, Neutrons, and Electrons

1. Start *Virtual ChemLab* and select *Counting Protons, Neutrons, and Electrons* from the list of assignments. The lab will open in the Calorimetry laboratory.

2. Enter the stockroom by clicking inside the *Stockroom* window. Once inside the stockroom, click on the *Metals* cabinet and then open the top drawer by clicking on it. When you open the drawer, a Petri dish will appear on the counter next to the cabinet. Place the sample of bismuth (Bi) found in the drawer into the sample dish by double-clicking on the sample or by clicking and dragging it to the dish. Return to the stockroom view by clicking on the green *Zoom Out* arrow. Place the Petri dish on the stockroom counter by double-clicking on it or by clicking and dragging it to the counter. Click on the *Return to Lab* arrow to return to the laboratory.

3. Drag the Petri dish to the spotlight near the balance. Click on the *Balance* area to zoom in. Drag a piece of weighing paper to the balance pan, *Tare* the balance and drag the bismuth sample to the balance pan.

   Record the mass of the sample. *Mass = 30.1509 g Bi (Answers will vary slightly.)*

4. *Calculate the moles of Bi contained in the sample.*

$$30.1509 \text{ g Bi} \cdot \frac{1 \text{ mol Bi}}{208.9804 \text{ g Bi}} = 0.14427 \text{ mol Bi}$$

5. *Calculate the atoms of Bi contained in the sample.*

$$0.14427 \text{ mol Bi} \cdot \frac{6.022 \times 10^{23} \text{ atoms Bi}}{1 \text{ mol Bi}} = 8.69 \times 10^{22} \text{ atoms Bi}$$

6. ^{209}Bi is the only naturally occurring isotope of bismuth.

   How many protons, neutrons and electrons are there in one atom of ^{209}Bi? **There are 83 protons, 126 neutrons, and 83 electrons.**

7. *How many protons, neutrons and electrons are there in one ion of* $^{209}Bi^{5+}$? **There are 83 protons, 126 neutrons, and 78 electrons.**

8. *Calculate the number of protons, neutrons, and electrons in a sample of* $^{209}Bi^{5+}$ *that has the same mass as the bismuth sample you weighed.*

$$8.69 \times 10^{22} \text{ ions } ^{209}\text{Bi}^{5+} \left(\frac{83 \text{ protons}}{1 \text{ ion } ^{209}\text{Bi}^{5+}} \right) = 7.21 \times 10^{24} \text{ protons}$$

$$8.69 \times 10^{22} \text{ ions } ^{209}\text{Bi}^{5+} \left(\frac{126 \text{ neutrons}}{1 \text{ ion } ^{209}\text{Bi}^{5+}} \right) = 1.09 \times 10^{25} \text{ neutrons}$$

$$8.69 \times 102 \text{ ions } ^{209}\text{Bi}^{5+} \left(\frac{78 \text{ electrons}}{1 \text{ ion } ^{209}\text{Bi}^{5+}} \right) = 6.78 \times 10^{24} \text{ electrons}$$

2-12: Creating a Solution of Known Molality

In this assignment, you will weigh out a sample of solid NH_4Cl and create a solution of known molality.

1. Start *Virtual ChemLab* and select *Creating a Solution of Known Molality* from the list of assignments. The lab will open in the Titration laboratory.

2. In the laboratory, a bottle of ammonium chloride (NH_4Cl) will be next to the balance and an empty beaker will be on the stir plate. Drag the beaker to the spotlight next to the balance, and click in the balance area to zoom in. Place the beaker on the balance and tare the balance. Click on the green *Zoom Out* arrow to return to the laboratory.

3. Drag the beaker to the sink and fill it with water until the beaker is approximately one-quarter full. Return the beaker to the balance and click in the *Balance* area to zoom in. Record the mass of the water in the data table. Drag the beaker off the balance to the spotlight on the right.

4. Place a weigh paper on the balance and tare the balance. Open the bottle by clicking on the lid (*Remove Lid*). Pick up the *Scoop* and scoop out some sample by first dragging the scoop to the mouth of the bottle and then pulling the scoop down the face of the bottle. As the scoop is dragged down the face of the bottle it will pickup different quantities of solid. Select the largest sample possible and drag the scoop to the weighing paper on the balance until it snaps in place and then let go. This will put approximately 1 g of sample on the balance. Repeat with a second *Scoop*. Record the mass of the NH_4Cl in the data table.

5. Drag the weigh paper to the beaker of water and add the NH_4Cl sample to the water to make an aqueous solution of NH_4Cl.

6. *Determine the kilograms of solvent (water) in the beaker and record the data in the data table.*

7. *Determine the moles of NH_4Cl in the sample and record the data in the data table.*

Data Table

mass NH_4Cl	1.9395 g
moles NH_4Cl	0.03625 mol
mass water	74.7007 g
kg water	0.0747007 kg

8. The molality is calculated using the formula:

$$molality = \frac{moles\ solute}{kg\ solvent} = \frac{mass\ solute / molar\ mass\ solute}{kg\ solvent}$$

Calculate the molality of the NH$_4$Cl solution in units of mol/kg.

$$\text{molality} = \frac{0.03625 \text{ mol}}{0.0747007 \text{ kg}} = 0.0485 \text{ m}$$

OR

$$\text{molality} = \frac{1.9395 \text{ g} \Big/ 53.5 \text{ g/mol}}{0.0747007 \text{ kg}} = 0.0485 \text{ m}$$

2-13: Creating a Solution of Known Molarity

In this assignment, you will weigh out a sample of baking soda ($NaHCO_3$) and create a solution of known molarity.

1. Start *Virtual ChemLab* and select *Creating a Solution of Known Molarity* from the list of assignments. The lab will open in the Titration laboratory.

2. In the laboratory, a bottle of baking soda (sodium bicarbonate, $NaHCO_3$) will be next to the balance, and an empty beaker will be on the stir plate. Drag the empty beaker to the spotlight next to the balance, click in the *Balance* area to zoom in, place a weigh paper on the balance, and tare the balance.

3. Open the bottle by clicking on the lid (*Remove Lid*). Pick up the *Scoop* and scoop out some sample by first dragging the scoop to the mouth of the bottle and then pulling the scoop down the face of the bottle. As the scoop is dragged down the face of the bottle it will pickup different quantities of solid. Select the largest sample possible and drag the scoop to the weighing paper on the balance until it snaps in place and then let go. This will put approximately 1 g of sample on the balance. Repeat with a second *Scoop*. Record the mass of the $NaHCO_3$ in the data table.

4. Drag the weigh paper to the beaker and add the $NaHCO_3$ sample to the beaker. Click on the green *Zoom Out* arrow to return to the laboratory.

5. Drag the beaker to the 50 mL graduated cylinder (the largest one) by the sink and empty the sample into the cylinder. Hold the cylinder under the tap until it fills with water to make an aqueous solution of $NaHCO_3$. (When the graduated cylinder is full it will automatically snap back into place.) Note that the solid is added and dissolved before the volume is measured when making a molar solution. Chemists normally use a volumetric flask for making molar solutions, but this is not available in the simulation.

6. *Determine the liters of solution in the cylinder and record the data in the data table.*

7. *Determine the moles of NaHCO₃ in the sample and record the data in the data table.*

Data Table

mass $NaHCO_3$	1.9733 g
moles $NaHCO_3$	0.02349 mol
liters solution	0.050 L

8. The molarity is calculated using the formula:

$$\text{molarity} = \frac{\text{moles solute}}{\text{L solution}} = \frac{\text{mass solute}/\text{molar mass solute}}{\text{L solution}}$$

Calculate the molarity of the NaHCO$_3$ solution in units of mol/L.

$$molarity = \frac{0.02349 \, mol}{0.050 \, L} = 0.4698 \, M$$

OR

$$molarity = \frac{1.9733 \, g \Big/ 84 \, g/mol}{0.050 \, L} = 0.4698 \, M$$

2-14: Converting Concentrations to Different Units

Occasionally, when making solutions in the laboratory, it is convenient to make a solution with a certain concentration unit, such as molarity, and then convert the concentration to a different unit. In this assignment, you will make a sodium bicarbonate (baking soda) solution of a certain molarity and then convert that concentration to molality, mass percent, and mole fraction.

1. Start *Virtual ChemLab* and select *Converting Concentrations to Different Units* from the list of assignments. The lab will open in the Titration laboratory.

2. In the laboratory, a bottle of baking soda (sodium bicarbonate, $NaHCO_3$) will be next to the balance, and an empty beaker will be on the stir plate. Drag the empty beaker to the spotlight next to the balance, click in the *Balance* area to zoom in, place a weigh paper on the balance, and tare the balance.

3. Open the bottle by clicking on the lid (*Remove Lid*). Pick up the *Scoop* and scoop out some sample by first dragging the scoop to the mouth of the bottle and then pulling the scoop down the face of the bottle. As the scoop is dragged down the face of the bottle, it will pick up different quantities of solid. Select the largest sample possible and drag the scoop to the weighing paper on the balance until it snaps in place and then let go. This will put approximately 1 g of sample on the balance. Repeat this process six additional times so there is approximately 7.0 g of sample. Record the mass of the $NaHCO_3$ in the data table.

4. Drag the weigh paper to the beaker and add the $NaHCO_3$ sample to the beaker. Click on the green *Zoom Out* arrow to return to the laboratory.

5. Drag the beaker to the 50 mL graduated cylinder (the largest one) by the sink and empty the sample into the cylinder. Hold the cylinder under the tap until it fills with water to make an aqueous solution of $NaHCO_3$. (When the graduated cylinder is full, it will automatically snap back into place.) Note that the solid is added and dissolved before the volume is measured when making a molar solution. Chemists normally use a volumetric flask for making molar solutions, but this is not available in the simulation. Record the volume of the solution, in L, in the data table.

6. *Calculate the moles of $NaHCO_3$ in the sample and record the data in the data table.*

Data Table

mass $NaHCO_3$	7.0000 g
moles $NaHCO_3$	0.08333 mol
liters $NaHCO_3$	0.050 L

7. The molarity is calculated using the formula:

$$\text{molarity} = \frac{\text{moles solute}}{\text{L solution}} = \frac{\text{mass solute}\big/\text{molar mass solute}}{\text{L solution}}$$

Calculate the molarity of the $NaHCO_3$ solution in units of mol/L.

$$\text{molarity} = \frac{0.08333 \text{ mol}}{0.050 \text{ L}} = 1.66 \text{ M}$$

OR

$$\text{molarity} = \frac{7.0000 \text{ g}\Big/84 \text{ g/mol}}{0.050 \text{ L}} = 1.66 \text{ M}$$

8. *If the density of the solution is 1.047 g/mL, calculate the molality of the solution in units of mol/kg.*

$$50 \text{ mL solution} \left(\frac{1.047 \text{ g}}{1 \text{ mL}} \right) = 52.35 \text{ g solution}$$

52.35 g solution - 7.0000 g sodium bicarbonate = 45.35 g water

$$\text{molality} = \frac{\text{mass solute}\Big/\text{molar mass solute}}{\text{kg solvent}} = \frac{7.0000 \text{ g sodium bicarbonate}\Big/84 \text{ g/mol}}{0.04535 \text{ kg water}} = 1.84 \text{ m}$$

9. *Calculate the mass percent of sodium bicarbonate in the solution.*

$$\text{mass\% } NaCO_3 = \frac{\text{mass sodium bicarbonate}}{\text{total mass}} \times 100 = \frac{7.0000 \text{ g sodium bicarbonate}}{52.35 \text{ g solution}} \times 100 = 13.37\%$$

10. *Calculate the mole fraction of sodium bicarbonate in the solution.*

$$7.0000 \text{ g sodium bicarbonate} \left(\frac{1 \text{ mol sodium bicarbonate}}{84 \text{ g sodium bicarbonate}} \right) = 0.08333 \text{ mol sodium bicarbonate}$$

$$45.35 \text{ g water} \left(\frac{1 \text{ mol water}}{18 \text{ g water}} \right) = 2.519 \text{ mol water}$$

total moles = 0.08333 mol sodium bicarbonate + 2.519 mol water = 2.603 mol

$$x_{NaHCO_3} = \frac{0.08333 \text{ mol sodium bicarbonate}}{2.603 \text{ mol total}} = 0.03201$$

3-1: Endothermic vs. Exothermic

In various chemical processes such as reactions and the dissolving of salts, heat is either absorbed or given off. We call these events either an endothermic (heat in) or exothermic (heat out) process. It is usual to detect these heat events by measuring the temperature change associated with the process. In this problem, you will dissolve several salts in water, measure the resulting temperature change, and then make deductions about the nature of the process.

1. Start *Virtual ChemLab* and select *Endothermic vs. Exothermic* from the list of assignments. The lab will open in the Calorimetry laboratory.

2. There will be a bottle of sodium chloride (NaCl) on the lab bench. A weigh paper will be on the balance with approximately 2 g of NaCl on the paper.

3. The calorimeter will be on the lab bench and filled with 100 mL water. Click the *Lab Book* to open it. Make certain the stirrer is *On* (you should be able to see the shaft rotating). In the thermometer window click *Save* to begin recording data. Allow 20-30 seconds to obtain a baseline temperature of the water.

4. Drag the weigh paper with the sample to the calorimeter until it snaps into place and then pour the sample into the calorimeter. Observe the change in temperature until it reaches a maximum and then record data for an additional 20-30 seconds. Click *Stop*. (You can click on the clock on the wall labeled *Accelerate* to accelerate the time in the laboratory.) A blue data link will appear in the lab book. Click the data link and record the temperature before adding the NaCl and the *highest* or *lowest* temperature after adding the NaCl in the data table.

5. Click the red disposal bucket to clear the lab. Click on the Stockroom to enter. Click on the clipboard and select Preset Experiment #7 and repeat the experiment with $NaNO_3$. Record the initial and final temperatures in the data table.

6. Click the red disposal bucket to clear the lab. Click on the Stockroom to enter. Click the clipboard and select Preset Experiment #8 and repeat the experiment with $NaCH_3COO$ (NaAc). Record the initial and final temperatures in the data table.

Data Table

Mixture	T_1	T_2	$\Delta T\ (T_2 T_1)$
NaCl (s) + H_2O (l)	25.00	24.90	-0.10
$NaNO_3$ (s) + H_2O (l)	25.00	24.00	-1.00
$NaCH_3COO$ + H_2O (l)	25.00	25.96	0.96

Use your experimental data to answer the following questions.

7. *Calculate ΔT ($\Delta T = T_2 - T_1$) for each mixture and record it in the data table.*

NaCl: -0.10
$NaNO_3$: -1.00
$NaCH_3COO$: 0.96

8. An exothermic process gives off heat (warms up). An endothermic process absorbs heat (cools off).

   Which solutions are endothermic and which are exothermic? What is the sign of the change in

   enthalpy (ΔH) in each case? **endothermic: NaNO₃: sign is positive (+)**

   exothermic: NaCH₃COO: sign is negative (-)

9. *Which solution(s) had little or no change in temperature?* **NaCl**

3-2: Enthalpy of Solution: NH_4NO_3

Have you ever used one of those "instant cold packs" that looks like a plastic bag filled with liquid? If you hit the bag and shake it up it gets extremely cold, but why does it do that? The liquid inside the cold pack is water, and in the water is another plastic bag or tube containing NH_4NO_3 fertilizer. When you hit the cold pack, it breaks the tube so that the water mixes with the fertilizer. The dissolving of a salt, such as NH_4NO_3, in water is called dissolution, and the heat associated with the dissolving process is called the Enthalpy of Solution. In this problem, you will take a sample of NH_4NO_3, dissolve it in water, and after measuring the change in temperature, calculate the enthalpy of solution for NH_4NO_3.

1. Start *Virtual ChemLab* and select *Enthalpy of Solution: NH_4NO_3* from the list of assignments. The lab will open in the Calorimetry laboratory.

2. There will be a bottle of ammonium nitrate (NH_4NO_3) on the lab bench. A weigh paper will be on the balance with approximately 2 g of NH_4NO_3 on the paper. Record the mass of the sample in the data table. If you cannot read the mass on the balance, click in the balance area to *Zoom In*. *Return to Lab* when you have recorded the mass.

3. The coffee cup calorimeter will be on the lab bench and filled with 100 mL water. Click the *Lab Book* to open it. Make certain the stirrer is *On* (you should be able to see the shaft rotating). In the thermometer window click *Save* to begin recording data. Allow 20-30 seconds to obtain a baseline temperature of the water.

4. Drag the weigh paper with the sample to the calorimeter until it snaps into place and then pour the sample into the calorimeter. Observe the change in temperature until it reaches a maximum and then record data for an additional 20-30 seconds. Click *Stop*. (You can click on the clock on the wall labeled *Accelerate* to accelerate the time in the laboratory.) A blue data link will appear in the lab book. Click the data link and record the temperature before adding the NH_4NO_3 and the *highest* or *lowest* temperature after adding the NH_4NO_3 in the data table.

Data Table

Mixture	mass	$T_{initial}$	T_{final}
NH_4NO_3 (s) + H_2O (l)	1.9989	25.00	23.61

5. *Calculate ΔT ($\Delta T = T_{initial} - T_{final}$) for the dissolving process.* **1.39 K**

6. An exothermic process gives off heat (warms up), and an endothermic process absorbs heat (cools off).

   Was the addition of NH_4NO_3 to the water an endothermic or exothermic process? What is the sign of

   the change in enthalpy (ΔH)? **endothermic; sign is positive (+).**

7. *Determine the moles of NH_4NO_3 in the sample.* The molecular weight of NH_4NO_3 is 80 g/mol.

$$1.9989 \text{ g NH}_4\text{NO}_3 \left(\frac{1 \text{ mol NH}_4\text{NO}_3}{80 \text{ g NH}_4\text{NO}_3} \right) = 0.02499 \text{ mol NH}_4\text{NO}_3$$

8. The heat absorbed or lost by the water can be calculated using $q = m \cdot C_{\text{water}} \cdot \Delta T$. Assume that the density of water is 1 g/mL.

    Calculate the mass of the water and substitute for m. ΔT is the change in the temperature of the water and C_{water} is the specific heat capacity for water (4.184 J/g·K). What is the heat absorbed or lost, in J,

    by the water? <u>**q = (100 g H₂O) (4.184 J/K·g)(1.39 K) = 581.6 J**</u>

9. The heat transferred from/to the NH_4NO_3 can be divided by the moles of NH_4NO_3 to obtain the molar heat of solution for NH_4NO_3.

    What is the molar heat of solution, in kJ, of NH_4NO_3? <u>**ΔH = 581.6 J/0.02499 mol = 23,271 J/mol =**</u>

    <u>**23.27 kJ/mol**</u>

10. *If the accepted value for the heat of solution for sugar is 25.69 kJ/mol, calculate the percent error.*

$$\% \ Error = \frac{|your \ answer - accepted \ answer|}{accepted \ answer} \times 100$$

    *% Error = **9.4%***

This experiment does not consider that all of the conditions are standard state conditions; therefore, you are calculating ΔH_{sol} **not** ΔH°_{sol}.

3-3: Specific Heat of Al

On a sunny day, the water in a swimming pool may warm up a degree or two while the concrete around the pool may become too hot to walk on with bare feet. This may seem strange since the water and concrete are being heated by the same source—the sun. This evidence suggests that it takes more heat to raise the temperature of some substances than others, which is true. The amount of heat required to raise the temperature of 1 g of a substance by 1 degree is called the *specific heat capacity* or *specific heat* of that substance. Water, for instance, has a specific heat of 4.18 J/K·g. This value is high in comparison with the specific heats for other materials, such as concrete or metals. In this experiment, you will use a simple calorimeter and your knowledge of the specific heat of water to measure the specific heat of aluminum (Al).

1. Start *Virtual ChemLab* and select *The Specific Heat of Al* from the list of assignments. The lab will open in the Calorimetry laboratory.

2. Click on the *Lab Book* to open it. Record the mass of Al on the balance. If it is too small to read click on the *Balance* area to zoom in, record the mass of Al in the data table below, and return to the laboratory.

3. Pick up the Al sample from the balance pan and place the sample in the oven. Click the oven door to close. The oven is set to heat to 200°C.

4. The calorimeter has been filled with 100 mL water. The density of water at 25°C is 0.998 g/mL. Use the density of the water to determine the mass of water from the volume and record the volume and mass in the data table.

   Make certain the stirrer is *On* (you should be able to see the shaft rotating). Click the thermometer window to bring it to the front and click *Save* to begin recording data. Allow 20-30 seconds to obtain a baseline temperature of the water. You can observe the temperature in the calorimeter as a function of time using the graph window.

5. Click on the *Oven* to open it. Drag the hot Al sample from the oven until it snaps into place above the calorimeter and drop it in. Click the thermometer and graph windows to bring them to the front again and observe the change in temperature in the graph window until it reaches a constant value and then wait an additional 20-30 seconds. Click *Stop* in the temperature window. (You can click on the clock on the wall labeled *Accelerate* to accelerate the time in the laboratory.) A blue data link will appear in the lab book. Click the blue data link and record the temperature before adding the Al and the *highest* temperature after adding the Al in the data table. (Remember that the water will begin to cool down after reaching the equilibrium temperature.)

Data Table

	Al
mass of metal (g)	7.3548
volume of water (mL)	100
mass of water (g)	98.8
initial temperature of water (°C)	25.00
initial temperature of metal (°C)	200.00
max temp of water + metal (°C)	27.39

Thermodynamics

6. *Calculate the change in temperature of the water (ΔT_{water}).* $\underline{\Delta T_{water} = 27.39°C - 25°C = 2.39°C = }$

   $\underline{2.39\text{ K.}}$

7. *Calculate the heat (q), in J, gained by the water using the following equation:*

$$q_{water} = m_{water} \times \Delta T_{water} \times C_{water}, \text{ given } C_{water} = 4.184 \text{ J/(K·g)}$$

   $\underline{q = 98.8\text{ g} \times 2.39\text{ K} \times 4.184\text{ J/(K·g)} = 987.98\text{ J}}$

8. *Calculate the changes in temperature of the Al (ΔT_{Al}).* $\underline{\Delta T_{Al} = 200°C - 25.43°C = 172.61°C = }$

   $\underline{172.61\text{ K.}}$

9. *Remembering that the heat gained by the water is equal to the heat lost by the metal, calculate the specific heat of aluminum in J/K·g.*

$$q_{water} = -q_{metal} = m_{Al} \times \Delta T_{Al} \times C_{Al} \text{ and } C_{Al} = \frac{q_{metal}}{(m_{metal})(\Delta T_{metal})}$$

   $\underline{C_{Al} = 987.98\text{ J/(7.3548 g)(172.69 K)} = 0.778\text{ J/K·g}}$

10. *Calculate the percent error in the specific heat value that you determined experimentally.* The accepted value for Al is 0.903 J/ K·g.

$$\% \text{ Error} = \frac{|your\ answer - accepted\ answer|}{accepted\ answer} \times 100$$

% Error = **13.8%**

3-4: Specific Heat of Pb

On a sunny day, the water in a swimming pool may warm up a degree or two while the concrete around the pool may become too hot to walk on with bare feet. This may seem strange since the water and concrete are being heated by the same source—the sun. This evidence suggests that it takes more heat to raise the temperature of some substances than others, which is true. The amount of heat required to raise the temperature of 1 g of a substance by 1 degree is called the *specific heat capacity* or *specific heat* of that substance. Water, for instance, has a specific heat of 4.18 J/K·g. This value is high in comparison with the specific heats for other materials, such as concrete or metals. In this experiment, you will use a simple calorimeter and your knowledge of the specific heat of water to measure the specific heat of lead (Pb).

1. Start *Virtual ChemLab* and select *The Specific Heat of Pb* from the list of assignments. The lab will open in the Calorimetry laboratory.

2. Click on the *Lab Book* to open it. Record the mass of Pb on the balance. If it is too small to read click on the *Balance* area to zoom in, record the mass of Pb in the data table below, and return to the laboratory.

3. Pick up the Pb sample from the balance pan and place the sample in the oven. Click the oven door to close. The oven is set to heat to 200°C.

4. The calorimeter has been filled with 100 mL water. The density of water at 25°C is 0.998 g/mL. Use the density of the water to determine the mass of water from the volume and record the volume and mass in the data table.

    Make certain the stirrer is *On* (you should be able to see the shaft rotating). Click the thermometer window to bring it to the front and click *Save* to begin recording data. Allow 20-30 seconds to obtain a baseline temperature of the water. You can observe the temperature in the calorimeter as a function of time using the graph window.

5. Click on the *Oven* to open it. Drag the hot Pb sample from the oven until it snaps into place above the calorimeter and drop it in. Click the thermometer and graph windows to bring them to the front again and observe the change in temperature in the graph window until it reaches a constant value and then wait an additional 20-30 seconds. Click *Stop* in the temperature window. (You can click on the clock on the wall labeled *Accelerate* to accelerate the time in the laboratory.) A blue data link will appear in the lab book. Click the blue data link and record the temperature before adding the Pb and the *highest* temperature after adding the Pb in the data table. (Remember that the water will begin to cool down after reaching the equilibrium temperature.)

Data Table

	Pb
mass of metal (g)	31.9812
volume of water (mL)	100
mass of water (g)	98.8
initial temperature of water (°C)	25.00
initial temperature of metal (°C)	200.00
max temp of water + metal (°C)	26.52

Thermodynamics

6. *Calculate the changes in temperature of the water (ΔT_{water}).* $\underline{\Delta T_{\text{water}} = 26.52°C - 25°C = 1.52°C =}$

   $\underline{\textbf{1.52 K.}}$

7. *Calculate the heat (q), in J, gained by the water using the following equation:*

$$q_{\text{water}} = m_{\text{water}} \times \Delta T_{\text{water}} \times C_{\text{water}} \text{ , given } C_{\text{water}} = 4.184 \text{ J/(K·g)}$$

   $\underline{q = 98.8 \text{ g} \times 1.52 \text{ K} \times 4.184 \text{ J/(K·g)} = 628.34 \text{ J}}$

8. *Calculate the changes in temperature of the Pb (ΔT_{Pb}).* $\underline{\Delta T_{\text{Pb}} = 200°C - 26.52°C = 173.48°C =}$

   $\underline{\textbf{173.48 K.}}$

9. *Remembering that the heat gained by the water is equal to the heat lost by the metal, calculate the specific heat of lead in J/K·g.*

$$q_{\text{water}} = -q_{\text{metal}} = m_{\text{Pb}} \times \Delta T_{\text{Pb}} \times C_{\text{Pb}} \text{ and } C_{\text{Pb}} = \frac{q_{\text{metal}}}{(m_{\text{metal}})(\Delta T_{\text{metal}})}$$

   $\underline{C_{\text{Pb}} = 628.34 \text{ J/(31.9812 g)(173.48 K)} = 0.113 \text{ J/K·g}}$

10. *Calculate the percent error in the specific heat value that you determined experimentally.* The accepted value for Pb is 0.130 J/ K·g.

$$\% \, Error = \frac{|your \, answer - accepted \, answer|}{accepted \, answer} \times 100$$

   % Error = **12.9%**

3-5: Heat of Combustion: Chicken Fat

The heat of combustion (ΔH_{comb}) is the heat of reaction for the complete burning (reacting with O_2) of one mole of a substance to form CO_2 and H_2O. Calorimetry experiments that measure the heat of combustion can be performed at constant volume using a device called a bomb calorimeter. In a bomb calorimeter a sample is burned in a constant-volume chamber in the presence of oxygen at high pressure. The heat that is released warms the water surrounding the chamber. By measuring the temperature increase of the water, it is possible to calculate the quantity of heat released during the combustion reaction. In this assignment you will calculate the heat of combustion of chicken fat. The calorimeter has already been calibrated by combusting benzoic acid.

1. Start *Virtual ChemLab* and select *Heat of Combustion: Chicken Fat* from the list of assignments. The lab will open in the Calorimetry laboratory with the bomb calorimeter out and disassembled and with a sample of chicken fat in the calorimeter cup on the balance. The balance has already been tared.

2. Click on the *Lab Book* to open it.

3. Record the mass of the chicken fat sample from the balance. If you cannot read it click on the *Balance* area to zoom in, record the mass in the data table below and return to the laboratory.

4. Double-click the following (in numerical order) to assemble the calorimeter: (1) the cup on the balance pan, (2) the bomb head, (3) the screw cap, and (4) the bomb. Click the calorimeter lid to close it. Combustion experiments can take a considerable length of time. Click the clock on the wall labeled *Accelerate* to accelerate the laboratory time.

5. Click the bomb control panel and the plot window to bring them to the front. Click on the *Save* button to save data to the lab book. Allow the graph to proceed for 20-30 seconds to establish a baseline temperature.

6. Click *Ignite* and observe the graph. When the temperature has leveled off (up to 5 minutes of laboratory time), click *Stop*. A blue data link will appear in the lab book. Click the blue data link to view the collected data. Record the temperature before and after ignition of the chicken fat sample in the data table.

Data Table

	chicken fat
mass of sample (g)	0.8991
initial temperature (°C)	25.004
final temperature (°C)	28.294

7. *Calculate ΔT for the water using $\Delta T = |T_f - T_i|$.* $\underline{\Delta T = 28.294°C - 25.004°C = 3.290°C = 3.290\ K}$

8. *Calculate the moles of chicken fat in the sample (MW_{fat} = 797.7 g/mol).*

$$0.8991\ \text{g chicken fat} \times \left(\frac{1\ \text{mol chicken fat}}{797.7\ \text{g chicken fat}} \right) = 0.001127\ \text{mol chicken fat}$$

9. ΔH_{comb} for chicken fat can be calculated using $\Delta H_{comb} = \left(C_{system}\Delta T\right)/n$, where n is the moles of chicken fat in the sample and C_{system} is the heat capacity of the calorimetric system.

    Use 10.310 kJ/K for C_{system} and calculate the heat of combustion, in kJ/mol, for chicken fat.

    $$\Delta H_{comb} = \left(C_{system}\Delta T\right)/n = (10.310 \times 3.290)/0.001127 = 30{,}098 \text{ kJ/mol}$$

10. *If the accepted value for the heat of combustion for chicken fat is 30,038 kJ/mol calculate the percent error.*

    $$\% \ Error = \frac{\left|your\ answer - accepted\ answer\right|}{accepted\ answer} \times 100$$

    *% Error = **0.20%***

    This experiment does not consider that all of the conditions are standard state conditions; therefore, you are calculating ΔH_{comb} **not** ΔH°_{comb}.

11. The "calorie" used to measure the caloric content of foods is actually a kilocalorie (kcal) or 4184 kJ.

    If the heat of combustion for sugar is 5639 kJ/mol, why are people who are on limited calorie diets advised to limit their fat intake? **The heat of combustion for chicken fat is 6 times larger than it is for sugar; consequently, the caloric content of fat is significantly larger than it is for sugar and should be avoided.**

12. The food that we ingest is certainly not "combusted" in the same manner as is done in a bomb calorimeter.

    Why can we compare the heats of combustion of sugar or chicken fat measured in a bomb calorimeter with the caloric content of those foods? **ΔH for the reaction of sugar or chicken fat to form H_2O and CO_2 is a state function or, in other words, it is path independent. Since the reaction of sugar or chicken fat by combustion or by some metabolic pathway ultimately forms the same products, ΔH for both processes must be the same.**

3-6: Heat of Combustion: Sugar

The heat of combustion (ΔH_{comb}) is the heat of reaction for the complete burning (reacting with O_2) of one mole of a substance to form CO_2 and H_2O. Calorimetry experiments that measure the heat of combustion can be performed at constant volume using a device called a bomb calorimeter. In a bomb calorimeter a sample is burned in a constant-volume chamber in the presence of oxygen at high pressure. The heat that is released warms the water surrounding the chamber. By measuring the temperature increase of the water, it is possible to calculate the quantity of heat released during the combustion reaction. In this assignment you will calculate the heat of combustion of sugar (sucrose, $C_{12}H_{22}O_{11}$). The calorimeter has already been calibrated by combusting benzoic acid.

1. Start *Virtual ChemLab* and select *Heat of Combustion: Sugar* from the list of assignments. The lab will open in the Calorimetry laboratory with the bomb calorimeter out and disassembled and with a sample of sugar in the calorimeter cup on the balance. The balance has already been tared.

2. Click on the *Lab Book* to open it.

3. Record the mass of the sugar sample from the balance. If you cannot read it click on the *Balance* area to zoom in, record the mass in the data table below and return to the laboratory.

4. Double-click the following (in numerical order) to assemble the calorimeter: (1) the cup on the balance pan, (2) the bomb head, (3) the screw cap, and (4) the bomb. Click the calorimeter lid to close it. Combustion experiments can take a considerable length of time. Click the clock on the wall labeled *Accelerate* to accelerate the laboratory time.

5. Click the bomb control panel and the plot window to bring them to the front. Click on the *Save* button to save data to the lab book. Allow the graph to proceed for 20-30 seconds to establish a baseline temperature.

6. Click *Ignite* and observe the graph. When the temperature has leveled off (up to 5 minutes of laboratory time), click *Stop*. A blue data link will appear in the lab book. Click the blue data link to view the collected data. Record the temperature before and after ignition of the sugar sample in the data table.

Data Table

	sucrose ($C_{12}H_{22}O_{11}$)
mass of sample (g)	0.9649
initial temperature (°C)	25.005
final temperature (°C)	26.548

7. *Write a complete balanced chemical equation for the combustion of sucrose.* $\underline{C_{12}H_{22}O_{11} + 12O_2 =}$

$\underline{12CO_2 + 11H_2O}$

8. *Calculate ΔT for the water using $\Delta T = |T_f - T_i|$.* $\underline{\Delta T = 26.548°C - 25.005°C = 1.543°C = 1.543\ K}$

Thermodynamics

9. *Calculate the moles of sucrose in the sample (MW$_{sucrose}$ = 342.3 g/mol).*

$$0.9649 \text{ g } C_{12}H_{22}O_{11} \times \left(\frac{1 \text{ mol } C_{12}H_{22}O_{11}}{342.3 \text{ g } C_{12}H_{22}O_{11}} \right) = 0.002819 \text{ mol } C_{12}H_{22}O_{11}$$

10. ΔH_{comb} for sucrose can be calculated using $\Delta H_{comb} = \left(C_{system} \Delta T \right)/n$, where n is the moles of sucrose in the sample and C_{system} is the heat capacity of the calorimetric system.

    Use 10.310 kJ/K for C$_{system}$ and calculate the heat of combustion, in kJ/mol, for sucrose.

$$\Delta H_{comb} = \left(C_{system} \Delta T \right)/n = (10.310 \times 1.543)/0.002819 = 5643 \text{ kJ/mol}$$

11. *If the accepted value for the heat of combustion for sugar is 5639 kJ/mol calculate the percent error.*

$$\% \text{ Error} = \frac{\left| your\ answer - accepted\ answer \right|}{accepted\ answer} \times 100$$

*% Error = **0.075%***

This experiment does not consider that all of the conditions are standard state conditions; therefore, you are calculating ΔH_{comb} **not** ΔH°_{comb}.

3-7: Heat of Combustion: TNT

The heat of combustion (ΔH_{comb}) is the heat of reaction for the complete burning (reacting with O_2) of one mole of a substance to form CO_2 and H_2O. Calorimetry experiments that measure the heat of combustion can be performed at constant volume using a device called a bomb calorimeter. In a bomb calorimeter a sample is burned in a constant-volume chamber in the presence of oxygen at high pressure. The heat that is released warms the water surrounding the chamber. By measuring the temperature increase of the water, it is possible to calculate the quantity of heat released during the combustion reaction. In this assignment you will calculate the heat of combustion of 2,4,6-trinitrotolune (TNT). The calorimeter has already been calibrated by combusting benzoic acid.

1. Start *Virtual ChemLab* and select *Heat of Combustion: TNT* from the list of assignments. The lab will open in the Calorimetry laboratory with the bomb calorimeter out and disassembled and with a sample of TNT in the calorimeter cup on the balance. The balance has already been tared.

2. Click on the *Lab Book* to open it.

3. Record the mass of the TNT sample from the balance. If you cannot read it click on the *Balance* area to zoom in, record the mass in the data table below and return to the laboratory.

4. Double-click the following (in numerical order) to assemble the calorimeter: (1) the cup on the balance pan, (2) the bomb head, (3) the screw cap, and (4) the bomb. Click the calorimeter lid to close it. Combustion experiments can take a considerable length of time. Click the clock on the wall labeled *Accelerate* to accelerate the laboratory time.

5. Click the bomb control panel and the plot window to bring them to the front. Click on the *Save* button to save data to the lab book. Allow the graph to proceed for 20-30 seconds to establish a baseline temperature.

6. Click *Ignite* and observe the graph. When the temperature has leveled off (up to 5 minutes of laboratory time), click *Stop*. A blue data link will appear in the lab book. Click the blue data link to view the collected data. Record the temperature before and after ignition of the TNT sample in the data table.

    Data Table

	2,4,6-trinitrotoluene (TNT)
mass of sample (g)	**1.0098**
initial temperature (°C)	**25.002**
final temperature (°C)	**26.518**

7. *Calculate ΔT for the water using $\Delta T = |T_f - T_i|$.* $\underline{\Delta T = 26.518°C - 25.002°C = 1.516°C = 1.516\ K}$

8. *Calculate the moles of TNT in the sample ($MW_{TNT} = 227.13\ g/mol$).*

$$\text{1.0098 g TNT} \times \left(\frac{\text{1 mol TNT}}{\text{227.13 g TNT}} \right) = 0.004446\ \text{mol TNT}$$

9. ΔH_{comb} for TNT can be calculated using $\Delta H_{comb} = \left(C_{system} \Delta T\right)/n$, where n is the moles of TNT in the sample and C_{system} is the heat capacity, in kJ/mol, of the calorimetric system.

   Use 10.310 kJ/K for C_{system} and calculate the heat of combustion for TNT.

$$\Delta H_{comb} = \left(C_{system} \Delta T\right)/n = (10.310 \times 1.516)/0.004446 = 3516 \text{ kJ/mol}$$

10. *If the accepted value for the heat of combustion for TNT is 3406 kJ/mol, calculate the percent error.*

$$\% \ Error = \frac{|your \ answer - accepted \ answer|}{accepted \ answer} \times 100$$

*% Error = **3.23%***

   This experiment does not consider that all of the conditions are standard state conditions; therefore, you are calculating ΔH_{comb} **not** $\Delta H°_{comb}$.

11. *The heat of combustion for sugar is 5639 kJ/mole, but that for TNT is 3406 kJ/mole. Why, if the heat of combustion for TNT is smaller than for sugar, is TNT an explosive?* **The "explosiveness" of TNT does not come from the heat of the reaction, but from the speed of the reaction and from the amount of gas produced in the reaction.**

3-8: Heat of Formation: Ethanol

The heat of formation is the heat of reaction for the formation of a compound from its elements. The heat of formation can be determined by measuring the heat of combustion for the compound and then using Hess's law to convert the heat of combustion to a heat of formation. Calorimetry experiments that measure the heat of combustion can be performed at constant volume using a device called a bomb calorimeter. In a bomb calorimeter a sample is burned in a constant-volume chamber in the presence of oxygen at high pressure. The heat that is released warms the water surrounding the chamber. By measuring the temperature increase of the water, it is possible to calculate the quantity of heat released during the combustion reaction. In this assignment you will first measure the heat of combustion of ethanol (ethyl alcohol, C_2H_5OH) and then convert the heat of combustion to a heat of formation.

1. Start *Virtual ChemLab* and select *Heat of Formation: Ethanol* from the list of assignments. The lab will open in the Calorimetry laboratory with the bomb calorimeter out and disassembled and with a sample of ethanol in the calorimeter cup on the balance. The balance has already been tared.

2. Click on the *Lab Book* to open it.

3. Record the mass of the ethanol sample from the balance. If you cannot read it click on the *Balance* area to zoom in, record the mass in the data table below and return to the laboratory.

4. Double-click the following (in numerical order) to assemble the calorimeter: (1) the cup on the balance pan, (2) the bomb head, (3) the screw cap, and (4) the bomb. Click the calorimeter lid to close it. Combustion experiments can take a considerable length of time. Click the clock on the wall labeled *Accelerate* to accelerate the laboratory time.

5. Click the bomb control panel and the plot window to bring them to the front. Click on the **Save** button to save data to the lab book. Allow the graph to proceed for 20-30 seconds to establish a baseline temperature.

6. Click **Ignite** and observe the graph. When the temperature has leveled off (up to 5 minutes of laboratory time), click **Stop**. A blue data link will appear in the lab book. Click the blue data link to view the collected data. Record the temperature before and after ignition of the ethanol sample in the data table.

Data Table

	ethanol (C_2H_5OH)
mass of sample (g)	0.7883
initial temperature (°C)	25.001
final temperature (°C)	27.282

7. *Write a complete balanced chemical equation for the combustion of ethanol.*

    $C_2H_5OH + 3O_2 = 2CO_2 + 3H_2O$

8. *Calculate ΔT for the water using $\Delta T = |T_f - T_i|$.* $\Delta T = 27.282°C - 25.001°C = 2.281°C = 2.281 K$

Thermodynamics

9. *Calculate the moles of ethanol in the sample (MW$_{enthanol}$ = 46.00 g/mol).*

$$0.7883 \text{ g C}_2\text{H}_5\text{OH} \times \left(\frac{1 \text{ mol C}_2\text{H}_5\text{OH}}{46.00 \text{ g C}_2\text{H}_5\text{OH}} \right) = 0.01714 \text{ mol C}_2\text{H}_5\text{OH}$$

10. ΔH_{comb} for ethanol can be calculated using $\Delta H_{comb} = \left(C_{system}\Delta T\right)/n$, where n is the moles of ethanol in the sample and C_{system} is the heat capacity of the calorimetric system.

    Use 10.310 kJ/K for C_{system} and calculate the heat of combustion, in kJ/mol, for ethanol. The heat of combustion will be negative since it is an exothermic reaction.

$$\Delta H_{comb} = \left(C_{system}\Delta T\right)/n = (10.310 \times 2.281)/0.01714 = -1372 \text{ kJ/mol}$$

11. *Write an equation for the combustion of ethanol in the form $\Delta H_{comb} = \Sigma n\Delta H_f \text{ (products)} - \Sigma m\Delta H_f$*

    (reactants). $\underline{\Delta H_{comb} = [2\Delta H_f(CO_2) + 3\Delta H_f(H_2O)] - [\Delta H_f(C_2H_5OH) + 3\Delta H_f(O_2)]}$

12. *Calculate the heat of formation for C_2H_5OH, given the standard enthalpies of formation for CO_2, H_2O, and O_2 are -393.5 kJ/mol, -285.83 kJ/mol, and 0 kJ/mol, respectively.*

$$\Delta H_f(C_2H_5OH) = [2\Delta H_f(CO_2) + 3\Delta H_f(H_2O)] - [\Delta H_{comb} + 3\Delta H_f(O_2)]$$
$$= 2(-393.5) + 3(-285.83) + (1372) + 3(0)$$
$$= -272.5 \text{ kJ/mol}$$

13. *If the accepted value for the enthalpy of formation for ethanol is -277.7 kJ/mol, calculate the percent error.*

$$\% \text{ Error} = \frac{|\text{your answer} - \text{accepted answer}|}{\text{accepted answer}} \times 100$$

$$\% \text{ Error} = \mathbf{1.87\%}$$

This experiment does not consider that all of the conditions are standard state conditions; therefore, you are calculating ΔH_f **not** ΔH°_f.

3-9: Heat of Formation: Aspirin

The heat of formation is the heat of reaction for the formation of a compound from its elements. The heat of formation can be determined by measuring the heat of combustion for the compound and then using Hess's law to convert the heat of combustion to a heat of formation. Calorimetry experiments that measure the heat of combustion can be performed at constant volume using a device called a bomb calorimeter. In a bomb calorimeter a sample is burned in a constant-volume chamber in the presence of oxygen at high pressure. The heat that is released warms the water surrounding the chamber. By measuring the temperature increase of the water, it is possible to calculate the quantity of heat released during the combustion reaction. In this assignment you will first measure the heat of combustion of aspirin ($C_9H_8O_4$) and then convert the heat of combustion to a heat of formation.

1. Start *Virtual ChemLab* and select *Heat of Formation: Aspirin* from the list of assignments. The lab will open in the Calorimetry laboratory with the bomb calorimeter out and disassembled and with a sample of asprin in the calorimeter cup on the balance. The balance has already been tared.

2. Click on the *Lab Book* to open it.

3. Record the mass of the aspirin sample from the balance. If you cannot read it click on the *Balance* area to zoom in, record the mass in the data table below and return to the laboratory.

4. Double-click the following (in numerical order) to assemble the calorimeter: (1) the cup on the balance pan, (2) the bomb head, (3) the screw cap, and (4) the bomb. Click the calorimeter lid to close it. Combustion experiments can take a considerable length of time. Click the clock on the wall labeled *Accelerate* to accelerate the laboratory time.

5. Click the bomb control panel and the plot window to bring them to the front. Click on the *Save* button to save data to the lab book. Allow the graph to proceed for 20-30 seconds to establish a baseline temperature.

6. Click *Ignite* and observe the graph. When the temperature has leveled off (up to 5 minutes of laboratory time), click *Stop*. A blue data link will appear in the lab book. Click the blue data link to view the collected data. Record the temperature before and after ignition of the aspirin sample in the data table.

Data Table

	aspirin ($C_9H_8O_4$)
mass of sample (g)	0.9994
initial temperature (°C)	25.001
final temperature (°C)	27.090

7. Write a complete balanced chemical equation for the combustion of aspirin. **$C_9H_8O_4 + 9O_2 =$** ___

   $9CO_2 + 4H_2O$ _____

8. Calculate ΔT for the water using $\Delta T = |T_f - T_i|$. **$\Delta T = 27.090°C - 25.001°C = 2.089°C = 2.089\ K$**

89

9. *Calculate the moles of aspirin in the sample (MW$_{aspirin}$ = 180.00 g/mol).*

$$0.9994 \text{ g C}_9\text{H}_8\text{O}_4 \times \left(\frac{1 \text{ mol C}_9\text{H}_8\text{O}_4}{180.00 \text{ g C}_9\text{H}_8\text{O}_4} \right) = 0.005552 \text{ mol C}_9\text{H}_8\text{O}_4$$

10. ΔH_{comb} for aspirin can be calculated using $\Delta H_{comb} = \left(C_{system} \Delta T \right)/n$, where n is the moles of aspirin in the sample and C_{system} is the heat capacity of the calorimetric system.

    Use 10.310 kJ/K for C_{system} and calculate the heat of combustion, in kJ/mol, for aspirin. The heat of combustion will be negative since it is an exothermic reaction.

$$\Delta H_{comb} = \left(C_{system} \Delta T \right)/n = (10.310 \times 2.089)/0.005552 = -3879 \text{ kJ/mol}$$

11. *Write an equation for the combustion of aspirin in the form $\Delta H_{comb} = \Sigma n \Delta H_f \text{ (products)} - \Sigma m \Delta H_f$ (reactants).*

$$\Delta H_{comb} = [9\Delta H_f (CO_2) + 4\Delta H_f (H_2O)] - [\Delta H_f (CH_3CH_2OH) + 9\Delta H_f (O_2)]$$

12. *Calculate the heat of formation for aspirin given the standard enthalpies of formation for CO_2, H_2O, and O_2 are -393.5 kJ/mol, -285.83 kJ/mol, and 0 kJ/mol, respectively.*

$$\begin{aligned} \Delta H_f (C_9H_8O_4) &= [9\Delta H_f (CO_2) + 4\Delta H_f (H_2O)] - [\Delta H_{comb} + 9\Delta H_f (O_2)] \\ &= 9(-393.5) + 4(-285.83) + (3879) + 9(0) \\ &= -805.8 \text{ kJ/mol} \end{aligned}$$

This experiment does not consider that all of the conditions are standard state conditions; therefore, you are calculating ΔH_f **not** $\Delta H°_f$.

3-10: Heat of Reaction: NaOH(aq) + HCl(aq)

Energy is either absorbed or released for all chemical reactions, and we call this energy the enthalpy of reaction (ΔH_{rxn}). If the enthalpy of reaction is positive, then we say that the energy was absorbed or that the reaction was *endothermic*. If the enthalpy of reaction is negative, then we say that energy was released or that the reaction was *exothermic*. Most chemical reactions are exothermic. In this problem, you will measure the amount of heat released when aqueous solutions of NaOH and HCl are mixed and react to form water and then you will calculate the heat of reaction.

$$NaOH(aq) + HCl(aq) = H_2O(l) + NaCl(aq)$$

1. Start *Virtual ChemLab* and select *Heat of Reaction: NaOH + HCl* from the list of assignments. The lab will open in the Calorimetry laboratory.

2. Click the *Lab Book* to open it. In the thermometer window click *Save* to begin recording data. Allow 20-30 seconds to obtain a baseline temperature of the water. Pour the first beaker containing 100 mL of 1.000 M HCl into the calorimeter and then pour the second beaker containing 100 mL of 1.000 M NaOH into the calorimeter. Observe the change in temperature until it reaches a maximum and then record data for an additional 20-30 seconds. Click *Stop* in the temperature window. (You can click on the clock on the wall labeled *Accelerate* to accelerate the time in the laboratory.) A blue data link will appear in the lab book. Click the blue data link and record the temperature before adding the NaOH and the *highest* temperature after adding the NaOH in the data table. (Remember that the water will begin to cool down after reaching the equilibrium temperature.)

Data Table

	NaOH/HCl
initial temperature (°C)	**25.00**
final temperature (°C)	**30.86**

3. *Is the observed reaction endothermic or exothermic? What will be the sign of ΔH_{rxn}?* **exothermic:**

    negative

4. *Calculate the change in temperature, ΔT. Record your results in the results table on the following page.*

5. *Calculate the mass of the reaction mixture in the calorimeter.* (To do this, first determine the total volume of the solution based on the assumption that the volumes are additive and that the density of the solution is the same as that of pure water, 1.0 g/mL.) Record your results in the results table.

    100 mL HCl + 100 mL NaOH = 200 mL solution (1 g/mL) = 200 g solution

6. *Calculate the total heat released in the reaction, assuming that the specific heat capacity of the solution is the same as that of pure water, 4.184 J/K·g. Record the result in the results table.* Remember: heat of reaction = $m \times C \times \Delta T$

    heat of reaction = 200 g × 4.184 J/K·g × 5.86 K = 4904 J

7. *Calculate the number of moles of NaOH used in the reaction by multiplying the volume of NaOH times the molarity (1.000 mol/L). Record the results in the results table.*

100 mL NaOH = 0.100 L NaOH × 1.000 mol/L = 0.100 mol NaOH

8. *Calculate ΔH_{rxn}, in kJ/mol, of NaOH for the reaction and record the results in the results table.* Make sure the sign of ΔH_{rxn} is correct.

$$\Delta H_{rxn} = \left(\frac{-4904 \text{ J}}{0.100 \text{ mol}} \right) \cdot \left(\frac{1 \text{ kJ}}{1000 \text{ J}} \right) = -49.04 \text{ kJ}$$

Results Table

Mass of Rxn Mixture	ΔT	Total Heat Released	mol NaOH	ΔH_{rxn}/mol
200 g	5.86 K	4904 J	0.100	-49.04 kJ

3-11: Heat of Reaction: MgO(s) + HCl(aq)

Energy is either absorbed or released for all chemical reactions, and we call this energy the enthalpy of reaction (ΔH_{rxn}). If the enthalpy of reaction is positive, then we say that the energy was absorbed or that the reaction was *endothermic*. If the enthalpy of reaction is negative, then we say that energy was released or that the reaction was *exothermic*. Most chemical reactions are exothermic. In this problem, you will measure the amount of heat released when solid MgO is reacted with aqueous HCl to form water and then you will calculate the heat of reaction.

$$MgO(s) + 2HCl(aq) = H_2O(l) + MgCl_2(aq)$$

1. Start *Virtual ChemLab* and select *Heat of Reaction: MgO + HCl* from the list of assignments. The lab will open in the Calorimetry laboratory.

2. There will be a bottle of MgO near the balance. A weigh paper will be on the balance with approximately 2.81 g MgO on the paper. Record the mass of MgO in the data table.

3. The calorimeter will be on the lab bench and filled with 100 mL 1.000 M HCl. Make certain the stirrer is *On* (you should be able to see the shaft rotating). Click the *Lab Book* to open it. In the thermometer window click *Save* to begin recording data. Allow 20-30 seconds to obtain a baseline temperature of the HCl solution. Drag the weigh paper containing the MgO sample over to the calorimeter and drop the sample in. Observe the change in temperature until it reaches a maximum and then record data for an additional 20-30 seconds. Click *Stop* in the temperature window. (You can click on the clock on the wall labeled *Accelerate* to accelerate the time in the laboratory.) A blue data link will appear in the lab book. Click the blue data link and record the temperature before adding the MgO and the *highest* temperature after adding the MgO in the data table. (Remember that the water will begin to cool down after reaching the equilibrium temperature.)

Data Table

	MgO/HCl
Mass MgO	2.8037
initial temperature (°C)	25.00
final temperature (°C)	42.84

4. *Is the observed reaction endothermic or exothermic? What will be the sign of ΔH_{rxn}?* **exothermic:**

    negative

5. *Calculate the change in temperature, ΔT. Record your results in the results table on the following page.*

6. *Calculate the mass of the reaction mixture in the calorimeter.* (To do this, assume that the density of the HCl solution originally in the calorimeter can be approximated with the density of water (1.0 g/mL). Record your results in the results table.

    100 mL HCl × 1.0 g/mL + 2.80 g MgO = 102.80 g solution

7. *Calculate the total heat released in the reaction, in J, assuming that the specific heat capacity of the solution is the same as that of pure water, 4.184 J/K·g. Record the result in the results table.*
    Remember: heat of reaction = $m \times C \times \Delta T$

__heat of reaction = 102.80 g × 4.184 J/K·g × 17.84 K = 7673 J__

8. *Calculate the number of moles of MgO used in the reaction.* The molar mass of MgO is 56.305 g/mole. Record the results in the results table.

__2.8037 g MgO/56.305 g/mol = 0.04979 mol MgO__

9. *Calculate ΔH_{rxn}, in kJ/mol, of MgO for the reaction and record the results in the results table.* Make sure the sign of ΔH_{rxn} is correct.

$$\Delta H_{rxn} = \left(\frac{-7673 \text{ J}}{0.04979 \text{ mol}} \right) \cdot \left(\frac{1 \text{ kJ}}{1000 \text{ J}} \right) = -154.09 \text{ kJ}$$

Results Table

Mass of Rxn Mixture	ΔT	Total Heat Released	mol MgO	ΔH_{rxn}/mol
102.8 g	17.84 K	7673 J	0.04979	-154.09 kJ

3-12: Hess's Law

In this experiment, you will measure the amount of heat released in these three related exothermic reactions:

1. $NaOH (s) = Na^+ (aq) + OH^- (aq) + \Delta H_1$
2. $NaOH (s) + H^+ (aq) + Cl^- (aq) = H_2O + Na^+ (aq) + Cl^- (aq) + \Delta H_2$
3. $Na^+ (aq) + OH^- (aq) + H^+ (aq) + Cl^- (aq) = H_2O + Na^+ (aq) + Cl^- (aq) + \Delta H_3$

After determining the heats of reaction (ΔH_1, ΔH_2 and ΔH_3), you will then analyze your data and verify Hess's Law or $\Delta H_1 + \Delta H_3 = \Delta H_2$.

1. Start *Virtual ChemLab* and select *Hess's Law* from the list of assignments. The lab will open in the Calorimetry laboratory.

Reaction 1

2. There will be a bottle of NaOH near the balance. A weigh paper will be on the balance with approximately 4 g NaOH on the paper. Record the mass of NaOH in the data table on the following page.

3. The calorimeter will be on the lab bench and filled with 200 mL water. Click the *Lab Book* to open it. Make certain the stirrer is *On* (you should be able to see the shaft rotating). In the thermometer window click *Save* to begin recording data. Allow 20-30 seconds to obtain a baseline temperature of the water.

4. Drag the weigh paper with the sample to the calorimeter until it snaps into place and then pour the sample into the calorimeter. Observe the change in temperature until it reaches a maximum and then record data for an additional 20-30 seconds. Click *Stop*. (You can click on the clock on the wall labeled *Accelerate* to accelerate the time in the laboratory.) A blue data link will appear in the lab book. Click the data link and record the initial and final water temperatures in the data table. If you need to repeat this part of the experiment, enter the Stockroom and select Preset Experiment #6 on the clipboard.

Reaction 2

5. Click the red disposal bucket to clear the lab. Click on the Stockroom to enter. Click on the clipboard and select Preset Experiment #5. Return to the laboratory.

6. There will be a bottle of NaOH near the balance. A weigh paper will be on the balance with approximately 4 g NaOH on the paper. Record the mass of NaOH in the data table. The calorimeter will be on the lab bench filled with 100 mL water, and there will be a beaker containing 100 mL of 1.000 M HCl on the lab bench. In the thermometer window click *Save* to begin recording data. Allow 20-30 seconds to obtain a baseline temperature of the water.

7. Make sure the beaker of HCl is visible and drag it to the calorimeter and pour it into the calorimeter. The HCl and the water are at the same temperature so there should be no temperature change. Now drag the weigh paper with the NaOH to the calorimeter until it snaps into place and pour the sample into the calorimeter. It is important that the HCl be added first and the NaOH added second. Observe the change in temperature until it reaches a maximum and then record data for an additional 20-30

seconds. Record the temperature before adding the HCl and the temperature after adding the NaOH in the data table.

Reaction 3

8. Click the red disposal bucket to clear the lab. Click on the Stockroom to enter. Click on the clipboard and select Preset Experiment #4. Return to the laboratory.

9. In the thermometer window click *Save* to begin recording data. Allow 20-30 seconds to obtain a baseline temperature of the water. Pour the first beaker containing the HCl into the calorimeter and then pour the second beaker containing the NaOH into the calorimeter. Observe the change in temperature until it reaches a maximum and then record data for an additional 20-30 seconds. Record the initial and final temperatures in the data table.

Data Table

Parameter	Reaction 1	Reaction 2	Reaction 3
Mass NaOH	3.9982	3.9958	
initial temperature (°C)	25.00	25.00	24.99
final temperature (°C)	30.05	36.05	30.84

10. *Determine the change in temperature, ΔT, for each reaction. Record your results in the results table on the following page.*

11. *Calculate the mass of the reaction mixture in each reaction.* (To do this, first determine the total volume of the solution. Then calculate the mass of the solution, based on the assumption that the added solid does not change the volume and that the density of the solution is the same as that of pure water, 1.0 g/mL.) Remember to add the mass of the solid. Record your results in the result table.

Reaction 1 200 g H_2O + 3.9982 g NaOH = 203.9982 g solution
Reaction 2 200 g H_2O + 3.9958 g NaOH = 203.9958 g solution
Reaction 3 100 g HCl + 100 g NaOH = 200 g solution

12. *Calculate the total heat released in each reaction, in J, assuming that the specific heat capacity of the solution is the same as that of pure water, 4.184 J/K·g. Record the result in the results table.*
Remember: heat of reaction $= m \times C \times \Delta T$

Reaction 1 heat = 203.9982 g × 4.184 J/K·g × 5.05 K = 4310 J
Reaction 2 heat = 203.9958 g × 4.184 J/ K·g × 11.05 K = 9431 J
Reaction 3 heat = 200.00 g × 4.184 J/ K·g × 5.85 K = 4895 J

13. *Calculate the number of moles of NaOH used in reactions 1 and 2 where n = m/MW. Record the results in the results table.*

Reaction 1 3.9982 g/(40.0 g/mol) = 0.099956 mol NaOH
Reaction 2 3.9958 g/(40.0 g/mol) = 0.099895 mol NaOH

14. *Calculate the number of moles of NaOH used in reaction 3 by multiplying the volume of NaOH times the molarity (1.000 mol/L). Record the results in the results table.*

Reaction 3 100 mL NaOH = 0.100 L NaOH (1 mol/L) = 0.100 mol NaOH

15. *Calculate the energy released, in kJ/mol, of NaOH for each reaction and record the results in the results table.*

Reaction 1
$$\frac{4310 \text{ J}}{0.099956 \text{ mol}}\left(\frac{1 \text{ kJ}}{1000 \text{ J}}\right) = 43.12 \text{ kJ/mol}$$

Reaction 2
$$\frac{9431 \text{ J}}{0.099895 \text{ mol}}\left(\frac{1 \text{ k J}}{1000 \text{ J}}\right) = 94.41 \text{ kJ/mol}$$

Reaction 3
$$\frac{4895 \text{ J}}{0.100 \text{ mol}}\left(\frac{1 \text{ k J}}{1000 \text{ J}}\right) = 48.95 \text{ kJ/mol}$$

Results Table

Rxn #	Mass of Rxn Mixture	ΔT	Total Heat Released	mol NaOH	Heat Released per mol NaOH
1	203.9982 g	5.05	4310 J	0.099956	43.12 kJ
2	203.9958 g	11.05	9431 J	0.099895	94.41 kJ
3	200 g	5.85	4895 J	0.100	48.95 kJ

16. *Show that the equations for reactions 1 and 3, which are given in the background section, add up to equal the equation for reaction 2. Include the energy released per mole of NaOH in each equation.*

1. $NaOH \text{ (s)} \rightarrow Na^+ \text{ (aq)} + OH^- \text{ (aq)} + 43.12 \text{ kJ}$
3. $Na^+ \text{ (aq)} + OH^- \text{ (aq)} + H^+ \text{ (aq)} + Cl^- \text{ (aq)} \rightarrow H_2O + Na^+ \text{ (aq)} + Cl^- \text{ (aq)} + 48.95 \text{ kJ}$

2. $NaOH \text{ (s)} + H^+ \text{ (aq)} + Cl^- \text{ (aq)} \rightarrow H_2O + Na^+ \text{ (aq)} + Cl^- \text{ (aq)} + 92.07 \text{ kJ}$

17. *Calculate the percent difference between the heat given off in reaction 2 and the sum of the heats given off in reactions 1 and 3. Assume that the heat given off in reaction 2 is correct.*

$$\% \text{ Difference} = \frac{|heat_2 - (heat_1 + heat_3)|}{heat_2} \times 100$$

$$\% \text{ Difference} = (94.41 - 92.07)/94.41 \times 100 = 2.48\%$$

18. *State in your own words what is meant by the additive nature of heats of reaction.* **If the equations for two reactions can be algebraically added together to form the equation for a third chemical reaction, then the heat of reaction for the third reaction is the sum for the heats of reaction for the first two equations.**

3-13: The Balance Between Enthalpy and Entropy

For chemical reactions, we say that a reaction proceeds to the right when ΔG is negative and that the reaction proceeds to the left when ΔG is positive. At equilibrium ΔG is zero. The Gibbs-Helmholtz equation specifies that at constant temperature $\Delta G = \Delta H - T \Delta S$ or, in other words, that the sign and size of ΔG is governed by the balance between enthalpic (ΔH) and entropic (ΔS) considerations. In this assignment, you will dissolve several different salts in water, measure the resulting temperature changes, and then make some deductions about the thermodynamic driving forces behind the dissolving process.

1. Start *Virtual ChemLab* and select *The Balance Between Enthalpy and Entropy* from the list of assignments. The lab will open in the Calorimetry laboratory.

2. There will be a bottle of sodium chloride (NaCl) on the lab bench. A weigh paper will be on the balance with approximately 2 g of NaCl on the paper.

3. The calorimeter will be on the lab bench and filled with 100 mL water. Click on the *Lab Book* to open it. Make certain the stirrer is *On* (you should be able to see the shaft rotating). In the thermometer window click *Save* to begin recording data. Allow 20-30 seconds to obtain a baseline temperature of the water.

4. Drag the weigh paper with the sample to the calorimeter until it snaps into place and then pour the sample in the calorimeter. Observe the change in temperature until it reaches a maximum (or minimum) and then record data for an additional 20-30 seconds. (You can click the clock on the wall labeled *Accelerate* to accelerate the time in the laboratory.) Click *Stop*. A blue data link will appear in the Lab Book. Click the data link and record the temperature before adding the NaCl and the *highest* or *lowest* temperature after adding the NaCl in the data table.

5. Click the red disposal bucket to clear the lab. Click on the *Stockroom* to enter. Click on the clipboard and select Preset Experiment #7 and repeat the experiment with $NaNO_3$. Record the initial and final temperatures in the data table.

6. Click the red disposal bucket to clear the lab. Click on the *Stockroom* to enter. Click the clipboard and select Preset Experiment #8 and repeat the experiment with $NaCH_3COO$ (NaAc). Record the initial and final temperatures in the data table.

Data Table

Mixture	T_1	T_2	$\Delta T \; (T_2 - T_1)$
NaCl (s) + H_2O (l)	25.00	24.90	-0.10
$NaNO_3$ (s) + H_2O (l)	25.00	24.00	-1.00
$NaCH_3COO$ + H_2O (l)	25.00	25.96	0.96

Use your experimental data to answer the following questions:

7. *Calculate ΔT ($\Delta T = T_2 - T_1$) for each mixture and record the results in the data table.*

8. An exothermic process releases heat (warms up), and an endothermic process absorbs heat (cools down).

    Which solutions are endothermic and which are exothermic? What is the sign of the change in enthalpy, ΔH, in each case?

    endothermic: $NaNO_3$, sign is positive (+): exothermic: $NaCH_3COO$, sign is negative (-)

9. *Which solution(s) had little or no change in temperature?* **NaCl**

10. When sodium chloride dissolves in water, the ions dissociate:

    $$NaCl\ (s)\ =\ Na^+\ (aq)\ +\ Cl^-\ (aq)$$

    Write ionic equations, similar to the one above, that describe how $NaNO_3$ and $NaCH_3COO$ each dissociate as they dissolve in water. Include heat as a reactant or product in each equation.

    heat $+$ $NaNO_3$ (s) $\rightarrow$ Na^+ (aq) $+$ NO_3^- (aq)

    $NaCH_3COO$ (s) $\rightarrow$ Na^+ (aq) $+$ CH_3COO^- (aq) $+$ heat

11. *What is the sign of the change in Gibbs free energy (ΔG) for each process?*

    Spontaneous reactions have a negative (-) sign for ΔG and these were all spontaneous reactions.

12. *Consider the Gibbs-Helmholtz equation, $\Delta G = \Delta H - T\Delta S$. For each dissolving process, substitute the signs of ΔG and ΔH into the equation and predict the sign for the entropy (ΔS). Does the sign for entropy change seem to make sense? Explain.*

    $NaNO_3$: Since ΔH is positive and ΔG is negative, the sign for ΔS has to be positive.
    $NaCH_3COO$: Since ΔH is negative and the ΔG is negative, the sign for ΔS could be negative or positive but is likely to be positive since the dissolving process is similar to $NaNO_3$. The signs for the entropy change should both be positive since the dissolving process creates more disorder.

13. *If the sign for ΔG is negative (spontaneous process) and the sign for ΔS is positive (more disorder) for both dissolving processes, how could one be endothermic (positive ΔH) and one be exothermic (negative ΔH)? Is there more to consider than just the dissolving process?*

    Both $NaNO_3$ and $NaCH_3COO$ are salts that dissolve in water. The nitrate ion (NO_3^-) is the anion of a strong acid. Strong acids ionize 100%; hence NO_3^- does not react in aqueous solution. The acetate ion (CH_3COO^-), however, is the conjugate base of a weak acid and in aqueous solutions reacts with water to make the weak acid CH_3COOH. This additional acid-base reaction is exothermic and makes the total dissolving process exothermic. The $NaNO_3$ process is endothermic since there are no exothermic reactions and we are left with just the endothermic process of breaking the bonds in the crystal. Consequently, the $NaNO_3$ dissolution process is entropy driven.

4-1: Heat of Fusion of Water

The molar heat of fusion for a substance, ΔH_{fus}, is the heat required to transform one mole of the substance from the solid phase into the liquid phase. In this assignment, you will use a simple coffee cup calorimeter and a thermometer to measure the molar heat of fusion for water.

1. Start *Virtual ChemLab* and select *Heat of Fusion of Water* from the list of assignments. The lab will open in the Calorimetry laboratory with a beaker of ice on the balance and a coffee cup calorimeter on the lab bench.

2. Click on the *Lab Book* to open it. Record the mass of the ice on the balance in the data table. If the mass is too small to read, click on the *Balance* area to zoom in. Note that the balance has already been tared for the mass of the empty beaker.

3. 100 mL of water is already in the coffee cup. Use the density of water at 25°C (0.998 g/mL) to determine the mass of water from the volume. Record the mass in the data table. Make certain the stirrer is *On* (you should be able to see the shaft rotating). Click the thermometer window to bring it to the front and click *Save* to begin recording data to the lab book. Allow 20-30 seconds to obtain a baseline temperature of the water.

4. Drag the beaker from the balance area until it snaps into place above the coffee cup and then pour the ice into the calorimeter. Click the thermometer and graph windows to bring them to the front again and observe the change in temperature in the graph window until it reaches a minimum value and begins to warm again. Click *Stop* in the temperature window. (You can click on the clock on the wall labeled *Accelerate* to accelerate the time in the laboratory.) A blue data link will appear in the lab book. Click the blue data link and record the temperature before adding the ice and the *lowest* temperature after adding ice in the data table. (Remember that the water will begin to warm back up after all of the ice has melted.)

5. If you want to repeat the experiment, click on the red disposal bucket to clear the lab, click on the Stockroom, click on the clipboard, and select Preset Experiment #3, Heat of Fusion of Water.

Data Table

volume of water in calorimeter (mL)	100
mass of water in calorimeter (g)	98.8
mass of ice (g)	24.7036
initial temperature (°C)	25.00
final temperature (°C)	5.58

6. *Calculate ΔT for the water using $\Delta T = |T_f - T_i|$.* __**19.13°C = 19.13 K**__

7. *Calculate the heat (q) transferred, in kJ, from the water to the ice using $q = m \times C \times \Delta T$ where the heat capacity (C) for water is 4.18 J/K·g and the mass, m, is for the water in the calorimeter.*

__$q = m \times C \times \Delta T = 99.8\ \text{g} \times (4.184\ \text{J/K·g}) \times 19.13\ \text{K} = 7988\ \text{J} = 7.988\ \text{kJ}$__

8. *Convert the mass of ice to moles.* **24.7036 g ice × (1 mol/18.0 g ice) = 1.372 mol ice**

9. *Calculate ΔH$_{fus}$ of water, in kJ/mol, by dividing the heat transferred from the water by the moles of*

    ice melted. **7.988 kJ/1.372 mole = 5.822 kJ/mol**

10. *Compare your experimental value of ΔH$_{fus}$ of ice with the accepted value of 6.01 kJ/mol and calculate the % error using the formula:*

$$\% \ Error = \frac{|your \ answer - accepted \ answer|}{accepted \ answer} \times 100$$

    % Error = **3.13%**

11. *What are some possible sources of error in this laboratory procedure? ?* **(1) The calorimeter**

    absorbs some of the heat from the water. (2) After the ice melts, the water from the ice

    absorbed some heat as it warms from 0°C to the equilibrium temperature. (3) After the ice

    melts, the water contributes to the heat capacity of the calorimeter.

4-2: Heat of Vaporization of Water

A graph of the vapor pressure of a liquid as a function of temperature has a characteristic shape that can be represented fairly accurately with the *Clausius-Clapeyron* equation. In this assignment you will measure the vapor pressure of water at several temperatures and then use this data to estimate the heat of vaporization of water using the *Clausius-Clapeyron* equation.

1. Start *Virtual ChemLab* and select *Heat of Vaporization of Water* from the list of assignments. The lab will open in the Gases laboratory.

2. The balloon is filled with 0.10 moles of water vapor at a pressure of 140 kPa and a temperature of 400 K. Pull down the lever on the Temperature LCD controller until the temperature stops decreasing. This temperature represents the equilibrium temperature where water as a gas exists in equilibrium with water as a liquid. The pressure at this temperature is the vapor pressure. Record the vapor pressure (in kPa) and the temperature (in K) in the data table.

3. Change the pressure from 140 kPa to 120 kPa using the lever on the Pressure LCD controller or by clicking on the tens place and typing "2." Pull down the lever on the Temperature controller until the temperature stops decreasing. Record the vapor pressure (in kPa) and the temperature (in K) in the data table. Continue this process with pressures of 100 kPa, 80 kPa, 60 kPa, and 40 kPa. Do not forget to decrease the temperature until the temperature stops decreasing after each pressure change. Record all vapor pressure and temperatures in the data table.

Data Table

Vapor Pressure (kPa)	Temperature (K)
140	382.47
120	377.97
100	372.79
80	366.67
60	359.11
40	349.03

4. The *Clausius-Clapeyron* equation has the form $\ln\dfrac{P_2}{P_1} = -\dfrac{\Delta H_{vap}}{R}\left(\dfrac{1}{T_2} - \dfrac{1}{T_1}\right)$. If you plot ln *P* (natural log of the vapor pressure) as a function of $1/T$, the data should form a straight line. Using a spreadsheet program and the data you collected, plot $1/T$ (reciprocal temperature) on the *x*-axis and ln *P* (natural log of the vapor pressure) on the *y*-axis.

Describe the curve. **The curve is a straight line with a negative slope.**

5. Graphically or using the spreadsheet program, determine the best linear fit for your curve and find the slope of the line. From the *Clausius-Clapeyron* equation, $\Delta H_{vap} = $ -slope $\times R$ where $R = 8.314$ $J{\cdot}K^{-1}{\cdot}mol^{-1}$.

Based on your slope, calculate the heat of vaporization of water in kJ/mol.

$\underline{\Delta H_{vap} = \text{-slope} \times R = -(-5.00 \times 10^3)(\, 8.314\ J{\cdot}K^{-1}{\cdot}mol^{-1}) = 4.16 \times 10^4\ J/mol = 41.6\ kJ/mol}$

6. The accepted value for the heat of vaporization of water is 40.7 kJ/mol.

    Calculate the percent error using the formula:

    $$\% \, Error = \frac{\left| your \; answer - accepted \; answer \right|}{accepted \; answer} \times 100$$

    % Error = **2.21%**

4-3: The Boiling Point of Water at High Altitude

The relationship between the equilibrium vapor pressure of a liquid or solid and temperature is given by the *Clausius-Clapeyron* equation. In this assignment you will measure the vapor pressure of water at a given temperature and use this data and the *Clausius-Clapeyron* equation to calculate the boiling point of water on the top of Mt. Denali in Alaska.

1. Start *Virtual ChemLab* and select *The Boiling Point of Water at High Altitude* from the list of assignments. The lab will open in the Gases laboratory.

2. The balloon is filled with 0.40 moles of water vapor at a pressure of 1500 Torr and a temperature of 400 K. Pull down the lever on the Temperature LCD controller until the temperature stops decreasing. This temperature represents the equilibrium temperature where water as a gas exists in equilibrium with water as a liquid. The pressure at this temperature is the vapor pressure. Record the vapor pressure (in Torr) and the temperature (in K) in the data table.

Data Table

Vapor Pressure (Torr)	Temperature (K)
1500	393.38

3. The *Clausius-Clapeyron* equation may be written in several forms. For this assignment, the most useful form can be written as

$$\ln\frac{P_2}{P_1} = -\frac{\Delta H_{vap}}{R}\left(\frac{1}{T_2} - \frac{1}{T_1}\right)$$

If P_1 and T_1 are the experimental vapor pressure and temperature that you measured and the pressure at the top of Mt. Denali, P_2, is 340 Torr, the boiling point of water, T_2, at the top of the mountain can be calculated by solving the *Clausius-Clapeyron* equation for T_2.

Calculate the boiling point of water at the top of Mt. Denali. The value of R is 8.314 J·K^{-1}·mol^{-1} and ΔH_{vap} for water is 40.67 kJ/mol

$$\ln\left(\frac{340\text{ torr}}{1500\text{ torr}}\right) = \frac{-40{,}670\text{ J}}{8.314\text{ J}\cdot\text{K}^{-1}\cdot\text{mol}^{-1}}\left(\frac{1}{T_2} - \frac{1}{393.38\text{ K}}\right)$$

$$T_2 = 351\text{ K} = 78°\text{C}$$

4-4 Boiling Point Elevation

If you dissolve a substance such as ordinary table salt (NaCl) in water, the boiling point of the water will increase relative to the boiling point of the pure water. In this assignment, you will dissolve a sample of NaCl in water and then measure the boiling point elevation for the solution.

1. Start *Virtual ChemLab* and select *Boiling Point Elevation* from the list of assignments. The lab will open in the Calorimetry laboratory with a calorimeter on the lab bench and a sample of sodium chloride (NaCl) on the balance.

2. Record the mass of the sodium chloride in the data table. If it is too small to read, click on the *Balance* area to zoom in, record the reading, and then return to the laboratory.

3. 100 mL of water is already in the calorimeter. Use the density of water at 25°C (0.998 g/mL) to determine the mass from the volume and record it in the data table. Make certain the stirrer is *On* (you should be able to see the shaft rotating). Click on the green heater light on the control panel to turn on the heater and begin heating the water. Click the clock on the wall labeled *Accelerate* to accelerate the laboratory time if necessary.

4. Observe the temperature until the first appearance of steam comes from the calorimeter. Immediately click the red light on the heater to turn it off and then record the temperature as the boiling point of pure water in the data table. Letting the water boil will decrease the mass of the water present in the calorimeter. Note that the boiling point may be different than 100°C if the atmospheric pressure is *not* 760 Torr. The current atmospheric pressure for the day can be checked by selecting *Pressure* on the LED meter on the wall.

5. Drag the weigh paper to the calorimeter and add the NaCl. Wait 30 seconds for the salt to dissolve and then turn on the heater. When steam first appears observe and record the temperature in the data table.

6. If you want to repeat the experiment, click on the red disposal bucket to clear the lab, click on the Stockroom, click on the clipboard, and select Preset Experiment #2, Boiling Point Elevation – NaCl.

Data Table

mass NaCl	4.0865 g
mass water	99.8 g
boiling temp of pure water	99.49°C
boiling temp of solution	100.24°C

7. The boiling point elevation can be predicted using the equation $\Delta T = K_b \times m \times i$, where ΔT is the change in boiling point, i is the number of ions in the solution per mole of dissolved NaCl ($i = 2$), m is the molality of the solution, and K_b is the molal boiling point constant for water which is 0.51°C/m.

Calculate the predicted change in boiling point, in °C for your solution.

$$\Delta T = i \times \left(\frac{mass\ solute / molar\ mass}{kg\ solvent} \right) \times K_b = 2 \times \left(\frac{4.0865\ g / 58.5\ g/mol}{0.0998\ kg} \right) \times 0.51°\ C/m = 0.71°\ C$$

8. The change in boiling point must be added to the boiling point of pure water in your experiment in order to compare the predicted boiling point with the actual boiling point.

    What is the calculated boiling point of the solution? Compare this with the actual boiling point.

    predicted: 99.49°C + 0.71°C = 100.20°C: The experimental boiling point is 100.24°C. This is

    pretty good agreement.

4-5: Freezing Point Depression

If you dissolve a substance such as ordinary table salt (NaCl) in water, the freezing point of the water will decrease relative to the freezing point of the pure water. This property is used to melt the snow or ice on roads during the winter or to make homemade ice cream. In this assignment, you will dissolve a sample of NaCl in water, add some ice, and then measure the freezing point depression.

1. Start *Virtual ChemLab* and select *Freezing Point Depression* from the list of assignments. The lab will open in the Calorimetry laboratory with a beaker containing 45.00 g of ice and a coffee cup calorimeter on the lab bench. A sample of sodium chloride (NaCl) will also be on the balance.

2. Click on the *Lab Book* to open it. Record the mass of the sodium chloride in the data table. If it is too small to read, click on the *Balance* area to zoom in, record the mass, and then return to the laboratory.

3. 100 mL of water is already in the calorimeter. Use the density of water at 25°C (0.998 g/mL) to determine the mass from the volume and record it in the data table. Make certain the stirrer is *On* (you should be able to see the shaft rotating). Click the thermometer window to bring it to the front and click *Save* to begin recording data in the lab book. Allow 20-30 seconds to obtain a baseline temperature of the water. Click the clock on the wall labeled *Accelerate* to accelerate the laboratory time if necessary.

4. Drag the beaker of ice until it snaps into place above the calorimeter and then pour the ice into the calorimeter. Click the thermometer and graph windows to bring them to the front again and observe the change in temperature in the graph window until it reaches zero. Drag the weigh paper from the balance to the calorimeter and then pour it into the calorimeter. Observe the change in temperature until it reaches a stable minimum and click *Stop* in the temperature window. A blue data link will appear in the lab book. Click the blue data link and record the *lowest* temperature after adding the salt in the data table. (Remember that the water may have begun to warm back up.)

5. If you want to repeat the experiment, click on the red disposal bucket to clear the lab, click on the Stockroom, click on the clipboard, and select Preset Experiment #1, Freezing Point Depression – NaCl.

Data Table

mass NaCl	4.0240 g
mass water	99.80 g
mass ice	45.00 g
mass water + ice	144.8 g
minimum temperature	-1.76°C

6. The freezing point depression can be predicted using the equation $\Delta T = K_f \times m \times i$, where ΔT is the change in freezing point, i is the number of ions in the solution per mole of dissolved NaCl ($i = 2$), m is the molality of the solution, and K_f is the molal freezing point constant for water which is 1.86°C/m.

Colligative Properties

Calculate the predicted change in freezing point for your solution.

$$\Delta T = i \times \left(\frac{\text{mass solute} / \text{molar mass}}{\text{kg solvent}} \right) \times K_f = 2 \times \left(\frac{4.0240\text{ g} / 58.5\text{ g/mol}}{0.1448\text{ kg}} \right) \times 1.86^\circ\text{ C/m} = 1.76^\circ\text{ C}$$

7. The change in freezing point must be subtracted from the freezing point of pure water, which is 0.0 °C, in order to compare the predicted freezing point with the actual freezing point.

What is the calculated freezing point of the solution? Compare this to the actual freezing point.

0°C – 1.76°C = -1.76°C: The experimental freezing point is also –1.76°C.

4-6: Molar Mass Determination by Boiling Point Elevation

If you dissolve a substance such as ordinary table salt (NaCl) in water, the boiling point of the water will increase relative to the boiling point of the pure water. You can use this property to calculate the molar mass of an unknown. In this assignment, you will dissolve a sample of NaCl in water, measure the boiling point elevation for the solution, and then calculate the molar mass for NaCl as if it were an unknown.

1. Start *Virtual ChemLab* and select *Boiling Point Elevation* from the list of assignments. The lab will open in the Calorimetry laboratory with a calorimeter on the lab bench and a sample of sodium chloride (NaCl) on the balance.

2. Record the mass of the sodium chloride in the data table. If it is too small to read, click on the *Balance* area to zoom in, record the reading, and then return to the laboratory.

3. 100 mL of water is already in the calorimeter. Use the density of water at 25°C (0.998 g/mL) to determine the mass from the volume and record it in the data table. Make certain the stirrer is *On* (you should be able to see the shaft rotating). Click on the green heater light on the control panel to turn on the heater and begin heating the water. Click the clock on the wall labeled *Accelerate* to accelerate the laboratory time if necessary.

4. Observe the temperature until the first appearance of steam comes from the calorimeter. Immediately click the red light on the heater to turn it off and then record the temperature as the boiling point of pure water in the data table. Letting the water boil will decrease the mass of the water present in the calorimeter. Note that the boiling point may be different than 100°C if the atmospheric pressure is *not* 760 Torr. The current atmospheric pressure for the day can be checked by selecting *Pressure* on the LED meter on the wall.

5. Drag the weigh paper to the calorimeter and add the NaCl. Wait 30 seconds for the salt to dissolve and then turn on the heater. When steam first appears, observe and record the temperature in the data table.

6. If you want to repeat the experiment, click on the red disposal bucket to clear the lab, click on the Stockroom, click on the clipboard, and select Preset Experiment #2, Boiling Point Elevation – NaCl.

Data Table

mass NaCl	4.0865 g
mass water	99.8 g
boiling temp of pure water	99.49°C
boiling temp of solution	100.24°C

7. *Calculate the boiling point elevation, ΔT, caused by adding NaCl to the water.*

$\Delta T = 100.24°C - 99.49 °C = 0.75°C$

8. The boiling point elevation can be calculated using the equation $\Delta T = K_b \times m \times i$, where ΔT is the change in boiling point, i is the number of ions in the solution per mole of dissolved NaCl ($i = 2$), m is the molality of the solution, and K_b is the molal boiling point constant for water which is 0.51°C/m.

Using this equation and the data recorded in the data table, calculate the molar mass for NaCl and compare it with the actual value.

$$\Delta T = i \times m \times K_b = i \times \left(\frac{\text{mass solute}\big/ \text{molar mass}}{\text{kg solvent}} \right) \times K_b$$

$$\text{mass solute}\big/ \text{molar mass} = \frac{\text{kg solvent} \times \Delta T}{i \times K_b}$$

$$\text{molar mass} = \frac{\text{mass solute} \times i \times K_b}{\text{kg solvent} \times \Delta T}$$

$$\text{molar mass} = \frac{4.0865 \text{ g} \times 2 \times 0.51^\circ \text{C}/m}{0.0998 \text{ kg} \times 0.75^\circ \text{C}} = 55.69 \text{ g/mol}$$

The actual molar mass of NaCl is 58.44 g/mol.

4-7: Molar Mass Determination by Freezing Point Depression

If you dissolve a substance such as ordinary table salt (NaCl) in water, the freezing point of the water will decrease relative to the freezing point of the pure water. You can use this property to calculate the molar mass of an unknown. In this assignment, you will dissolve a sample of NaCl in water, measure the freezing point depression for the solution, and then calculate the molar mass for NaCl as if it were an unknown.

1. Start *Virtual ChemLab* and select *Freezing Point Depression* from the list of assignments. The lab will open in the Calorimetry laboratory with a beaker containing 45.00 g of ice and a coffee cup calorimeter on the lab bench. A sample of sodium chloride (NaCl) will also be on the balance.

2. Click on the *Lab Book* to open it. Record the mass of the sodium chloride in the data table. If it is too small to read, click on the *Balance* area to zoom in, record the mass, and then return to the laboratory.

3. 100 mL of water is already in the calorimeter. Use the density of water at 25°C (0.998 g/mL) to determine the mass from the volume and record it in the data table. Make certain the stirrer is *On* (you should be able to see the shaft rotating). Click the thermometer window to bring it to the front and click *Save* to begin recording data in the lab book. Allow 20-30 seconds to obtain a baseline temperature of the water. Click the clock on the wall labeled *Accelerate* to accelerate the laboratory time if necessary.

4. Drag the beaker of ice until it snaps into place above the calorimeter and then pour the ice into the calorimeter. Click the thermometer and graph windows to bring them to the front again and observe the change in temperature in the graph window until it reaches zero. Drag the weigh paper from the balance to the calorimeter and then pour it into the calorimeter. Observe the change in temperature until it reaches a stable minimum and click *Stop* in the temperature window. A blue data link will appear in the lab book. Click the blue data link and record the *lowest* temperature after adding the salt in the data table. (Remember that the water may have begun to warm back up.)

5. If you want to repeat the experiment, click on the red disposal bucket to clear the lab, click on the Stockroom, click on the clipboard, and select Preset Experiment #1, Freezing Point Depression – NaCl.

Data Table

mass NaCl	4.0240 g
mass water	99.80 g
mass ice	45.00 g
mass water + ice	144.8 g
minimum temperature	-1.76°C

6. *What is the freezing point depression caused by adding NaCl to the water?* $\underline{\Delta T = 1.76°C}$

7. The freezing point depression can be calculated using the equation $\Delta T = K_f \times m \times i$, where ΔT is the change in freezing point, i is the number of ions in the solution per mole of dissolved NaCl ($i = 2$), m is the molality of the solution, and K_f is the molal freezing point constant for water which is 1.86°C/m.

Using this equation and the data recorded in the data table, calculate the molar mass for NaCl and compare it with the actual value.

$$\Delta T = i \times m \times K_f = i \times \left(\frac{mass\ solute\big/molar\ mass}{kg\ solvent} \right) \times K_f$$

$$mass\ solute\big/molar\ mass = \frac{kg\ solvent \times \Delta T}{i \times K_f}$$

$$molar\ mass = \frac{mass\ solute \times i \times K_f}{kg\ solvent \times \Delta T}$$

$$molar\ mass = \frac{4.0240\ g \times 2 \times 1.86^{\circ}C/m}{0.1448\ kg \times 1.76^{\circ}C} = 58.74\ g/mol$$

The actual molar mass of NaCl is 58.44 g/mol.

4-8: Changes in the Boiling Point

If you dissolve a substance such as ordinary table salt (NaCl) in water, the boiling point of the water will increase relative to the boiling point of the pure water. In this assignment, you will dissolve a sample of NaCl in water and then observe what happens when you continue to boil the water until the water boils away.

1. Start *Virtual ChemLab* and select *Changes in the Boiling Point* from the list of assignments. The lab will open in the Calorimetry laboratory with a calorimeter on the lab bench and a sample of sodium chloride (NaCl) on the balance.

2. 100 mL of water is already in the calorimeter. Make certain the stirrer is **On** (you should be able to see the shaft rotating). Drag the weigh paper to the calorimeter and add the NaCl. Wait 30 seconds for the salt to dissolve and then turn on the heater by clicking on the green heater light on the control panel. Click the clock on the wall labeled *Accelerate* to accelerate the laboratory time if necessary.

3. When steam first appears, observe the temperature. Allow the solution to continue boiling and observe the temperature until all of the water boils away and the heater burns out. (The water level is shown on the right side of the calorimeter control panel.)

   What observations did you make about the temperature as the solution continued to boil?

   The water level decreased and the boiling point continued to climb until the heater burned out.

4. *Explain the observations described in question # 3. Why does this occur?*

   As the solution boils the water is evaporating and the amount of water decreases causing the
   molality of the solution to increase. As the molality increases, the boiling point elevation also
   increases until the heater burns out.

5-1: Boyle's Law: Pressure and Volume

Robert Boyle, a philosopher and theologian, studied the properties of gases in the 17th century. He noticed that gases behave similarly to springs; when compressed or expanded, they tend to 'spring' back to their original volume. He published his findings in 1662 in a monograph entitled *The Spring of the Air and Its Effects*. You will make observations similar to those of Robert Boyle and learn about the relationship between the pressure and volume of an ideal gas.

1. Start *Virtual ChemLab* and select *Boyle's Law: Pressure and Volume* from the list of assignments. The lab will open in the Gases laboratory.

2. Note that the balloon in the chamber is filled with 0.300 moles of an ideal gas (MW = 4 g/mol) at a temperature of 298 K, a pressure of 1.00 atm, and a volume of 7.336 L. To the left of the Pressure LCD controller is a lever that will decrease and increase the pressure as it is moved up or down; the digit changes depending on how far the lever is moved. Digits may also be clicked directly to type in the desired number. You may want to practice adjusting the lever so that you can decrease and increase the pressure accurately. Make sure the moles, temperature, and pressure are returned to their original values before proceeding.

3. Click on the *Lab Book* to open it. Back in the laboratory, click on the *Save* button to start recording *P, V, T,* and *n* data to the lab book. Increase the pressure from 1 atm to 10 atm one atmosphere at a time. Click *Stop* to stop recording data, and a blue data link will appear in the lab book. To help keep track of your data links, enter 'Ideal Gas 1' next to the link.

4. *Zoom Out* by clicking the green arrow next to the *Save* button. Click *Return Tank* on the gas cylinder. On the table underneath the experimental chamber is a switch to choose Real gases or Ideal gases. Click on the *Ideal Gases* and choose the cylinder labeled *Ideal 8* (Ideal 8 MW = 222 g/mol). Click on the balloon chamber to *Zoom In* and set the temperature, pressure, and moles to 298 K, 1.00 atm, and 0.300 moles, respectively. Repeat the experiment with this gas labeling the data link as 'Ideal Gas 8.'

5. *Zoom Out* by clicking on the green arrow next to the *Save* button. Click on the *Stockroom* and then on the *Clipboard* and select *Balloon Experiment N2*. Again, set the temperature, pressure, and moles to 298 K, 1.00 atm, and 0.300 moles, respectively. You may have to click on the *Units* button to change some of the variables to the correct units. Repeat the experiment with this gas labeling the data link 'Real Gas N2.'

6. Select the lab book and click on the data link for Ideal Gas 1. In the *Data Viewer* window, select all the data by clicking on the *Select All* button and copy the data using CTRL-C for Windows or CMD-C for Macintosh. Paste the data into a spreadsheet program and create a graph with volume on the *x*-axis and pressure on the *y*-axis. Also create a graph for your data from Ideal Gas 8 and Real Gas N2.

7. *Based on your data, what relationship exists between the pressure and the volume of a gas (assuming a constant temperature)?* **Pressure varies inversely with volume—i.e., as pressure increases, volume decreases.**

Gas Properties

8. *Look up a statement of Boyle's Law in your textbook. Do your results further prove this?* **yes**

9. Complete the tables from the data saved in your lab book. Use only a sampling of the data for pressures at 1, 3, 6, and 9 atm.

Ideal Gas 1 MW = 4 g/mol

Volume (L)	Pressure (atm)	PV Product ($P \times V$)
7.335895	1	7.335895
2.445298	3	7.335894
1.222649	6	7.335894
0.8150995	9	7.335895

Ideal Gas 8 MW = 222 g/mol

Volume (L)	Pressure (atm)	PV Product ($P \times V$)
7.335895	1	7.335895
2.445298	3	7.335894
1.222649	6	7.335894
0.8150995	9	7.335895

Real Gas N2

Volume (L)	Pressure (atm)	PV Product ($P \times V$)
7.334204	1	7.334204
2.443806	3	7.331418
1.221250	6	7.327500
0.8137625	9	7.323863

10. *What conclusions can you make about the PV product with Ideal Gas 1, MW = 4 g/mol?*

    The *PV* product does not change. It is constant.

    How is the PV product affected using an ideal gas with a different molecular weight (Ideal Gas 8)?

    It is not affected. The *PV* product is still a constant.

11. *How are your results affected using a Real Gas (N2)?* **It is affected. As the pressure increases, the**

    PV product decreases slightly. It is essentially the same number, but it does vary.

12. You may want to repeat the experiment several times using different size pressure changes.

118

5-2: Charles' Law: Temperature and Volume

Charles' Law was discovered by Joseph Louis Gay-Lussac in 1802; it was based on unpublished work done by Jacques Charles in about 1787. Charles had found that a number of gases expand to the same extent over the same 80 degree temperature interval. You will be observing the relationship between the temperature and volume of a gas similar to that studied by Charles.

1. Start *Virtual ChemLab* and select *Charles's Law: Temperature and Volume* from the list of assignments. The lab will open in the Gases laboratory.

2. Note that the balloon in the chamber is filled with 0.050 moles of an ideal gas (MW = 4 g/mol) at a temperature of 100°C, a pressure of 1.00 atm, and a volume of 1.531 L. To the left of the Temperature LCD controller is a lever that will decrease and increase the temperature as it is moved up or down; the digit changes depending on how far the lever is moved. Digits may also be clicked directly to type in the desired number, or they can be rounded by clicking on the *R* button. You may want to practice adjusting the lever so that you can decrease and increase the temperature accurately. Make sure the moles, temperature, and pressure are returned to their original values before proceeding.

3. Click on the *Lab Book* to open it. Back in the laboratory, click on the *Save* button to start recording *P, V, T,* and *n* data to the lab book. Increase the temperature from 100°C to 1000°C 100 degrees at a time. Click *Stop* to stop recording data, and a blue data link will appear in the lab book. To help keep track of your data links, enter 'Ideal Gas 1' next to the link.

4. *Zoom Out* by clicking on the green arrow next to the *Save* button. Click on the *Stockroom* and then on the *Clipboard* and select *Balloon Experiment N2*. Again, set the temperature, pressure, and moles to 100°C, 1.00 atm, and 0.050 moles, respectively. You may have to click on the *Units* button to change some of the variables to the correct units. Repeat the experiment with this gas labeling the data link 'Real Gas N2.'

5. Select the lab book and click on the data link for Ideal Gas 1. In the *Data Viewer* window, select all the data by clicking on the *Select All* button and copy the data using CTRL-C for Windows or CMD-C for Macintosh. Paste the data into a spreadsheet program and create a graph with temperature on the *x*-axis and volume on the *y*-axis. Also create a graph for the data labeled Real Gas N2.

6. *Based on your data, what relationship exists between the temperature and the volume of a gas (assuming a constant pressure)?* <u>**Temperature varies directly with volume—i.e., as temperature**</u>

    <u>**increases, volume increases.**</u>

7. *Look up a statement of Charles' Law in your textbook. Do your results further prove this?* <u>**yes**</u>

8. Using the spreadsheet program, fit the ideal gas data to a line or printout the graph and use a ruler to draw the best line through the data. The lowest possible temperature is reached when an ideal gas has zero volume. This temperature is the *x*-intercept for the plotted line.

    What is this temperature? <u>**-273°C**</u>

9. *Now do the same analysis with the real gas data (N2). What temperature did you find?* <u>**-273°C**</u>

10. *Under these conditions, does N_2 behave like an ideal gas?* <u>**yes**</u>

5-3: Avogadro's Law: Moles and Volume

In 1808, Joseph Gay-Lussac observed the *law of combining values,* which states that the volumes of gases that react with one another react in the ratio of small whole numbers. Three years later, Amedeo Avogadro built upon this observation by proposing what is now known as *Avogadro's hypothesis*: Equal volumes of gases at the same temperature and pressure contain equal numbers of molecules. Avogadro's Law, which states the relationship between moles and volume, followed from his hypothesis. You will be observing the same principle that Avogadro stated two hundred years ago.

1. Start *Virtual ChemLab* and select *Avogadro's Law: Moles and Volume* from the list of assignments. The lab will open in the Gases laboratory. You will see LCD controllers on the left for volume, pressure, temperature and number of moles. You may change the units for volume, pressure, and temperature by clicking on the *Units* buttons. The balloon has been filled with 0.100 moles of an ideal gas and the pressure is 2.00 atm. Record the number of moles and the volume (in L) in the data table below.

2. Click on the tenths digit on the Moles LCD controller and change the moles of gas in the balloon from 0.1 to 0.2 mole. Record the number of moles and volume in the data table. Repeat for 0.3, 0.4, and 0.5 moles.

Data Table

n (moles)	V (L)
0.10	1.223
0.20	2.445
0.30	3.668
0.40	4.891
0.50	6.113

3. *Based on your observations, what can you state about the relationship between moles and volume*

    of a gas? **When the moles of gas increases the volume increases. The volume is directly**

    proportional to the number of moles of gas.

4. *Write a mathematical equation using a proportionality constant (k) with units of L/mol that expresses what you have learned about Avogadro's Law. Determine the value of k.*

$$V = kn$$
$$k = \frac{V}{n} = \frac{6.113\,\text{L}}{0.50\,\text{mol}} = 12.225\,\text{L/mol}$$

5-4: Derivation of the Ideal Gas Law

An ideal gas is a hypothetical gas whose pressure, volume, and temperature follow the relationship $PV = nRT$. Ideal gases do not actually exist, although all real gases can behave like an ideal gas at certain temperatures and pressures. All gases can be described to some extent using the Ideal Gas Law, and it is important in our understanding of how all gases behave. In this assignment, you will derive the Ideal Gas Law from experimental observations.

The state of any gas can be described using the four variables: pressure (P), volume (V), temperature (T), and the number of moles of gas (n). Each experiment in *Virtual ChemLab: Gases* allows three of these variables (the independent variables) to be manipulated or changed and shows the effect on the remaining variable (the dependent variable).

1. Start *Virtual ChemLab* and select *Ideal Gas Law* from the list of assignments. The lab will open in the Gases laboratory.

2. Use the balloon experiment already setup in the laboratory to describe the relationship between pressure (P) and volume (V). Increase and decrease the pressure using the lever on the Pressure LCD controller to determine the effect on volume.

    What can you conclude about the effect of pressure on volume? Write a mathematical relationship using the proportionality symbol ($\propto$).

    <u>**Volume is inversely proportional to pressure ($V \propto 1/P$).**</u>

3. Use this same experiment to describe the relationship between temperature (T) and volume by increasing and decreasing the temperature.

    What can you conclude about the effect of temperature on volume? Write a mathematical relationship using the proportionality symbol ($\propto$).

    <u>**Volume is directly proportional to temperature ($V \propto T$).**</u>

4. Use this same experiment to describe the relationship between moles of gas and volume by increasing and decreasing the number of moles (n).

    What can you conclude about the effect of moles on volume? Write a mathematical relationship using the proportionality symbol ($\propto$).

    <u>**Volume is directly proportional to the number of moles ($V \propto n$).**</u>

5. Since volume is inversely proportional to pressure and directly proportional to temperature and moles, we can combine these three relationships into a single proportionality by showing how V is proportional to $1/P$, T, and n.

Write one combined proportion to show the relationship of volume to pressure, temperature and moles.

$V \propto nT/P$

6. This proportional relationship can be converted into a mathematical equation by inserting a proportionality constant (*R*) into the numerator on the right side.

    Write this mathematical equation and rearrange with P on the left side with V.

    $PV = nRT$

7. This equation is known as the Ideal Gas Law.

    Using data for volume, temperature, pressure and moles from one of the gas experiments, calculate the value for R with units of L·atm·K^{-1}·mol^{-1}. (Show all work and round to three significant digits.)

    0.0821 L·atm·K^{-1}·mol^{-1}

8. *Using the conversion between atmospheres and mm Hg (1 atm = 760 mm Hg), calculate the value for R with units of L·mm Hg·K^{-1}·mol^{-1}. (Show all work and round to three significant digits.)*

    62.4 L·mm Hg·K^{-1}·mol^{-1}

9. *Using the conversion between atmospheres and kPa (1 atm = 101.3 kPa), calculate the value for R with units of L·kPa·K^{-1}·mol^{-1}. (Show all work and round to three significant digits.)*

    8.31 L·kPa·K^{-1}·mol^{-1}

5-5: Dalton's Law of Partial Pressures

Dalton's Law of Partial Pressures, named after its discoverer John Dalton, describes the behavior of gas mixtures. It states that the total pressure of the gas, P_{tot}, is the sum of the partial pressures of each gas, or the sum of the pressures that each gas would exert if it were alone in the container. In this assignment you will become more familiar with Dalton's law.

1. Start *Virtual ChemLab* and select *Dalton's Law of Partial Pressures* from the list of assignments. The lab will open in the Gases laboratory. You will see a gas experiment with eight gas cylinders on the right. Make certain that the switch on the lower right of the lab bench is set to Ideal Gases. Note that the Ideal Gases each have a different molecular weight.

2. Select one of the Ideal Gas cylinders by clicking on the white label. Click the red arrow on the brass cylinder valve until the meter reads 400. Add this Ideal Gas to the balloon by clicking the green *Open Valve* switch once to add gas and again to stop. Add an amount of your choice but do not fill the balloon too full since you will be adding two additional gases. Click *Return Tank*.

3. Repeat step # 2 for two additional Ideal Gases of your choice. Make certain that you do not explode the balloon. If you do, click the *Reset* button located on the upper right of the gas chamber and repeat the experiment.

4. Click on the experimental apparatus to *Zoom In*. There are four LCD controllers on the left for volume, pressure, temperature, and number of moles. You can change the units for volume, pressure, and temperature by clicking on the *Units* button on each controller. Under pressure and number of moles are numbers 1-8 that correspond to Ideal Gases 1-8. The three gases that you selected will be highlighted. Clicking on each highlighted number will display the pressure or moles for that gas alone. Find the Ideal Gas number, the number of moles, and the partial pressure for each of your three Ideal Gases. Record this in the data table.

Data Table

Ideal Gas Number	Moles (n)	Partial Pressure (P_i)
2	0.089	28.01 kPa
5	0.146	45.92 kPa
6	0.083	26.08 kPa

5. *Using the information from the data table, determine the total pressure in the balloon.*

28.01 + 45.92 + 26.08 = 100.01 kPa (answers will vary)

6. Click *Total* on the Pressure controller. Compare your answer from # 5 to the total pressure on the meter.

Write both pressures below and write a mathematical equation to represent what you have learned about Dalton's Law.

$$P_1 + P_2 + P_3 = 100.01 \text{ kPa}$$
$$P_{total} = 100.01 \text{ kPa}$$
$$P_{total} = P_1 + P_2 + P_3$$

7. Another way of expressing Dalton's Law of Partial Pressures is with the expression $P_i = x_i P_{total}$ where P_i is the partial pressure of gas i, x_i is the mole fraction of that gas in the gas mixture, and P_{total} is the total pressure.

    Verify that this relationship holds using the data you have collected and record you results in the data table below.

Data Table

Ideal Gas Number	x_i	P_i (Calculated)	P_i (Measured)
2	0.280	28.00	28.01
5	0.459	45.91	45.92
6	0.261	26.10	26.08

5-6: Ideal vs. Real Gases

At room temperature and normal atmospheric pressures, real gases behave similarly to ideal gases, but real gases can deviate significantly from ideal gas behavior at extreme conditions such as high temperatures and high pressures. It is not always easy to find an effective means to show the deviation from ideal gas behavior for real gases. An effective but simple method to see these deviations is to calculate the value of R, the ideal gas constant, for real gases *assuming* they follow the ideal gas law and then compare the value of R with the actual value of 0.08205 L·atm·K^{-1}·mol^{-1}. In this assignment, you will measure P, V, T, and n for various real gases under different conditions and then you will calculate the value of R and compare it with its actual value.

1. Start *Virtual ChemLab* and select *Ideal vs. Real Gases* from the list of assignments. The lab will open in the Gases laboratory with the balloon filled with 0.100 moles of Ideal Gas 1.

2. Click on the ***Units*** buttons to change the units to L or mL for volume, atm for pressure, and K for temperature. On the left of the gas chamber are LCD controllers for the volume, pressure, temperature, and moles. On the left of the Pressure, Temperature, and Moles LCD controllers is a lever that will decrease and increase the pressure, temperature, or moles as the lever is moved up or down; the digit changes depending on how far the lever is moved. Digits may also be clicked directly to type in the desired number. Clicking to the left of the farthest left digit will add the next place; for example, if you have 1.7 atm you can click left of the 1 and enter 2 to make it 21.7 atm or click left of the 2 and enter 5 to make it 521.7 atm. The small ***R*** button in the upper left corner rounds the number. Clicking several times will round from ones to tens to hundreds.

    The green arrow to the left of the ***Save*** button will *Zoom Out*. Clicking ***Return Tank*** on the gas cylinder will return the tank to the rack and allow you to select a different gas. Clicking the gas chamber will *Zoom In* to allow you to change parameters. Be careful not to make the balloon so large that it bursts. If it does, click the red ***Reset*** button in the top right and then reset your units and values for each parameter. Remember that volume must be in L. If mL appears, you must convert to L in your calculations.

3. *Complete the data table for the following gases and conditions (all with 0.100 mole):*

    a. Ideal gas at low $T = 10$ K, high $T = 1000$ K, low $P = 1$ atm, high $P = 15$ atm
    b. Methane gas (CH$_4$) at low $T = 160$ K, high $T = 400$ K, low $P = 1$ atm, high $P = 15$ atm
    c. Carbon dioxide gas (CO$_2$) at low $T = 250$ K, high $T = 1000$ K, low $P = 1$ atm, high $P = 15$ atm

Data Table

Gas	V (L)	P (atm)	T (K)	n (mol)
Ideal, low T, low P	0.08206	1	10	0.1
Ideal, low T, high P	5.471	15	10	0.1
Ideal, high T, low P	8.206	1	1000	0.1
Ideal, high T, high P	0.547	15	1000	0.1
CH$_4$, low T, low P	1.297	1	160	0.1
CH$_4$, low T, high P	0.06752	15	160	0.1
CH$_4$, high T, low P	3.281	1	400	0.1
CH$_4$, high T, high P	0.2172	15	400	0.1

CO_2, low T, low P	2.033	1	250	0.1
CO_2, low T, high P	.1154	15	250	0.1
CO_2, high T, low P	8.207	1	1000	0.1
CO_2, high T, high P	.5487	15	1000	0.1

4. If $PV = nRT$ then $R = PV/nT$.

    Complete the results table for each experiment above. Use four significant digits.

Results Table

Gas	Calculated R $(L \cdot atm \cdot K^{-1} \cdot mol^{-1})$
Ideal, low T, low P	0.08206
Ideal, low T, high P	0.08205
Ideal, high T, low P	0.08206
Ideal, high T, high P	0.08205
CH_4, low T, low P	0.08106
CH_4, low T, high P	0.06330
CH_4, high T, low P	0.08203
CH_4, high T, high P	0.08145
CO_2, low T, low P	0.08132
CO_2, low T, high P	0.06924
CO_2, high T, low P	0.08207
CO_2, high T, high P	0.08231

5. *Which gases and conditions show significant deviation from the actual value of R? Explain.*

    <u>CH_4 at low T and high P and CO_2 at low T and high P show deviation from the actual value of</u>

    <u>R. At low temperatures and high pressures, molecules are close together and molecular</u>

    <u>interactions and molecular volume become significant. The Ideal Gas Law disregards the</u>

    <u>molecular interactions and volume.</u>

5-7: The Effect of Mass on Pressure

An understanding of pressure is an integral part of our understanding of the behavior of gases. Pressure is defined as the force per unit area exerted by a gas or other medium. The pressure of a gas is affected by many variables, such as temperature, external pressure, volume, moles of a gas, and other factors. This assignment will help you become more familiar with pressure and the effect of adding mass to a frictionless, massless piston.

1. Start *Virtual ChemLab* and select *The Effect of Mass on Pressure* from the list of assignments. The lab will open in the Gases laboratory.

2. This experiment consists of a cylinder with a frictionless-massless piston. When the experiment starts, the chamber is filled with the selected gas. Clicking on the **Piston** button moves the piston onto the cylinder and traps the gas in the cylinder. The moles of gas trapped in the cylinder and the volume of gas are measured using the Moles/Volume LCD controller. Pressure can be exerted on the gas in the cylinder by adjusting the external pressure in the chamber and by adding mass to the top of the piston (or $P_{int} = P_{mass} + P_{ext}$ where P_{int} is the internal pressure or the pressure of the gas in the cylinder, P_{mass} is the pressure being exerted on the gas by adding weights to the piston, and P_{ext} is the pressure being exerted on the piston by the gas in the chamber). If there is no mass on the piston, then $P_{int} = P_{ext}$.

3. Click the green **Piston** button to move the piston onto the cylinder. Record the mass (force, in tons) and the internal pressure (in psi) in the data table.

4. Click on the tenths place for mass and add 0.5 tons of mass to the piston. Record the mass and internal pressure in the Data Table. Repeat this for 2.5 tons (the weight of a small car).

Data Table

Mass (tons)	External Pressure (psi)	Calculated Internal Pressure (psi)	Measured Internal Pressure (psi)
0	14.7		14.7
0.5	14.7	51.2	51.2
2.5	14.7	197.2	197.3

5. You must now calculate the pressure being exerted by the 0.5 tons or, P_{mass}. First, convert tons to psi (pounds per square inch).

How many pounds is 0.5 tons? **1000 lbs**

The diameter of the piston is 15 cm. What is the radius (in cm)? **7.5 cm**

1 inch = 2.54 cm.

What is the radius of the piston in inches? **2.95 inches**

The area of the circular piston is found by $A = \pi r^2$.

What is the area of the piston in square inches (in²)? **27.39 in²**

The pressure exerted on the piston by the added mass in pounds per square inch (psi) can be determined by dividing the mass in pounds by the area in square inches.

What is the pressure exerted by the added mass in psi? **36.5 psi**

The internal pressure is the sum of the external pressure and the added mass.

What is the calculated internal pressure? Compare your calculated answer with the internal pressure meter answer. How do they compare?

14.7 psi + 36.5 = 51.20 psi, which is same as the measured pressure.

6. *Predict the internal pressure (in psi) when 2.5 tons are added.* **14.7 psi + 182.5 = 197.2 psi**

How does your calculated answer compare with the internal pressure meter when you add 2.5 tons of mass? Record your data in the data table.

Calculated = 197.2; the meter reads 197.3; these are very similar answers.

6-1: Acid-Base Classification of Salts

In this assignment you will be asked to classify aqueous solutions of salts as to whether they are acidic, basic, or neutral. This is most easily done by first identifying how both the cation and anion affect the pH of the solution and then by combining the effects. After predicting the acid-base properties of these salts, you will then test your predictions in the laboratory.

1. *State whether 0.1 M solutions of each of the following salts are acidic, basic, or neutral. Explain your reasoning for each by writing a balanced net ionic equation to describe the behavior of each non-neutral salt in water: NaCN, KNO$_3$, NH$_4$Cl, NaHCO$_3$, and Na$_3$PO$_4$.*

    NaCN: **Sodium is neutral because it is the cation from a strong base. Cyanide is basic because it is the anion from a weak acid and acts as a weak base. The solution is basic. CN^- (aq) + H_2O (aq) = HCN (aq) + OH^- (aq)**

    KNO$_3$:   **Potassium is neutral because it is the cation from a strong base and nitrate is neutral because it is the anion from a strong acid. The solution is neutral.**

    NH$_4$Cl: **Chloride is neutral because it is the anion from a strong acid and the ammonium ion is a weak acid with $K_a = 5.6 \times 10^{-10}$. The solution is acidic. NH_4^+ (aq) = NH_3 (aq) + H^+ (aq)**

    NaHCO$_3$:   **Sodium is neutral because it is the cation of a strong base and hydrogen carbonate is a weak base with $K_b = 2.3 \times 10^{-8}$. The solution is basic. Equation: HCO_3^- + H_2O = H_2CO_3 + OH^-**

    Na$_3$PO$_4$:   **Sodium is neutral because it is the cation from a strong base and phosphate is a weak base with $K_b = 2.2 \times 10^{-2}$. The solution is basic. Equation: PO_4^{-3} + H_2O = HPO_4^{-2} + OH^-**

Once you have predicted the nature of each salt solution, you will use *Virtual ChemLab* to confirm your prediction. Each solution must be approximately 0.1 M for your comparisons to be valid. Most of the solutions in the Stockroom are approximately 0.1 M already. Three solutions must be prepared from solid salts. One of these salt solutions is already prepared and on the lab bench ready for you to measure the pH.

2. Start *Virtual ChemLab* and select *Acid-Base Classification of Salts* from the list of assignments. The lab will open in the Titrations laboratory.

3. On the stir plate, there will be a beaker of 0.10 M ammonium chloride (NH$_4$Cl) that has already been prepared. The pH meter has been calibrated and is in the beaker. Record the pH of the NH$_4$Cl solution in the data table on the following page. When finished, drag the beaker to the red disposal bucket, and drag the bottle of NH$_4$Cl to the stockroom counter.

4. Click in the *Stockroom* to enter. Double-click on the NH$_4$Cl bottle to return it to the shelf and then double-click on the NaHCO$_3$ and KNO$_3$ bottles to move them to the *Stockroom* counter. Return to the laboratory.

5. Open the beaker drawer (click on it) and drag a beaker to the spotlight next to the *Balance*. Click and drag the bottle of $NaHCO_3$ and place it on the spot light near the balance. Click in the *Balance* area to zoom in. Place a weigh paper on the balance and tare the balance. Open the bottle by clicking on the lid (*Remove Lid*). Pick up the *Scoop* and scoop up some salt by dragging the *Scoop* to the mouth of the bottle and then down the face of the bottle. Each scoop position on the face of the bottle represents a different size scoop. Pull the scoop down from the top to the second position (approximately 0.20 g) and drag it to the weigh paper in the balance until it snaps into place. Releasing the scoop places the sample on the weigh paper. Now drag the weigh paper from the balance to the beaker until it snaps into place and then empty the salt into the beaker. Return to the laboratory and drag the beaker to the stir plate.

6. Drag the 25 mL graduated cylinder to the sink under the tap until it fills. When filled, it will return to the lab bench and will indicate that it is full when you place the cursor over the cylinder. Drag the 25 mL cylinder to the beaker on the stir plate and empty it into the beaker. Place the pH probe in the beaker and record the pH in the data table. Drag the beaker to the red disposal bucket. Double-click the bottle of $NaHCO_3$ to move it to the *Stockroom* counter. Repeat steps 5 and 6 for KNO_3.

7. Click in the *Stockroom*. The stock solutions of NaCN and Na_3PO_4 are already approximately 0.1 M. Double-click each bottle to move them to the counter and return to the laboratory. With these solutions you can pour a small amount into a beaker that you have placed on the stir plate and place the pH probe in the solution. Record each pH in the data table. Drag each beaker to the red disposal bucket when you have finished. Were your predictions correct?

Data Table

solution	pH	acidic, basic or neutral
NH_4Cl	5.20	acidic
$NaHCO_3$	8.16	basic
KNO_3	7.01	neutral
NaCN	11.00	basic
Na_3PO_4	12.08	basic

6-2: Ranking Salt Solutions by pH

In this assignment you will be asked to rank aqueous solutions of acids, bases, and salts in order of increasing pH. This is most easily done by first identifying the strong acids that have the lowest pH, the strong bases that have the highest pH, and the neutral solutions that have a pH near 7. The weak acids will have a pH between 1 and 6 and the weak bases between 8 and 14. The exact order of weak acids and weak bases is determined by comparing the ionization constants (K_a for the weak acids and K_b for the weak bases). After ranking the pH of these solutions, you will then test your predictions in the laboratory.

1. *Arrange the following 0.1 M solutions in order of increasing pH and state why you placed each solution in that position: NaCH$_3$COO, HCl, HCN, NaOH, NH$_3$, NaCN, KNO$_3$, H$_2$SO$_4$, NH$_4$Cl, H$_2$SO$_3$, NaHCO$_3$, Na$_3$PO$_4$ and CH$_3$COOH.*

   In order of increasing pH:

   H$_2$SO$_4$: **The first hydrogen is strong and ionizes 100% and the second is weak and ionizes a small amount. This is a lower pH than HCl because of the small amount of ionization from the second hydrogen.**

   HCl: **This is a strong acid with 100% ionization.**

   H$_2$SO$_3$: **This is a weak acid with $K_{a1} = 1.7 \times 10^{-2}$.**

   CH$_3$COOH: **This is a weak acid with $K_a = 1.8 \times 10^{-5}$.**

   HCN: **This is a weak acid with $K_a = 5.8 \times 10^{-10}$.**

   NH$_4$Cl: **The ammonium ion is a weak acid with $K_{a1} = 5.6 \times 10^{-10}$.**

   KNO$_3$: **This is a neutral salt.**

   NaCH$_3$COO: **The acetate ion is a weak base with $K_b = 5.6 \times 10^{-10}$.**

   NaHCO$_3$: **Hydrogen carbonate is a weak base with $K_b = 2.3 \times 10^{-8}$.**

   NaCN: **The cyanide ion is a weak base with $K_b = 1.7 \times 10^{-5}$.**

   NH$_3$: **This is a weak base with $K_b = 1.8 \times 10^{-5}$.**

   Na$_3$PO$_4$: **The phosphate ion is a weak base with $K_b = 2.2 \times 10^{-2}$.**

   NaOH: **This is a strong base with 100% ionization.**

Once you have predicted the nature of each salt solution, you will use *Virtual ChemLab* to confirm your prediction. Each solution must be approximately 0.1 M for your comparisons to be valid. Most of the solutions in the Stockroom are approximately 0.1 M already. Two solutions will need to be diluted and three solutions will need to be prepared from solid salts. One of these salt solutions is already prepared and on the lab bench ready for you to measure the pH.

2. Start *Virtual ChemLab* and select *Ranking Salt Solutions by pH* from the list of assignments. The lab will open in the Titrations laboratory.

3. On the stir plate, there will be a beaker of 0.10 M ammonium chloride (NH$_4$Cl) that has already been prepared. The pH meter has been calibrated and is in the beaker. Record the pH of the NH$_4$Cl solution in the data table on the following page. When finished, drag the beaker to the red disposal bucket, and drag the bottle of NH$_4$Cl to the stockroom counter.

4. Click in the *Stockroom* to enter. Double-click on the NH_4Cl bottle to return it to the shelf and then double-click on the $NaHCO_3$ and KNO_3 bottles to move them to the *Stockroom* counter. Return to the laboratory

5. Open the beaker drawer (click on it) and drag a beaker to the spotlight next to the *Balance*. Click and drag the bottle of $NaHCO_3$ and place on the spot light near the balance. Click in the *Balance* area to zoom in. Place a weigh paper on the balance and tare the balance. Open the bottle by clicking on the lid (*Remove Lid*). Pick up the *Scoop* and scoop up some salt by dragging the *Scoop* to the bottle and then down the face of the bottle. Each scoop position on the face of the bottle represents a different size scoop. Pull the scoop down from the top to the second position (approximately 0.20 g) and drag it to the weigh paper in the balance until it snaps into place. Releasing the scoop places the sample on the weigh paper. Now drag the weigh paper from the balance to the beaker until it snaps into place and then empty the salt into the beaker. Return to the laboratory and drag the beaker to the stir plate.

6. Drag the 25 mL graduated cylinder to the sink under the tap until it fills. When filled, it will return to the lab bench and will indicate that it is full when you place the cursor over the cylinder. Drag the 25 mL cylinder to the beaker on the stir plate and empty it into the beaker. Place the pH probe in the beaker and record the pH in the data table. Drag the beaker to the red disposal bucket. Double-click the bottle of $NaHCO_3$ to move it to the *Stockroom* counter. Repeat steps 5 and 6 for KNO_3.

7. Click in the *Stockroom*. Double-click on the bottles of NH_3 and H_2SO_4 to move them from the shelf to the counter and return to the laboratory. Drag the bottle of NH_3 to one of the three spotlights on the lab bench. Place a beaker from the drawer on the stir plate. Drag the bottle of NH_3 to the 5 mL graduated cylinder (the smallest one) by the sink and fill the cylinder by dropping the bottle on the cylinder. Now drag the 5 mL graduated cylinder to the beaker on the stir plate and add the 5 mL of NH_3. Add 20 mL water to the beaker by filling and emptying the 10 mL cylinder into the beaker twice. Place the pH probe in the beaker and record the pH in the data table. Drag the beaker to the red disposal bucket. Double-click on the NH_3 bottle to move it back to the counter.

8. Repeat step 7 with H_2SO_4, *except* that you should use a 10 mL graduated cylinder of H_2SO_4 and adding 15 mL water.

9. Each of the other solutions is already approximately 0.1 M. With these solutions you can pour a small amount into the beaker that you have placed on the stir plate and place the pH probe in the solution to measure the pH. Record the pH of each solution in the data table. Drag each beaker to the red disposal bucket when you have finished. You must determine the pH for HCl, H_2SO_3, CH_3COOH (HAc), HCN, NaOH, NaCN, Na_3PO_4, and $NaCH_3COO$ (NaAc). You may take two bottles at a time from the stockroom.

Data Table

solution	pH	solution	pH
NH_4Cl	5.20	CH_3COOH (HAc)	2.87
$NaHCO_3$	8.16	HCN	5.11
KNO_3	7.01	NaOH	12.91
NH_3	11.11	NaCN	11.00
H_2SO_4	1.01	$NaCH_3COO$ (NaAc)	8.80
HCl	1.08	Na_3PO_4	12.08
H_2SO_3	1.50		

6-3: Concepts in Acid-Base Titrations

Titrations provide a method of quantitatively measuring the concentration of an unknown solution. In an acid-base titration, this is done by delivering a titrant of known concentration into an analyte of known volume. (The concentration of an unknown titrant can also be determined by titration with an analyte of known concentration and volume.) Titration curves (graphs of volume vs. pH) have characteristic shapes. The graph can be used to determine the strength or weakness of an acid or base. The equivalence point of the titration, or the point where the analyte has been completely consumed by the titrant, is identified by the point where the pH changes rapidly over a small volume of titrant delivered. There is a steep incline or decline at this point of the titration curve. It is also common to use an indicator that changes color at or near the equivalence point. In this assignment, you will observe this titration curve by titrating the strong acid HCl with the strong base NaOH.

1. Start *Virtual ChemLab* and select *Concepts in Acid-Base Titrations* from the list of assignments. The lab will open in the Titration laboratory.

2. Click the *Lab Book* to open it. The buret will be filled with NaOH. The horizontal position of the orange handle is off for the stopcock. Click the *Save* button in the *Buret Zoom View* window. Open the stopcock by pulling down on the orange handle. The vertical position delivers solution the fastest with three intermediate rates in between. Turn the stopcock to one of the fastest positions. Observe the titration curve. When the volume reaches 35 mL, double-click the stopcock to stop the titration. Click *Stop* in the *Buret Zoom View*. A blue data link will be created in the lab book, click on it to view the data.

3. The beaker contains 0.3000 M HCl and the buret contains 0.3000 M NaOH.

4. *Write a complete balanced equation for the neutralization reaction between HCl and NaOH.*

    HCl (aq) + NaOH (aq) → H$_2$O (aq) + NaCl (aq)

    The following questions can be answered by examining the *Plot and Data Viewer* windows.

5. *What was the pH and color of the solution at the beginning of the titration?* **0.92 and yellow**

6. *What was the pH and color of the solution at the end of the titration?* **Answers may vary slightly**

    but they should be approximately 12 and blue.

7. Examine the graph of the pH vs. volume (blue line).

   Sketch the shape of the titration graph of pH vs. volume.

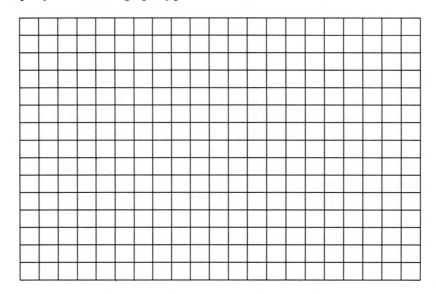

8. *What happens to the pH around 25 mL?* **The pH changes rapidly from low to high .**

9. *What would cause the change observed in question #4?* **At the beginning, the solution contains only acid (a low pH). When the amount of base equals the amount of acid the equivalence point is reached and only water and salt are in the solution at the equivalence point. Water is neutral with a pH of 7. After the equivalence point NaOH has been added which has a high pH.**

6-4: Predicting the Equivalence Point

Titrations provide a method of quantitatively measuring the concentration of an unknown solution. In an acid-base titration, this is done by delivering a titrant of known concentration into an analyte of known volume. To make a titration more efficient and more accurate, it is often important to be able to predict the equivalence point for the titration. In this assignment, you will be given 0.3000 M HCl and 0.3000 M NaOH, you will predict the equivalence point, and then perform the titration to check your prediction.

1. Start *Virtual ChemLab* and select *Predicting the Equivalence Point* from the list of assignments. The lab will open in the Titrations laboratory.

2. Click the *Lab Book* to open it. Click the *Buret Zoom View* window to bring it to the front. The buret is filled with 0.3000 M NaOH. The beaker has 25.00 mL of 0.3000 M HCl. The pH meter is turned on and has been calibrated. The indicator is bromocresol green.

3. *Predict what volume (mL) of 0.3000 M NaOH is required to titrate the 25.00 mL of 0.3000 M HCl to the equivalence point.*

$$0.02500 \text{ L HCl} \left(\frac{0.3000 \text{ mol HCl}}{1 \text{ L HCl}} \right) \left(\frac{1 \text{ mol NaOH}}{1 \text{ mol HCl}} \right) \left(\frac{1 \text{ L NaOH}}{0.3000 \text{ mol NaOH}} \right) = 0.02500 \text{ L NaOH}$$

4. *Perform the titration.* Click the **Save** button in the *Buret Zoom View* window so the titration data can be saved. The horizontal position of the orange handle is off for the stopcock. Open the stopcock by pulling down on the orange handle. The vertical position delivers solution the fastest with three intermediate rates in between. Turn the stopcock to one of the fastest positions. Observe the titration curve. When the blue line in the graph window (the pH curve) begins to turn up, double-click the stopcock to turn it off. Move the stopcock down one position to add volume drop by drop.

    There are two methods for determining the volume at the equivalence point: (1) Stop the titration (close the stopcock) when a color change occurs, and then click the **Stop** button in the *Buret Zoom View*. A blue data link will appear in the lab book. Click the blue data link to open the *Data View* window. Scroll down to the last data entry and record the volume at the equivalence point. OR (2) Add drops slowly through the equivalence point until the pH reaches approximately 12. Click the **Stop** button in the *Buret Zoom View*. A blue data link will appear in the lab book. Click the blue data link to open the *Data View* window. Click **Select All** button to copy and paste the data to a spreadsheet program. Plot the first derivative of pH vs. volume. The peak will indicate the volume of the equivalence point since this is where the pH is changing the most rapidly as the volume changes.

5. *What volume of 0.3000 M NaOH was required by the titration to reach the equivalence point?*

    Answers should be between 24.95 and 25.05 mL.

6. *Calculate the percent error of the predicted volume using the formula:*

$$\% \text{ Error} = \frac{\left| your \ predicted \ answer - your \ actual \ answer \right|}{your \ predicted \ answer} \times 100$$

    % Error = **Answers should be < 0.25 %**

137

If you want to repeat the titration, click *Exit*, select this problem from the workbook again, and repeat the experiment.

6-5: Predicting the Equivalence Point

Titrations provide a method of quantitatively measuring the concentration of an unknown solution. In an acid-base titration, this is done by delivering a titrant of known concentration into an analyte of known volume. To make a titration more efficient and more accurate, it is often important to be able to predict the equivalence point for the titration. In this assignment, you will be given 0.1276 M HCl and 0.1475 M NaOH, you will predict the equivalence point, and then perform the titration to check your prediction.

1. Start *Virtual ChemLab* and select *Predicting the Equivalence Point* from the list of assignments. The lab will open in the Titrations laboratory.

2. Click the *Lab Book* to open it. Click the *Buret Zoom View* window to bring it to the front. The buret is filled with 0.1475 M NaOH. The beaker has 25.00 mL of 0.1276 M HCl. The pH meter is turned on and has been calibrated. The indicator is bromocresol green.

3. *Predict what volume (mL) of 0.1475 M NaOH is required to titrate the 25.00 mL of 0.1276 M HCl to the equivalence point.*

$$25.00 \text{ mL HCl} \left(\frac{0.1276 \text{ mmol HCl}}{1 \text{ mmol HCl}} \right) \left(\frac{1 \text{ mmol NaOH}}{1 \text{ mmol HCl}} \right) \left(\frac{1 \text{ mL NaOH}}{0.1475 \text{ mmol NaOH}} \right) = 21.63 \text{ mL NaOH}$$

4. *Perform the titration.* Click the **Save** button in the *Buret Zoom View* window so the titration data can be saved. The horizontal position of the orange handle is off for the stopcock. Open the stopcock by pulling down on the orange handle. The vertical position delivers solution the fastest with three intermediate rates in between. Turn the stopcock to one of the fastest positions. Observe the titration curve. When the blue line in the graph window (the pH curve) begins to turn up, double-click the stopcock to turn it off. Move the stopcock down one position to add volume drop by drop.

   There are two methods for determining the volume at the equivalence point: (1) Stop the titration (close the stopcock) when a color change occurs, and then click the **Stop** button in the *Buret Zoom View*. A blue data link will appear in the lab book. Click the blue data link to open the *Data View* window. Scroll down to the last data entry and record the volume at the equivalence point. OR (2) Add drops slowly through the equivalence point until the pH reaches approximately 12. Click the **Stop** button in the *Buret Zoom View*. A blue data link will appear in the lab book. Click the blue data link to open the *Data View* window. Click **Select All** button to copy and paste the data to a spreadsheet program. Plot the first derivative of pH vs. volume. The peak will indicate the volume of the equivalence point since this is where the pH is changing the most rapidly as the volume changes.

5. *What volume of 0.1475 M NaOH was required by the titration to reach the equivalence point?*

   Answers should range between 21.58 and 21.68 mL.

6. *Calculate the percent error of the predicted volume using the formula:*

$$\% \, Error = \frac{|your \, predicted \, answer - your \, actual \, answer|}{your \, predicted \, answer} \times 100$$

   % Error = **Answers should be < 0.25 %**

If you want to repeat the titration, click *Exit*, select this problem from the workbook again, and repeat the experiment.

6-6: Predicting the Equivalence Point

Titrations provide a method of quantitatively measuring the concentration of an unknown solution. In an acid-base titration, this is done by delivering a titrant of known concentration into an analyte of known volume. To make a titration more efficient and more accurate, it is often important to be able to predict the equivalence point for the titration. In this assignment, you will be given 0.1033 M CH_3COOH (acetic acid or HAc) and 0.1104 M NaOH, you will predict the equivalence point, and then perform the titration to check your prediction.

1. Start *Virtual ChemLab* and select *Predicting the Equivalence Point* from the list of assignments. The lab will open in the Titrations laboratory.

2. Click the *Lab Book* to open it. Click the *Buret Zoom View* window to bring it to the front. The buret is filled with 0.1104 M NaOH. The beaker has 15.00 mL of 0.1033 M HAc. The pH meter is turned on and has been calibrated. The indicator is methyl orange.

3. *Predict what volume (mL) of 0.1104 M NaOH is required to titrate the 15.00 mL of 0.1033 M HAc to the equivalence point.*

$$15.00 \text{ mL HAc}\left(\frac{0.1033 \text{ mmol HAc}}{1 \text{ mmol HAc}}\right)\left(\frac{1 \text{ mmol NaOH}}{1 \text{ mmol HAc}}\right)\left(\frac{1 \text{ mL NaOH}}{0.1104 \text{ mmol NaOH}}\right) = 14.04 \text{ mL NaOH}$$

4. *Perform the titration.* Click the *Save* button in the *Buret Zoom View* window so the titration data can be saved. The horizontal position of the orange handle is off for the stopcock. Open the stopcock by pulling down on the orange handle. The vertical position delivers solution the fastest with three intermediate rates in between. Turn the stopcock to one of the fastest positions. Observe the titration curve. When the blue line in the graph window (the pH curve) begins to turn up, double-click the stopcock to turn it off. Move the stopcock down one position to add volume drop by drop.

   There are two methods for determining the volume at the equivalence point: (1) Stop the titration (close the stopcock) when a color change occurs, and then click the *Stop* button in the *Buret Zoom View*. A blue data link will appear in the lab book. Click the blue data link to open the *Data View* window. Scroll down to the last data entry and record the volume at the equivalence point. OR (2) Add drops slowly through the equivalence point until the pH reaches approximately 12. Click the *Stop* button in the *Buret Zoom View*. A blue data link will appear in the lab book. Click the blue data link to open the *Data View* window. Click *Select All* button to copy and paste the data to a spreadsheet program. Plot the first derivative of pH vs. volume. The peak will indicate the volume of the equivalence point since this is where the pH is changing the most rapidly as the volume changes.

5. *What volume of 0.1104 M NaOH was required by the titration to reach the equivalence point?*

   Answers should range between 14.00 and 14.08 mL.

6. *Calculate the percent error of the predicted volume using the formula:*

$$\% \text{ Error} = \frac{|your\ predicted\ answer - your\ actual\ answer|}{your\ predicted\ answer} \times 100$$

% Error = **Answers should be < 0.25 %**

If you want to repeat the titration, click *Exit*, select this problem from the workbook again, and repeat the experiment.

6-7: Ionization Constants of Weak Acids

An acid-base indicator is usually a weak acid with a characteristic color in the protonated and deprotonated forms. In this assignment, you will monitor the color of an acetic acid solution containing *Bromocresol Green* as an indicator, as the pH is changed and then you will estimate the ionization constant, K_a, for the indicator.

1. Start *Virtual ChemLab* and select *Ionization Constants of Weak Acids* from the list of assignments. The lab will open in the Titration laboratory. Bottles of 0.1104 M NaOH and 0.1031 M HAc (acetic acid) will be on the lab bench. The buret will be filled with the NaOH solution and a beaker containing 10.00 mL of the HAc solution will be on the stir plate. The stir plate will be on, *Bromocresol Green* indicator will have been added to the beaker, and a calibrated pH probe will also be in the beaker so the pH of the solution can be monitored.

2. *What is the color and pH of the solution?* **yellow; 2.87** _____

3. On the buret, the horizontal position of the orange handle is off for the stopcock. Open the stopcock by pulling down on the orange handle. The vertical position delivers solution the fastest with three intermediate rates in between (slow drop-wise, fast drop-wise, and slow stream). Turn the stopcock to the second position or fast drop-wise addition. Observe the color of the solution and close the stopcock when the color turns green by double clicking on the center of the stopcock.

4. *What is the color and pH of the solution now?* **It is green; pH will vary but should be 3.80 – 4.10.**

5. Continue to add NaOH as before or at a faster rate.

   What is the final color of the solution? **blue** _____

6. An acid-base indicator is usually a weak acid with a characteristic color in the protonated and deprotonated forms. Because bromocresol green is an acid, it is convenient to represent its rather complex formula as HBCG. HBCG ionizes in water according to the following equation:

$$\text{HBCG} + \text{H}_2\text{O} = \text{BCG}^- + \text{H}_3\text{O}^+$$
   (yellow)   (blue)

   The K_a (the equilibrium constant for the acid) expression is:

$$K_a = \frac{\left[\text{BCG}^-\right]\left[\text{H}_3\text{O}^+\right]}{\left[\text{HBCG}\right]}$$

   When $[\text{BCG}^-] = [\text{HBCG}]$, then $K_a = [\text{H}_3\text{O}^+]$. If you know the pH of the solution, then the $[\text{H}_3\text{O}^+]$ and K_a can be determined.

   What would be the color of the solution if there were equal concentrations of HBCG and BCG⁻?

   green _____

7. *What is the pH at the first appearance of this color?* <u>**Answers will vary, but they should be**</u>

    <u>**between 3.80 - 4.10.**</u>

8. *What is an estimate for the K_a for bromocresol green?* <u>**Answers will vary, but they should be**</u>

    <u>**between $1.58 \times 10^{-4} - 7.94 \times 10^{-5}$.**</u>

6-8: Acid-Base Titration: Practice

Titrations provide a method of quantitatively measuring the concentration of an unknown solution. In an acid-base titration, this is done by delivering a titrant of known concentration into an analyte of known volume. In this assignment, you will titrate a 0.3000 M solution of NaOH into 25 mL of 0.3000 M HCl. Although in this case you know the concentration of both NaOH and HCl, this will give you practice in performing a titration and calculating the concentration of the analyte, which in this case is HCl.

1. Start *Virtual ChemLab* and select *Acid-Base Titration: Practice* from the list of assignments. The lab will open in the Titrations laboratory.

2. Click the *Lab Book* to open it. Click the *Buret Zoom View* window to bring it to the front. The buret is filled with 0.3000 M NaOH. The beaker has 25.00 mL of 0.3000 M HCl. The pH meter is turned on and has been calibrated. The indicator is bromocresol green.

3. *Perform the titration.* Click the *Save* button in the *Buret Zoom View* window so the titration data can be saved. The horizontal position of the orange handle is off for the stopcock. Open the stopcock by pulling down on the orange handle. The vertical position delivers solution the fastest with three intermediate rates in between. Turn the stopcock to one of the fastest positions. Observe the titration curve. When the blue line in the graph window (the pH curve) begins to turn up, double-click the stopcock to turn it off. Move the stopcock down one position to add volume drop by drop.

   There are two methods for determining the volume at the equivalence point: (1) Stop the titration (close the stopcock) when a color change occurs, and then click the *Stop* button in the *Buret Zoom View*. A blue data link will appear in the lab book. Click the blue data link to open the *Data View* window. Scroll down to the last data entry and record the volume at the equivalence point. OR (2) Add drops slowly through the equivalence point until the pH reaches approximately 12. Click the *Stop* button in the *Buret Zoom View*. A blue data link will appear in the lab book. Click the blue data link to open the *Data View* window. Click *Select All* button to copy and paste the data to a spreadsheet program. Plot the first derivative of pH vs. volume. The peak will indicate the volume of the equivalence point since this is where the pH is changing the most rapidly as the volume changes.

4. *What volume of 0.3000 M NaOH was required by the titration to reach the equivalence point?*

   Answers should be between 24.95 and 25.05 mL.

5. *Calculate the molarity of the HCl using 25.00 mL of HCl solution and the volume of the 0.3000 M NaOH from your titration.*

$$24.96 \text{ mL NaOH} \left(\frac{0.3000 \text{ mmol NaOH}}{1 \text{ mL}} \right) \left(\frac{1 \text{ mmol HCl}}{1 \text{ mmol NaOH}} \right) \left(\frac{1}{25.00 \text{ mL HCl}} \right) = 0.2995 \text{ M NaOH}$$

6. *Remember that the concentration of your HCl solution is 0.3000 M. Calculate the percent error using the formula:*

$$\% \ Error = \frac{|your \ calculated \ answer - the \ actual \ answer|}{the \ predicted \ answer} \times 100$$

$$\% \ Error = \textbf{Answers should be} < \textbf{0.25 \%}$$

If you want to repeat the titration, click *Exit*, select this problem from the workbook again, and repeat the experiment.

6-9: Acid-Base Titration: Unknown HCl

Titrations provide a method of quantitatively measuring the concentration of an unknown solution. In an acid-base titration, this is done by delivering a titrant of known concentration into an analyte of known volume. In this assignment, you will titrate a 0.2564 M solution of NaOH into 25 mL of an unknown concentration of HCl and calculate the concentration of the HCl solution.

1. Start *Virtual ChemLab* and select *Acid-Base Titration: Unknown HCl* from the list of assignments. The lab will open in the Titrations laboratory.

2. Click the *Lab Book* to open it. Click the *Buret Zoom View* window to bring it to the front. The buret is filled with 0.2564 M NaOH. The beaker has 25.00 mL of unknown HCl. The pH meter is turned on and has been calibrated. The indicator is bromocresol green.

3. *Perform the titration.* Click the **Save** button in the *Buret Zoom View* window so the titration data can be saved. The horizontal position of the orange handle is off for the stopcock. Open the stopcock by pulling down on the orange handle. The vertical position delivers solution the fastest with three intermediate rates in between. Turn the stopcock to one of the fastest positions. Observe the titration curve. When the blue line in the graph window (the pH curve) begins to turn up, double-click the stopcock to turn it off. Move the stopcock down one position to add volume drop by drop.

   There are two methods for determining the volume at the equivalence point: (1) Stop the titration (close the stopcock) when a color change occurs, and then click the **Stop** button in the *Buret Zoom View*. A blue data link will appear in the lab book. Click the blue data link to open the *Data View* window. Scroll down to the last data entry and record the volume at the equivalence point. OR (2) Add drops slowly through the equivalence point until the pH reaches approximately 12. Click the **Stop** button in the *Buret Zoom View*. A blue data link will appear in the lab book. Click the blue data link to open the *Data View* window. Click **Select All** button to copy and paste the data to a spreadsheet program. Plot the first derivative of pH vs. volume. The peak will indicate the volume of the equivalence point since this is where the pH is changing the most rapidly as the volume changes.

4. *What is your unknown sample number?* **Answers will vary from #1 to #15 depending on the random sample dispensed.**

5. *What volume of 0.2564 M NaOH was required by the titration to reach the equivalence point?*

   Answers will depend on the unknown sample. Sample # 5 should be between 14.56 and 14.62 mL.

6. *Calculate the molarity of the HCl using 25.00 mL of HCl solution and the volume of the 0.2564 M NaOH from your titration.* **Sample response is for unknown #5.**

$$14.59 \text{ mL NaOH} \left(\frac{0.2564 \text{ mmol NaOH}}{1 \text{ mL}} \right) \left(\frac{1 \text{ mmol HCl}}{1 \text{ mmol NaOH}} \right) \left(\frac{1}{25.00 \text{ mL HCl}} \right) = 0.1496 \text{ M HCl}$$

Answers for Unknowns

Unknown #1: 0.1611 M

Unknown #2: 0.1552 M

Unknown #3: 0.1518 M

Unknown #4: 0.1501 M

Unknown #5: 0.1496 M

Unknown #6: 0.1503 M

Unknown #7: 0.1516 M

Unknown #8: 0.1535 M

Unknown #9: 0.1559 M

Unknown #10: 0.1587 M

Unknown #11: 0.1619 M

Unknown #12: 0.1654 M

Unknown #13: 0.1692 M

Unknown #14: 0.1732 M

Unknown #15: 0.1774 M

6-10: Study of Acid-Base Titrations – Monoprotic Acids

Titrations provide a method of quantitatively measuring the concentration of an unknown solution. In an acid-base titration, this is done by delivering a titrant of known concentration into an analyte of known volume. (The concentration of an unknown titrant can also be determined by titration with an analyte of known concentration and volume.) Titration curves (graphs of volume vs. pH) have characteristic shapes. The graph can be used to determine the strength or weakness of an acid or base. The equivalence point of the titration, or the point where the analyte has been completely consumed by the titrant, is identified by the point where the pH changes rapidly over a small volume of titrant delivered. In this assignment, you will observe this titration curve by titrating the strong acid HCl with the strong base NaOH.

1. Start *Virtual ChemLab* and select *Study of Acid-Base Titrations – Monoprotic Acids* from the list of assignments. The lab will open in the Titration laboratory.

2. Click the *Lab Book* to open it. The buret will be filled with NaOH and 25.00 mL of HCl will be in the beaker with bromocresol green as an indicator. Click the *Save* button in the *Buret Zoom View* window. The horizontal position of the orange handle is off for the stopcock. Open the stopcock by pulling down on the orange handle. The vertical position delivers solution the fastest with three intermediate rates in between. Turn the stopcock to one of the fastest positions. Observe the titration curve. When the volume reaches 35 mL, double-click the stopcock to stop the titration. Click *Stop* in the *Buret Zoom View*. A blue data link will be created in the lab book. Click on it to view the titration data.

    If you need to repeat the titration, click in the *Stockroom* to enter, click on the clipboard, and select Preset Experiment #1 *Strong Acid-Strong Base*.

3. The beaker contains 0.3000 M HCl and the buret contains 0.3000 M NaOH.

    Write a complete balanced equation for the neutralization reaction between HCl and NaOH.

    $HCl\ (aq)\ +\ NaOH\ (aq)\ =\ H_2O\ (aq)\ +\ NaCl\ (aq)$

    The following questions can be answered by examining the *Plot* window and the *Data Viewer* window.

4. *What was the pH and color of the solution at the beginning of the titration?* **0.92: yellow**

5. *What was the pH and color of the solution at the end of the titration?*

    pH may vary slightly, but should be approximately 12. The color should be blue.

6. *Examine the graph of pH vs. volume (blue line) and sketch the titration curve below.*

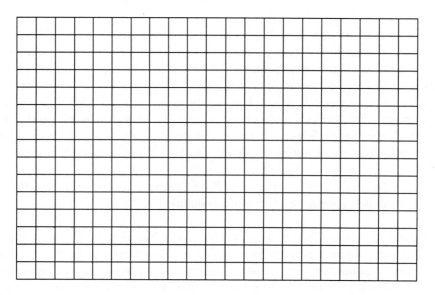

7. *What happens to the pH around 25 mL and what causes this?*

   The pH changes rapidly from low to high. At the beginning, the solution contains only acid (a low pH). When the amount of base equals the amount of acid the equivalence point is reached and only water and salt are in the solution at the equivalence point. Water is neutral with a pH of 7. After the equivalence point NaOH has been added, which has a high pH.

8. *Examine the graph of conductivity vs. volume (red line) and sketch the titration curve on the graph above.*

9. *What happens to the conductivity during the titration?* **The graph has a negative slope, reaches a minimum at 25 mL, and then has a positive slope after 25 mL.**

10. *What would cause the change observed in question #9?*

   In the beginning of the titration the $[H^+] = 0.3000$ M. As the OH^- is added the reaction produces   water and the concentration of ions decreases, hence less and less conductivity from the beginning until the equivalence point is reached. After the equivalence point, no H^+ exists in solution and the concentration of ions (OH^-) increases and so does the conductivity.

6-11: Weak Acid-Strong Base Titrations

Titrations provide a method of quantitatively measuring the concentration of an unknown solution. In an acid-base titration, this is done by delivering a titrant of known concentration into an analyte of known volume. Titration curves (graphs of volume vs. pH) have characteristic shapes. The equivalence point of the titration, or the point where the analyte has been completely consumed by the titrant, is identified by the point where the pH changes rapidly over a small volume of titrant delivered. In this assignment, you will observe this titration curve by titrating the weak acid CH_3COOH (acetic acid) with the strong base NaOH. You will also predict the pH at the equivalence point, validate your prediction experimentally, and then calculate the equilibrium constant for the neutralization reaction.

1. Start *Virtual ChemLab* and select *Weak Acid-Strong Base Titrations* from the list of assignments. The lab will open in the Titration laboratory.

2. Click the *Lab Book* to open it. The buret will be filled with NaOH and 25.00 mL of CH_3COOH will be in the beaker with phenolphthalein as the indicator. Click the *Save* button in the *Buret Zoom View* window. The horizontal position of the orange handle is off for the stopcock. Open the stopcock by pulling down on the orange handle. The vertical position delivers solution the fastest with three intermediate rates in between. Turn the stopcock to one of the fastest positions. Observe the titration curve. When the volume reaches 40 mL, double-click the stopcock to stop the titration. Click *Stop* in the *Buret Zoom View*. A blue data link will be created in the lab book. Click on it to view the data.

    If you need to repeat the titration, click in the *Stockroom* to enter, click on the clipboard, and select Preset Experiment # 3 *Weak Acid-Strong Base*.

2. The beaker contains 0.1894 M CH_3COOH and the buret contains 0.2006 M NaOH.

    Write a complete balanced equation for the neutralization reaction between CH_3COOH and NaOH and then write a balanced net ionic equation for this chemical reaction.

    CH_3COOH (aq) + NaOH (aq) = H_2O (aq) + $NaCH_3COO$ (aq)
    CH_3COOH (aq) + OH^- (aq) = H_2O (aq) + CH_3COO^- (aq)

    The following questions can be answered by examining the *Plot* window, the *Data Viewer* window, and the balanced net ionic equation.

4. *Indicate the species present at the equivalence point, and predict whether the pH at the equivalence point will be pH > 7, pH < 7, or pH ≈ 7. Explain why you made this prediction.*

    pH > 7. At the equivalence point the solution contains only water and the acetate ion, which is a

    weak base. The pH of a weak base will be greater than 7.

5. *Examine the graph of pH vs. volume (blue line) and sketch the titration curve on the following page. Mark the equivalence point as halfway between the top and bottom "shoulders" of the curve. Based on your graph, what is the pH at the equivalence point? How does it compare with your predicted pH?*

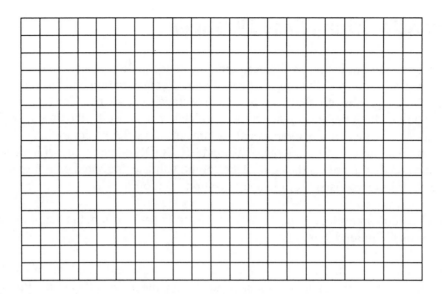

The experimental pH is 9. It is the same as predicted.

6. *Calculate the value of the equilibrium constant for the balanced net ionic equation for the weak acid-strong base titration.*

The balanced net ionic equation is CH_3COOH (aq) + OH^- (aq) = H_2O (aq) + CH_3COO^- (aq)

and is the reverse of the weak base equation for the acetate ion. The equilibrium constant is the

reciprocal of K_b. K_b for the acetate is 5.6×10^{-10}. The reciprocal of K_b is K_{eq} for the

neutralization of the weak acid CH_3COOH and the strong base NaOH and has a value of

1.79×10^9.

6-12: Strong Acid-Weak Base Titrations

Titrations provide a method of quantitatively measuring the concentration of an unknown solution. In an acid-base titration, this is done by delivering a titrant of known concentration into an analyte of known volume. Titration curves (graphs of volume vs. pH) have characteristic shapes. The equivalence point of the titration, or the point where the analyte has been completely consumed by the titrant, is identified by the point where the pH changes rapidly over a small volume of titrant delivered. In this assignment, you will observe this titration curve by titrating the strong acid HCl with the weak base sodium hydrogen carbonate ($NaHCO_3$). You will also predict the pH at the equivalence point, validate your prediction experimentally, and then calculate the equilibrium constant for the neutralization reaction.

1. Start *Virtual ChemLab* and select *Strong Acid-Weak Base Titrations* from the list of assignments. The lab will open in the Titration laboratory.

2. Click the *Lab Book* to open it. The buret will be filled with HCl and 25 mL of $NaHCO_3$ solution will be in the beaker with methyl orange as the indicator. Click the *Save* button in the *Buret Zoom View* window. The horizontal position of the orange handle is off for the stopcock. Open the stopcock by pulling down on the orange handle. The vertical position delivers solution the fastest with three intermediate rates in between. Turn the stopcock to one of the fastest positions. Observe the titration curve. When the volume reaches 40 mL, double-click the stopcock to stop the titration. Click *Stop* in the *Buret Zoom View*. A blue data link will be created in the lab book. Click on it to view the data.

    If you need to repeat the titration, click in the *Stockroom* to enter, click on the clipboard, and select Preset Experiment # 5 *Strong Acid-Weak Base*.

3. The beaker contains 0.40 M $NaHCO_3$ and the buret contains 0.30 M HCl.

    Write a complete balanced equation for the neutralization reaction between HCl and NaHCO₃ and then write a balanced net ionic equation for this chemical reaction.

    HCl (aq) + NaHCO₃ (aq) = H₂CO₃ (aq) + NaCl (aq)
    H⁺ (aq) + HCO₃⁻ (aq) = H₂CO₃ (aq)

    The following questions can be answered by examining the *Plot* window, the *Data Viewer* window, and the balanced net ionic equation.

4. *Indicate the species present at the equivalence point, and predict whether the pH at the equivalence point will be pH > 7, pH < 7, or pH ≈ 7. Explain why you made this prediction.*

    pH < 7. At the equivalence point the solution contains only carbonic acid, which is a weak acid.

    The pH of a weak acid will be less than 7.

5. *Examine the graph of pH vs. volume (blue line) and sketch the titration curve on the following page. Mark the equivalence point as halfway between the top and bottom "shoulders" of the curve. Based on your graph, what is the pH at the equivalence point? How does it compare with your predicted pH?*

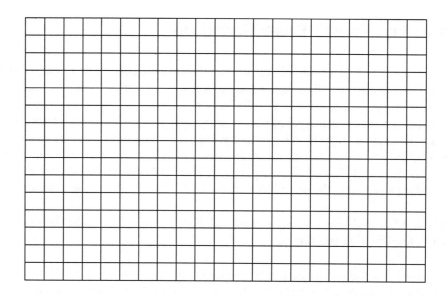

The experimental pH is 4. It is the same as predicted.

6. *Calculate the value of the equilibrium constant for the balanced net ionic equation for the strong acid-weak base titration.*

The balanced net ionic equation is H^+ (aq) + HCO_3^- (aq) = H_2CO_3 (aq) and is the reverse of

the ionization of carbonic acid. The equilibrium constant is the reciprocal of K_a. K_a for the

carbonic acid is 4.3×10^{-7}. The reciprocal of K_a is K_{eq} for the neutralization of the strong acid

HCl and the weak base HCO_3^- and has the value of 2.33×10^6.

6-13: Weak Acid-Weak Base Titrations

Titrations provide a method of quantitatively measuring the concentration of an unknown solution. In an acid-base titration, this is done by delivering a titrant of known concentration into an analyte of known volume. Titration curves (graphs of volume vs. pH) have characteristic shapes. The equivalence point of the titration, or the point where the analyte has been completely consumed by the titrant, is identified by the point where the pH changes rapidly over a small volume of titrant delivered. In this assignment, you will observe this titration curve by titrating the weak acid CH_3COOH (acetic acid) with the weak base NH_3. You will also predict the pH at the equivalence point, validate your prediction experimentally, and then calculate the equilibrium constant for the neutralization reaction.

1. Start *Virtual ChemLab* and select *Weak Acid-Weak Base Titrations* from the list of assignments. The lab will open in the Titration laboratory.

2. Click the *Lab Book* to open it. The buret will be filled with NH_3 and 50.00 mL of CH_3COOH is in the beaker with bromocresol purple as the indicator. Click the *Save* button in the *Buret Zoom View* window. The horizontal position of the orange handle is off for the stopcock. Open the stopcock by pulling down on the orange handle. The vertical position delivers solution the fastest with three intermediate rates in between. Turn the stopcock to one of the fastest positions. Observe the titration curve. When the volume reaches 25 mL, double-click the stopcock to stop the titration. Click *Stop* in the *Buret Zoom View*. A blue data link will be created in the lab book. Click on it to view the data.

   If you need to repeat the titration, exit the laboratory and select *Weak Acid-Weak Base Titrations* from the list of assignments.

3. The beaker contains 0.1033 M CH_3COOH and the buret contains 0.4949 M NH_3.

   Write a complete balanced equation for the neutralization reaction between CH_3COOH and NH_3.

   CH_3COOH (aq) + NH_3 (aq) = NH_4^+ (aq) + CH_3COO^- (aq)

   The following questions can be answered by examining the *Plot* window, the *Data Viewer* window, and the balanced equation.

4. *Indicate the species present at the equivalence point, and predict whether the pH at the equivalence point will be pH > 7, pH < 7, or pH ≈ 7. Explain why you made this prediction.*

   pH ≈ 7. At the equivalence point the solution contains the NH_4^+ ion which is a weak acid with K_a

   = 5.6×10^{-10} and the acetate ion which is a weak base with $K_b = 5.6\times10^{-10}$. Since the weak acid

   has the same strength as the weak base the pH = 7.

5. *Examine the graph of pH vs. volume (blue line) and sketch the titration curve on the following page. Mark the equivalence point as halfway between the top and bottom "shoulders" of the curve. Based on your graph, what is the pH at the equivalence point? How does it compare with your predicted pH?*

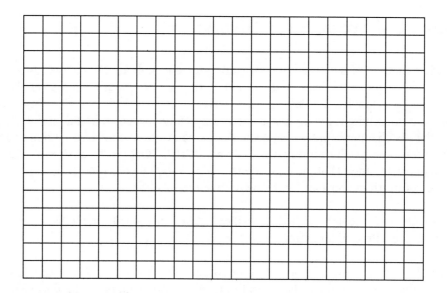

The experimental pH is 7. It is the same as predicted.

6. *Calculate the value of the equilibrium constant for the balanced net ionic equation for the weak acid-weak base titration.*

The balanced net ionic equation is CH_3COOH (aq) + NH_3 (aq) = NH_4^+ (aq) + CH_3COO^- (aq)

and is the combination of the ionization of acetic acid and the reverse of the ionization of

ammonium ion. The equilibrium constant is the K_a for acetic acid (1.8×10^{-5}) divided by the K_a

for the ammonium ion (5.6×10^{-10}) which is 3.21×10^4.

6-14: Study of Acid-Base Titrations – Polyprotic Acids

Titrations provide a method of quantitatively measuring the concentration of an unknown solution. In an acid-base titration, this is done by delivering a titrant of known concentration into an analyte of known volume. (The concentration of an unknown titrant can also be determined by titration with an analyte of known concentration and volume.) Titration curves (graphs of volume vs. pH) have characteristic shapes. The graph can be used to determine the strength or weakness of an acid or base. The equivalence point of the titration, or the point where the analyte has been completely consumed by the titrant, is identified by the point where the pH changes rapidly over a small volume of titrant delivered. For polyprotic acids, there will be multiple equivalence points. In this assignment, you will observe this titration curve by titrating the weak acid H_2SO_3 with the strong base NaOH.

1. Start *Virtual ChemLab* and select *Study of Acid-Base Titrations – Polyprotic Acids* from the list of assignments. The lab will open in the Titration laboratory.

2. Click the *Lab Book* to open it. The buret will be filled with NaOH and 25.00 mL of H_2SO_3 will be in the beaker with thymol blue as an indicator. Click the *Save* button in the *Buret Zoom View* window. The horizontal position of the orange handle is off for the stopcock. Open the stopcock by pulling down on the orange handle. The vertical position delivers solution the fastest with three intermediate rates in between. Turn the stopcock to one of the fastest positions. Observe the titration curve. When the volume reaches 40 mL, double-click the stopcock to stop the titration. Click *Stop* in the *Buret Zoom View*. A blue data link will be created in the lab book. Click on it to view the titration data.

    If you need to repeat the titration, click in the *Stockroom* to enter, click on the clipboard and select Preset Experiment #7 *Polyprotic Acid-Strong Base*.

3. The beaker contains 0.2556 M H_2SO_3 and the buret contains 0.3106 M NaOH.

    Write a complete balanced equation for the two-step neutralization reaction between H_2SO_3 and NaOH.

    H_2SO_3 (aq) + NaOH (aq) → H_2O (aq) + $NaHSO_3$ (aq)
    $NaHSO_3$ (aq) + NaOH (aq) → H_2O (aq) + Na_2SO_3 (aq)

    The following questions can be answered by examining the *Plot* window and the *Data Viewer* window.

4. *What was the pH and color of the solution at the beginning of the titration?* **1.31: orange**

5. *What was the pH and color of the solution at the end of the titration? Did any additional color changes occur during the titration?*

    12.41: blue: solution changed from orange to yellow

6. *Examine the graph of pH vs. volume (blue line) and sketch the titration curve on the following page.*

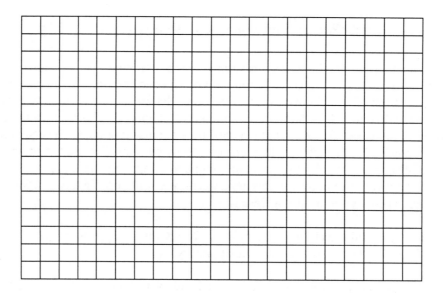

7. *What happens to the pH around 16 mL and 32 mL? What causes each to occur?*

    The pH changes rapidly from 3 to 6 at 16 mL and from 8 to 11 at 32 mL. At the beginning the solution contains only acid (a low pH). When the amount of base equals the amount of acid for the first proton (hydrogen) the first equivalence point is reached. Water and $NaHSO_3$ are the products. $NaHSO_3$ is a weak acid and the pH is slightly lower than neutral water which has a pH of 7. As NaOH is continued to be added the second proton (hydrogen) is neutralized and the resulting solution contains only water and Na_2SO_3. Na_2SO_3 is a weak base so the pH of the solution is approximately 12.

8. *Examine the graph of conductivity vs. volume (red line) and sketch the titration curve on the graph above.*

9. *What happens to the conductivity during the titration?*

    The graph has a negative slope, reaches a minimum at 16 mL and then has a positive slope after 16 mL. It changes slope again at 32 mL and the slope is steeper after 32 mL.

10. *What would cause the change observed in question #10?*

    In the beginning of the titration the $[H_2SO_3]$ = 0.2556 M. As the OH^- is added, the reaction produces water and the concentration of ions decreases, hence less and less conductivity from the beginning until the first equivalence point is reached at 16 mL. After the first equivalence point, $NaHSO_3$ is soluble in water as Na^+ and HSO_3^-. This increase in ions causes the conductivity to increase. After the second equivalence point is reached at 32 mL, SO_3^{2-} ions are produced along with excess OH^-. This combination produces an increase in conductivity, hence a steeper slope.

6-15: Acid-Base Standardization

Titrations provide a method of quantitatively measuring the concentration of an unknown solution. In an acid-base titration, this is done by delivering a titrant of known concentration into an analyte of known volume. (The concentration of an unknown titrant can also be determined by titration with an analyte of known concentration and volume.) Titration curves (graphs of volume vs. pH) have characteristic shapes. The graph can be used to determine the strength or weakness of an acid or base. The equivalence point of the titration, or the point where the analyte has been completely consumed by the titrant, is identified by the point where the pH changes rapidly over a small volume of titrant delivered. In this assignment, you will determine the molarity of an unknown solution of NaOH by titrating against a primary standard, potassium hydrogen phthalate (KHP).

1. Start *Virtual ChemLab* and select *Acid-Base Standardization* from the list of assignments. The lab will open in the Titrations laboratory.

2. Click the *Lab Book* to open it. Click the *Beakers* drawer and place a beaker in the spotlight next to the balance. Click on the *Balance* area to zoom in, open the bottle of KHP by clicking on the lid (*Remove Lid*). Drag the beaker to the balance to place it on the balance pan and tare the balance. Pick up the *Scoop* and scoop out some sample by first dragging the scoop to the mouth of the bottle and then pulling the scoop down the face of the bottle. As the scoop is dragged down the face of the bottle it will pickup different quantities of solid. Select the largest sample possible and drag the scoop to the beaker on the balance until it snaps in place and then let go. Repeat this one additional time so you have put two scoops (approximately 2 g) of KHP in the beaker. Record the mass of the sample in the data table on the following page and return to the laboratory.

3. Drag the beaker from the balance to the sink and hold it under the tap to add a small amount of water. Place it on the stir plate and drag the calibrated pH meter probe to the beaker. Add *Phenolphthalein* as the indicator.

4. The buret will be filled with NaOH. Click the ***Save*** button in the *Buret Zoom View* window so the titration data can be saved. The horizontal position of the orange handle is off for the stopcock. Open the stopcock by pulling down on the orange handle. The vertical position delivers solution the fastest with three intermediate rates in between. Turn the stopcock to one of the fastest positions. Observe the titration curve. When the blue line begins to turn up, double-click the stopcock to turn it off. Move the stopcock down one position to add volume drop by drop.

    There are two methods for determining the volume at the equivalence point: (1) Stop the titration when a color change occurs. Click the ***Stop*** button in the *Buret Zoom View*. A blue data link will appear in the lab book. Click the blue data link to open the *Data Viewer* window. Scroll down to the last data entry and record the volume at the equivalence point in the data table. OR (2) Add drops slowly through the equivalence point until the pH reaches approximately 12. Click the ***Stop*** button in the *Buret Zoom View*. A blue data link will appear in the lab book. Click the blue data link to open the *Data Viewer* window. Click the ***Select All*** button to copy and paste the data to a spreadsheet. Plot the first derivative of pH vs. volume. The peak will indicate the volume at the equivalence point since this is where the pH is changing the most rapidly as the volume changes.

    Repeat at least two additional times recording data in the data table. Do not forget to refill the buret with NaOH and place the pH meter and indicator in the beaker each time.

    The molecular weight of KHP is 204.22 g/mol.

Unknown # _____ **sample student data for #3**

Data Table

Trial	mass KHP (g)	volume NaOH (mL)	molarity NaOH (mol/L)
1		**(sample student data)**	
2	**2.0195**	**33.21**	**.2978**
3			
4			
5			

5. *Write a balanced chemical equation for the reaction of KHP and NaOH.*

$KHP + NaOH \rightarrow H_2O + P^{2-} + Na^+ + K^+$

6. *What is the average molarity of the unknown NaOH for your closest three titrations?*

Answers will vary according to assigned unknown—but they should be close.

Answers to Unknowns:

Unknown #1: 0.3209 M

Unknown #2: 0.3064 M

Unknown #3: 0.2978 M

Unknown #4: 0.2910 M

Unknown #5: 0.2879 M

Unknown #6: 0.2870 M

Unknown #7: 0.2880 M

Unknown #8: 0.2907 M

Unknown #9: 0.2948 M

Unknown #10: 0.3004 M

Unknown #11: 0.3073 M

Unknown #12: 0.3156 M

Unknown #13: 0.3253 M

Unknown #14: 0.3364 M

Unknown #15: 0.3491 M

6-16: Analysis of Baking Soda

Titrations provide a method of quantitatively measuring the concentration of an unknown solution. In an acid-base titration, this is done by delivering a titrant of known concentration into an analyte of known volume. (The concentration of an unknown titrant can also be determined by titration with an analyte of known concentration and volume.) Titration curves (graphs of volume vs. pH) have characteristic shapes. The graph can be used to determine the strength or weakness of an acid or base. The equivalence point of the titration, or the point where the analyte has been completely consumed by the titrant, is identified by the point where the pH changes rapidly over a small volume of titrant delivered. In this assignment, you will determine the mass % of an unknown sample of baking soda ($NaHCO_3$) by titrating it with an HCl solution of known concentration.

1. Start *Virtual ChemLab* and select *Analysis of Baking Soda* from the list of assignments. The lab will open in the Titration laboratory. The laboratory will open with a beaker on the stir plate with 1.5000 g of impure solid $NaHCO_3$ and with sufficient water added to make the total volume 25.00 mL. Methyl orange indicator will have also been added to the beaker, as well as the calibrated pH meter probe.

2. Click on the *Lab Book* to open it and click on the *Buret Zoom View* window and the pH meter window to bring them to the front. The buret will be filled with 0.3015 M HCl. Click the *Save* button in the *Buret Zoom View* window so the titration data can be saved. The horizontal position of the orange handle is off for the stopcock. Open the stopcock by pulling down on the orange handle. The vertical position delivers solution the fastest with three intermediate rates in between. Turn the stopcock to one of the fastest positions. Observe the titration curve. When the blue line begins to turn down, double-click the stopcock to turn it off. Move the stopcock down one position to add volume drop by drop.

    There are two methods for determining the volume at the equivalence point: (1) Stop the titration when a color change occurs. Click the *Stop* button in the *Buret Zoom View*. A blue data link will appear in the lab book. Click the blue data link to open the *Data Viewer* window. Scroll down to the last data entry and record the volume at the equivalence point in the data table below. OR (2) Add drops slowly through the equivalence point until the pH reaches approximately 2. Click the *Stop* button in the *Buret Zoom View*. A blue data link will appear in the lab book. Click the blue data link to open the *Data Viewer* window. Click the *Select All* button to copy and paste the data to a spreadsheet. Plot the first derivative of pH vs. volume. The peak will indicate the volume at the equivalence point since this is where the pH is changing the most rapidly as the volume changes.

    Unknown sample # ___9___ (**answers will vary depending on assigned unknown**)

Data Table

mass unknown sample (g)	volume HCl (mL)	molarity HCl (mol/L)
1.5000	38.35	0.3015

3. *Write a balanced chemical equation for the reaction between $NaHCO_3$ and HCl.*

    $NaHCO_3$ + HCl = NaCl + H_2CO_3

4. *Calculate the moles of HCl by multiplying the volume of HCl in liters and the molarity of HCl in mol/L. (Keep four significant digits in all of the calculations.)* **0.01156 moles HCl**

5. *The moles of HCl can be converted to moles of NaHCO₃ using the coefficients from the balanced equation. What is the mole to mole ratio of HCl to NaHCO₃? How many moles of NaHCO₃ are present in the sample?*

1:1: 0.01156 moles NaHCO₃ (Answers will vary depending on unknown sample #.)

6. *Calculate the grams of NaHCO₃ by multiplying the moles of NaHCO₃ by the molecular weight of NaHCO₃ (84.007 g/mol).*

0.9710 g NaHCO₃ (Answers will vary depending on unknown sample #.)

7. The mass % of NaHCO₃ present in the sample can be calculated by dividing the mass of NaHCO₃ from question #6 by the mass of the sample from the data table and multiplying by 100.

What is the mass % of NaHCO₃?

64.73% (Answers will vary depending on unknown sample #.)

Answers to Unknown Samples:

Unknown #1: 67.52%

Unknown #2: 66.94%

Unknown #3: 66.45%

Unknown #4: 66.05%

Unknown #5: 65.70%

Unknown #6: 65.40%

Unknown #7: 65.13%

Unknown #8: 64.91%

Unknown #9: 64.73%

Unknown #10: 64.62%

Unknown #11: 64.65%

Unknown #12: 65.02%

Unknown #13: 66.16%

Unknown #14: 68.96%

Unknown #15: 74.88%

7-1: Study of Oxidation-Reduction Titrations

Titrations provide a method of quantitatively measuring the concentration of an unknown solution. This is done by delivering a titrant of known concentration into an analyte of known volume. (The concentration of an unknown titrant can also be determined by titration with an analyte of known concentration and volume.) In oxidation-reduction (redox) titrations, the voltage resulting from the mixture of an oxidant and reductant can be measured as the titration proceeds. The equivalence point of the titration, or the point where the analyte has been completely consumed by the titrant, is identified by the point where the voltage changes rapidly over a small volume of titrant delivered. In this assignment, you will observe this titration curve by titrating $FeCl_2$ with $KMnO_4$.

1. Start *Virtual ChemLab* and select *Study of Oxidation-Reduction Titrations* from the list of assignments. The lab will open in the Titrations laboratory.

2. The buret will be filled with $KMnO_4$ and a solution containing $FeCl_2$ will be in the beaker on the stir plate. The horizontal position of the orange handle is off for the stopcock. Open the stopcock by pulling down on the orange handle. The vertical position delivers volume the fastest with three intermediate rates in between. Turn the stopcock to one of the fastest positions. Observe the titration curve. When the volume reaches 45 mL double-click the stopcock to turn it off.

3. Examine the graph of voltage vs. volume (blue line) and sketch the titration curve below. Label the axes.

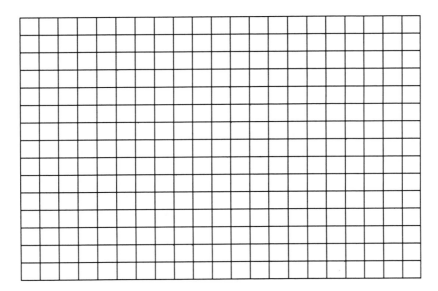

4. *Write a balanced net ionic equation for the reaction in acidic solution of $FeCl_2$ and $KMnO_4$ (Fe^{2+} becomes Fe^{3+} and MnO_4^- becomes Mn^{2+}).*

$$5Fe^{2+} + MnO_4^- + 8H^+ \rightarrow 5Fe^{3+} + Mn^{2+} + 4H_2O$$

5. The reduction potential of Fe^{2+} is 0.732 volts, and the reduction potential of MnO_4^- in acidic solution is 1.507 volts.

    If you titrate $KMnO_4$ into $FeCl_2$, what happens to the voltage of the solution as the titration starts and proceeds to the end?

    The voltage begins at approximately 0.73 V. At the equivalence point it jumps to 1.5 V.

7-2: Standardization of a Permanganate Solution

Titrations provide a method of quantitatively measuring the concentration of an unknown solution. This is done by delivering a titrant of known concentration into an analyte of known volume. (The concentration of an unknown titrant can also be determined by titration with an analyte of known concentration and volume.) In oxidation-reduction (redox) titrations, the voltage resulting from the mixture of an oxidant and reductant can be measured as the titration proceeds. The equivalence point of the titration, or the point where the analyte has been completely consumed by the titrant, is identified by the point where the voltage changes rapidly over a small volume of titrant delivered. In this assignment, you will determine the molarity of an unknown solution of $KMnO_4$ by titrating against a primary standard, solid As_2O_3.

1. Start *Virtual ChemLab* and select *Standardization of a Permanganate Solution* from the list of assignments. The lab will open in the Titrations laboratory.

2. Click the *Lab Book* to open it. Click the *Beakers* drawer and place a beaker in the spotlight next to the balance. Click on the *Balance* area to zoom in, open the bottle of As_2O_3 by clicking on the lid (*Remove Lid*). Drag the beaker to the balance to place it on the balance pan and tare the balance. Pick up the *Scoop* and scoop out some sample by first dragging the scoop to the mouth of the bottle and then pulling the scoop down the face of the bottle. As the scoop is dragged down the face of the bottle it will pick up different quantities of solid. Select the second sample size from the top and drag the scoop to the beaker on the balance until it snaps in place and then let go. You should have approximately 0.1 g of As_2O_3 in the beaker. Record the mass of the sample in the data table on the following page and return to the laboratory.

3. Drag the beaker from the balance to the sink and hold it under the tap to add a small amount of water. Place it on the stir plate and add the voltmeter probe to the beaker.

4. The buret will be filled with a solution of $KMnO_4$ of unknown concentration. A bottle of permanganate is on the lab bench. Record the unknown sample number. Click the *Save* button in the *Buret Zoom View* window so the titration data can be saved. The horizontal position of the orange handle is off for the stopcock. Open the stopcock by pulling down on the orange handle. The vertical position delivers solution the fastest with three intermediate rates in between. Turn the stopcock to one of the fastest positions. Observe the titration curve. When the blue line begins to turn up, double-click the stopcock to turn it off. Move the stopcock down one position to add volume drop by drop.

    There are two methods for determining the volume at the equivalence point: (1) Stop the titration when a color change occurs. Click the *Stop* button in the *Buret Zoom View*. A blue data link will appear in the lab book. Click the blue data link to open the *Data Viewer* window. Scroll down to the last data entry and record the volume at the equivalence point in the data table. OR (2) Add drops slowly through the equivalence point until the voltages reaches a maximum and levels off. Click the *Stop* button in the *Buret Zoom View*. A blue data link will appear in the lab book. Click the blue data link to open the *Data Viewer* window. Click the *Select All* button to copy and paste the data into a spreadsheet program. Plot the first derivative of voltage vs. volume. The peak will indicate the volume at the equivalence point since this is where the voltage is changing the most rapidly as the volume changes.

    To repeat the titration, drag the beaker to the red disposal bucket, move a new beaker from the beaker drawer next to the balance, and repeat the procedure. Do not forget to refill the buret with $KMnO_4$ and place the voltmeter in the beaker each time.

The molecular weight of As_2O_3 is 197.84 g/mol.

Unknown # _____ **sample student data for #5**

Data Table

Trial	mass As_2O_3 (g)	volume $KMnO_4$ (mL)	molarity $KMnO_4$ (mole/L)
1		(sample student data)	
2	0.0982	30.31	0.01310
3			
4			
5			

5. Upon the addition of water, As_2O_3 is converted to H_3AsO_3. During the titration H_3AsO_3 is oxidized to H_3AsO_4 and MnO_4^- is reduced to Mn^{2+}.

Write a balanced net ionic equation for the reaction.

$$2MnO_4^- + 5H_3AsO_3 + 6H^+ \longrightarrow 2Mn^{2+} + 5H_3AsO_4 + 3H_2O$$

6. *Using the information in the data table, calculate the molarity of the permanganate solution. (Note that 1 mole of As_2O_3 solid becomes 2 moles of H_3AsO_3 when dissolved in water.)*

$$0.0982 \text{ g As}_2O_3 \left(\frac{1 \text{ mol As}_2O_3}{197.84 \text{ g As}_2O_3} \right) \left(\frac{2 \text{ mol H}_3AsO_4}{1 \text{ mol As}_2O_3} \right) \left(\frac{2 \text{ mol MnO}_4^-}{5 \text{ mol H}_3AsO_4} \right) \left(\frac{1}{0.03031 \text{ L MnO}_4^-} \right) = 0.01310 \text{ M M}$$

Actual value for Unknown # 5 is 0.01308 M.
Answers will vary according to assigned unknown—but they should be close.

Unknown #1: 0.01333 M
Unknown #2: 0.01318 M
Unknown #3: 0.01310 M
Unknown #4: 0.01307 M
Unknown #5: 0.01308 M
Unknown #6: 0.01311 M
Unknown #7: 0.01316 M
Unknown #8: 0.01322 M
Unknown #9: 0.01330 M
Unknown #10: 0.01338 M
Unknown #11: 0.01348 M
Unknown #12: 0.01358 M
Unknown #13: 0.01369 M
Unknown #14: 0.01381 M
Unknown #15: 0.01393 M

7-3: Analysis of a Ferrous Chloride Sample

Titrations provide a method of quantitatively measuring the concentration of an unknown solution. This is done by delivering a titrant of known concentration into an analyte of known volume. (The concentration of an unknown titrant can also be determined by titration with an analyte of known concentration and volume.) In oxidation-reduction (redox) titrations, the voltage resulting from the mixture of an oxidant and reductant can be measured as the titration proceeds. The equivalence point of the titration, or the point where the analyte has been completely consumed by the titrant, is identified by the point where the voltage changes rapidly over a small volume of titrant delivered. In this assignment, you will determine the mass % of an unknown sample of ferrous chloride ($FeCl_2$) by titrating it with a $KMnO_4$ solution of known concentration.

1. Start *Virtual ChemLab* and select *Analysis of a Ferrous Chloride Sample* from the list of assignments. The lab will open in the Titrations laboratory.

2. Record the $FeCl_2$ Unknown number in the data table on the following page. Click the *Lab Book* to open it. Click the *Beakers* drawer and place a beaker in the spotlight next to the balance. Click on the *Balance* area to zoom in, open the bottle of unknown $FeCl_2$ by clicking on the lid (*Remove Lid*). Drag the beaker to the balance to place it on the balance pan and tare the balance. Pick up the *Scoop* and scoop out some sample by first dragging the scoop to the mouth of the bottle and then pulling the scoop down the face of the bottle. As the scoop is dragged down the face of the bottle it will pick up different quantities of solid. Select the largest sample size and drag the scoop to the beaker on the balance until it snaps in place and then let go. Repeat this again so you have approximately 2 g of unknown in the beaker. Record the unknown number and the mass of the sample in the data table. (You will have to drag the $FeCl_2$ bottle to the front of the lab bench to see the unknown number.) Return to the laboratory.

3. Place the beaker on the stir plate. Drag the 50 mL graduated cylinder under the tap in the sink and fill it with distilled water. It will automatically snap back into place when it is full. Drag the full 50 mL graduated cylinder to the beaker on the stir plate and then pour the water into the beaker. Now place the voltmeter probe in the beaker and make sure the voltmeter is on.

4. The buret will be filled with 0.0815 M $KMnO_4$. Click the **Save** button in the *Buret Zoom View* window so the titration data can be saved. The horizontal position of the orange handle is off for the stopcock. Open the stopcock by pulling down on the orange handle. The vertical position delivers solution the fastest with three intermediate rates in between. Turn the stopcock to one of the fastest positions. Observe the titration curve. When the blue line begins to turn up, double-click the stopcock to turn it off. Move the stopcock down one position to add volume drop by drop.

There are two methods for determining the volume at the equivalence point: (1) Stop the titration when a color change occurs. Click the **Stop** button in the *Buret Zoom View*. A blue data link will appear in the lab book. Click the blue data link to open the *Data Viewer* window. Scroll down to the last data entry and record the volume at the equivalence point in the data table. OR (2) Add drops slowly through the equivalence point until the voltage reaches a maximum and levels off. Click the **Stop** button in the *Buret Zoom View*. A blue data link will appear in the lab book. Click the blue data link to open the *Data Viewer* window. Click the **Select All** button to copy and paste the data into a spreadsheet program. Plot the first derivative of voltage vs. volume. The peak will indicate the volume at the equivalence point since this is where the voltage is changing the most rapidly as the volume changes.

5. Repeat the titration at least two additional times recording your data in the data table. Do not forget to refill the buret with $KMnO_4$, place the voltmeter probe in the beaker, and add water each time.

The molecular weight of $FeCl_2$ is 151.91 g/mol.

Unknown # _____ **sample student data for #4**

Data Table

Trial	mass $FeCl_2$ (g)	volume $KMnO_4$ (mL)	molarity $KMnO_4$ (mol/L)
1		**(sample student data)**	
2	**2.0436**	**25.57**	**.0815**
3			
4			
5			

6. *Write a balanced net ionic equation for the reaction in acidic solution of $FeCl_2$ and $KMnO_4$ (Fe^{2+} is oxidized to Fe^{3+} and MnO_4^- is reduced to Mn^{2+}).*

$$5Fe^{2+} + MnO_4^- + 8H^+ \rightarrow 5Fe^{3+} + Mn^{2+} + 4H_2O$$

7. The moles of MnO_4^- can be calculated by multiplying the volume of MnO_4^- required to reach the endpoint multiplied by the molarity of the MnO_4^- solution.

What are the moles of MnO_4^- used in the titration? **0.002084 mol (answers will vary)**

8. The moles of $FeCl_2$ can be calculated by using the mole ratio from the balanced equation.

How many moles of $FeCl_2$ were in the unknown? **0.01042 mol (answers will vary)**

9. The mass of $FeCl_2$ in the sample can be calculated by multiplying the moles of $FeCl_2$ by the molecular weight of $FeCl_2$.

What is the mass of $FeCl_2$ in the sample? **1.582 g (answers will vary)**

10. The mass % of $FeCl_2$ in the unknown sample can be calculated by dividing the mass of $FeCl_2$ in the sample by the total mass of the unknown sample.

What is the % $FeCl_2$ in your unknown sample? **77.45 % (answers will vary)**

11. *What is the average % iron in the unknown sample using your best three answers?*

Answers will vary depending on the unknown.

Answers to unknowns:

#1: 79.12%	*#5: 77.03%*	*#9: 75.72%*	*#13: 81.48%*
#2: 78.50%	*#6: 76.63%*	*#10: 75.62%*	*#14: 91.86%*
#3: 77.96%	*#7: 76.28%*	*#11: 75.92%*	*#15: 87.51%*
#4: 77.47%	*#8: 75.96%*	*#12: 77.29%*	

8-1: Flame Tests for Metals

Have you ever wondered why a candle flame is yellow? The characteristic yellow of the flame comes from the glow of burning carbon fragments. The carbon fragments are produced by the incomplete combustion reaction of the wick and the candle wax. When elements, such as carbon, are heated to high temperatures, some of their electrons are excited to higher energy levels. When these excited electrons fall back to lower energy levels, they release excess energy in packages of light called photons. The color of the emitted light depends on the individual energy level spacing in the atom. When heated, each element emits a characteristic pattern of photons, which is useful for identifying the element. The characteristic colors of light produced when substances are heated in the flame of a gas burner are the basis for flame tests of several elements. In this assignment, you will perform flame tests that are used to identify several metallic elements.

1. Start *Virtual ChemLab* and select *Flame Tests for Metals* from the list of assignments. The lab will open in the Inorganic laboratory.

2. Enter the stockroom by clicking inside the *Stockroom* window. Once inside the stockroom, drag a test tube from the box and place it on the metal test tube stand. Bottles containing solutions of metal cations are located on the shelves, and you can click on any of the bottles to add them to your test tube. Click on the Na^+ bottle and click **Done** to send the test tube back to the lab. Repeat this process for each new metal cation until you have created test tubes containing Na^+, K^+, Ca^{2+}, Ba^{2+}, Sr^{2+}, and Cu^{2+}.

3. On the right side of the stockroom is a shelf labeled *Unknowns*. Click on the *Unknowns* label to create a test tube with an unknown. Now click on each of the following bottles on the shelf: Na^+, K^+, Ca^{2+}, Ba^{2+}, Sr^{2+}, and Cu^{2+}. Do not change the maximum and minimum on the left side and click on the green *Save* arrow. An unknown test tube labeled *Practice* will show up in the blue unknown rack on the unknown shelf. Drag the practice unknown test tube from the blue rack and place it in the metal stand and click on the *Return to Lab* arrow.

4. When you return to the lab you should note that you have seven test tubes. You will use the two flame test buttons at the bottom of the screen to perform a regular flame test and a flame test with a cobalt filter (blue glass held in front of the flame.) A test tube must be moved from the blue test tube rack to the metal test tube stand in order to perform the flame test. Test tubes dragged from the test tube rack can also be dropped on a test tube in the stand to switch places. Just above the periodic table there is a handle that, when clicked, pulls down the TV monitor. With the monitor down you can mouse-over each test tube to identify what metal cation is present in the test tube. As you mouse over each test tube, you will also see a picture of the test tube in the lower left corner.

5. Select the test tube containing Na^+ and place it on the metal stand. Click the **Flame** button. Record your observations in the data table on the following page. Click the **Flame w/Cobalt** button and record your observations in the same table.

6. Drag the K^+ test tube to the metal stand to exchange it with the Na^+. Perform a flame test on K^+ with and without cobalt glass. Record your observations in the data table.

7. For the other four ions, perform a regular flame test only. Do not use the cobalt glass. Record your observations in the data table.

Data Table

Flame Tests	[Answers]
Ion	Flame Color
sodium, Na^+	yellow
sodium, Na^+ (cobalt glass)	none
potassium, K^+	violet and yellow
potassium, K^+ (cobalt glass)	violet
calcium, Ca^{2+}	dark red
barium, Ba^{2+}	green
strontium, Sr^{2+}	bright red
copper, Cu^{2+}	blue-green
unknown #1	response will vary with unknown
unknown #2	response will vary with unknown
unknown #3	response will vary with unknown
unknown #4	response will vary with unknown

8. Now perform a flame test on the practice unknown. Determine which of the six metal ions it most closely matches. You may repeat the flame test on any of the six metal ions if necessary. When you are confident that you have identified the unknown, open the *Lab Book* by clicking on it. On the left page, click the ***Report*** button. On the right page, click on the metal cation that you think is in the practice unknown. Click ***Submit*** and then ***OK***. If all of the cation buttons turn green, you have successfully identified the unknown. If any turn red then you are incorrect. Click on the red disposal bucket to clear all of your samples.

9. Return to the *Stockroom* and drag the practice unknown to the metal test tube stand. This will randomly create a new unknown. Click on the green *Return to lab* arrow and test and report this unknown. Continue until you have correctly identified four <u>different</u> practice unknowns.

10. The energy of colored light increases in the order red, yellow, green, blue, and violet.

    List the metallic elements used in the flame tests in increasing order of the energy of the light emitted.

Sr^{2+} and Ca^{2+} Na^+ Ba^{2+} and Cu^{2+} K^+

red   yellow   green   violet

low energy <--> high energy

11. *What is the purpose of using the cobalt glass in the identification of sodium and potassium?*

    <u>Cobalt glass filters out yellow allowing violet K^+ to be seen. The glass helps to distinguish Na^+</u>

    <u>from K^+. In fact, you should be able to distinguish the two even if mixed together.</u>

8-2: Identification of Cations in Solution – Flame Tests

The process of determining the composition of a sample by conducting chemical tests is called qualitative analysis. By using the appropriate tests and applying logic, the identities of the ions present in an unknown solution can be determined. A qualitative analysis scheme is typically made up of a systematic set of chemical reactions where a certain subset of the ions present in the solution are selectively precipitated and removed. The color of the precipitates and solutions provide the means to identify the ions present. Flame tests are also used to identify certain ions that are difficult to identify chemically. In this assignment, you will learn how flame tests are used to identify the cations Na^+ and K^+. As you complete this analysis, remember that careful observation and logical reasoning are the keys to a successful qualitative analysis.

1. Start *Virtual ChemLab* and select *Identification of Cations in Solution* from the list of assignments. The lab will open in the Inorganic laboratory.

2. Enter the stockroom by clicking inside the *Stockroom* window. Once inside the stockroom, drag a test tube from the box and place it on the metal test tube stand. Now click on the Na^+ bottle to add it to the test and click **Done** to send the test tube out to the laboratory. Repeat this process with K^+ and a Na^+/K^+ mixture. Fill one test tube with just water by clicking on the bottle of distilled water and return to the laboratory.

3. When you return to the lab you should note that you have four test tubes. Just above the periodic table there is a handle that, when clicked, pulls down the TV monitor. With the monitor down you can drag your cursor over each test tube to identify what cation is in each test tube and see a picture of what it looks like in the lower left corner of the laboratory.

4. In this assignment, you will use the **Flame** and **Flame w/ Cobalt** (cobalt glass held in front of the flame) buttons located at the bottom of the screen. Before performing any chemical test or flame test, a test tube must be moved from the blue test tube rack to the metal test tube stand. If a test tube is already present in the test tube stand, you can drag a test tube from the blue rack to the metal stand to automatically switch places.

5. *Perform a flame test with and without the cobalt filter for just the Na^+ solution. Record your observations.* **Sodium produces a yellow flame which cannot be seen with cobalt glass.**

6. *Now do the same for just the K^+ solution and record your observations.*

   Potassium produces a violet flame which can be seen using cobalt glass.

7. *Now do the same for the Na^+/K^+ mixture and record your observations.* **The yellow sodium flame masks the potassium but with cobalt glass the sodium is not seen and the potassium is.**

8. *Now do the same with just water to get a feel for what it looks like with no chemicals other than water. Record your observations.* **There is no change in the flame.**

9. Return to the *Stockroom* The bottom right shelf is called the Unknowns shelf. Click on the *Unknowns* label to reconfigure the stockroom to create a practice unknown. Click on Na^+ and K^+ and on the left

side make the minimum = 0 and maximum = 2. Click on the *Save* arrow to return to the regular stockroom. An unknown test tube labeled *Practice* will be placed in the blue unknown rack. Drag the practice unknown from the blue rack to the metal stand and then return to the laboratory.

10. Perform a flame test with and without the cobalt filter and determine if the practice unknown contains sodium or potassium or both or neither. To check your results, click on the *Lab Book* and on the left page, click the **Report** button, select the ions you think are present in the unknown, click **Submit**, then **Ok**. If the ion button is green, you correctly determined whether the ion was present or not. If the ion button is red you did not make the correct analysis. Return to the laboratory and click the red disposal bucket to clear the lab. If you want to repeat with a new practice unknown, return to the stockroom and retrieve it from the blue rack. Continue until you obtain only green buttons when submitted.

11. After you have finished with your practice unknowns, you are now ready to accept your assigned unknown. Clear the laboratory of any test tubes by clicking on the red disposal bucket. Return to the stockroom and then click on the clipboard hanging below the green arrow. The clipboard contains a list of test tubes containing known and unknown solutions. The unknowns are labeled with a list of possible cations followed by the unknown number. Select Preset #2, which will give you an unknown that could contain any combination of Na^+ and K^+ or both or neither. Test your assigned unknown and report the cations found in your unknown in the space below. Don't forget to record your unknown number.

Unknown _____   Cations found: **Answers for unknowns are listed in the back of this manual.**

8-3: Identification of Cations in Solution – Ag^+, Hg_2^{2+}, Pb^{2+}

The process of determining the composition of a sample by conducting chemical tests is called qualitative analysis. By using the appropriate tests and applying logic, the identities of the ions present in an unknown solution can be determined. A qualitative analysis scheme is typically made up of a systematic set of chemical reactions where a certain subset of the ions present in the solution are selectively precipitated and removed. The color of the precipitates and solutions provide the means to identify the ions present. Flame tests are also used to identify certain ions that are difficult to identify chemically. In this assignment, you will learn the basics of a qualitative analysis scheme by performing an analysis on a mixture of Ag^+, Hg_2^{2+}, and Pb^{2+}. As you complete this analysis, remember that careful observation and logical reasoning are the keys to a successful qualitative analysis.

1. Start *Virtual ChemLab* and select *Identification of Cations in Solution* from the list of assignments. The lab will open in the Inorganic laboratory.

2. Enter the stockroom by clicking inside the *Stockroom* window. Once inside the stockroom, drag a test tube from the box and place it on the metal test tube stand. Now click on the Ag^+, Hg_2^{2+}, and Pb^{2+} bottles to add these cations to the test tube and click **Done** to send the test tube out to the laboratory. (There is Hg^{2+} and Hg_2^{2+} on the shelf. Make sure you obtain Hg_2^{2+}.) Return to the laboratory and click on the TV monitor handle to pull it down. As you proceed with the chemical analysis watch the TV screen to see the chemistry involved in the chemical reactions. You may also want to make some copies of your original test tube by clicking on the **Divide** button in case you make a mistake and need to start over.

3. Move the test tube to the metal stand. Click the NaCl reagent bottle to add chloride to the test tube.

    What observations can you make? **The test tube turns white and cloudy.**

    Click the **Centrifuge** button. *What observations can you make?* **All the solid goes to the bottom.**

    Each of the three ions form insoluble precipitates (solids) with chloride. If the solution turns cloudy white it indicates that at least one of the three ions is present. Now, we must determine which one. (Remember we already know what is in the test tube, but for an unknown you won't.)

4. Turn the heat on with the **Heat** button. Observe the TV screen.

    What happened? If you cannot tell, turn the heat on and off while observing the TV screen.

    The lead ion becomes soluble with heat but the others do not.

    With the heat turned on, click **Centrifuge** again and then **Decant**. (Decanting separates the solids from the solution and places the solution in the test tube rack.) Drag your cursor over the new test tube in the rack.

    What appears on the TV screen? What appears in the picture window? **The TV screen has $PbCl_2$**

    and the picture is cloudy white.

    This is the test for Pb^{2+}. If heated, it is soluble. When cooled it becomes insoluble.

173

5. Turn off the *Heat*. With the test tube containing the two remaining ions in the metal stand, click the NH_3 bottle on the reagent shelf.

    What do you observe? **The TV screen shows $Ag(NH_3)_2^+$ and the picture shows a black precipitate.**

    Addition of ammonia produces a diammine silver complex ion that is soluble. The mercury produces a green/black solid. This is the test for mercury.

6. *Centrifuge* and then *Decant* to pour the silver ion into another test tube. Move the tube with the black mercury solid to the red disposal bucket. Move the test tube containing silver back to the metal stand. Click the pH 4 reagent bottle to make the solution slightly acidic.

    What do you observe? **The TV screen shows solid AgCl again and the picture shows a white**

    precipitate.

    The silver ion is soluble as the diammine silver complex ion in pH 10 and is insoluble as AgCl in pH 4. You can click alternately on each of the pH bottles to confirm this test for the silver ion.

7. Return to the *Stockroom* The bottom right shelf is called the Unknowns shelf. Click on the *Unknowns* label to reconfigure the stockroom to create a practice unknown. Click on the Ag^+, Hg_2^{2+}, and Pb^{2+} bottles and on the left side make the minimum = 0 and maximum = 3. Click on the *Save* arrow to return to the regular stockroom. An unknown test tube labeled *Practice* will be placed in the blue unknown rack. Drag the practice unknown from the blue rack to the metal stand and then return to the laboratory.

8. Test the *Practice* unknown and determine if it contains each of the ions Ag^+, Hg_2^{2+}, and Pb^{2+}. To check your results, click on the *Lab Book* and on the left page, click the *Report* button, select the ions you think are present in the unknown, click *Submit*, then *Ok*. If the ion button is green, you correctly determined whether the ion was present or not. If the ion button is red you did not make the correct analysis. Return to the laboratory and click the red disposal bucket to clear the lab. If you want to repeat with a new practice unknown, return to the stockroom and retrieve it from the blue rack. Continue until you obtain only green buttons when submitted.

9. After you have finished with your practice unknowns, you are now ready to accept your assigned unknown. Clear the laboratory of any test tubes by clicking on the red disposal bucket. Return to the stockroom and then click on the clipboard hanging below the green arrow. The clipboard contains a list of test tubes containing known and unknown solutions. The unknowns are labeled with a list of possible cations followed by the unknown number. Select Preset #4, which will give you an unknown that could contain any combination of Ag^+, Hg_2^{2+}, and Pb^{2+} or all of them or just water. Test your assigned unknown and report the cations found in your unknown in the space below. Don't forget to record your unknown number.

    Unknown _____   Cations found: **Answers for unknowns are listed in the back of this manual.**

8-4: Identification of Cations in Solution – Co^{2+}, Cr^{3+}, Cu^{2+}

The process of determining the composition of a sample by conducting chemical tests is called qualitative analysis. By using the appropriate tests and applying logic, the identities of the ions present in an unknown solution can be determined. A qualitative analysis scheme is typically made up of a systematic set of chemical reactions where a certain subset of the ions present in the solution are selectively precipitated and removed. The color of the precipitates and solutions provide the means to identify the ions present. Flame tests are also used to identify certain ions that are difficult to identify chemically. In this assignment, you will learn the basics of a qualitative analysis scheme by performing an analysis on a mixture of Co^{2+}, Cr^{3+}, and Cu^{2+}. As you complete this analysis, remember that careful observation and logical reasoning are the keys to a successful qualitative analysis.

1. Start *Virtual ChemLab* and select *Identification of Cations in Solution* from the list of assignments. The lab will open in the Inorganic laboratory.

2. Enter the stockroom by clicking inside the *Stockroom* window. Once inside the stockroom, drag a test tube from the box and place it on the metal test tube stand. Now click on the Co^{2+}, Cr^{3+}, and Cu^{2+} bottles to add these cations to the test tube and click ***Done*** to send the test tube out to the laboratory. Return to the laboratory and click on the TV monitor handle to pull it down. As you proceed with the chemical analysis watch the TV screen to see the chemistry involved in the chemical reactions. You may also want to make some copies of your original test tube by clicking on the ***Divide*** button in case you make a mistake and need to start over.

3. *Move the test tube to the metal stand. Click the NaOH bottle on the reagent shelf. What observations can you make?* **The TV screen shows that chromium makes a complex ion and is soluble. Cobalt and copper form insoluble precipitates. The picture is cloudy green.**

4. Click ***Centrifuge*** and ***Decant***. (Decanting separates the solids from the solution and places the solution in the test tube rack.)

    What observations can you make as you drag your cursor over each test tube? **The chromium tube is clear and green. The test tube with the other metal ions contains a green solid in the bottom.**

    This is the test for chromium. If the new test tube in the blue rack is green when decanted then chromium is present. You can confirm it by placing the clear green test tube in the metal stand and clicking pH 10 and then adding HNO_3.

    What observations can you make? **There is a black precipitate ($Cr(OH)_3$) at pH 10 and then a clear purple solution (Cr^{3+}) when HNO_3 is added.**

5. With the test tube containing the cobalt and copper precipitate in the metal stand, add NH_3.

    What observations can you make? **The TV screen shows copper forms a tetrammine copper (II) ion ($Cu(NH_3)_4^{2+}$) and the picture shows a cloudy blue-gray precipitate.**

6. *Centrifuge* and *Decant*. Add HNO_3 to the tube in the metal stand containing the precipitate.

   What observations can you make? **The TV screen shows Co^{2+} ion and the picture shows a clear pink solution.**

   This is the confirmatory test for cobalt ion (Co^{2+}).

7. Place the test tube from the blue rack, which is the solution from step # 5, in the metal stand. Add HNO_3.

   What observations can you make? **The deep blue copper ammine complex ion ($Cu(NH_3)_4^{2+}$) turns a baby blue (Cu^{2+}).**

   This is the confirmatory test for copper.

8. Return to the *Stockroom*. The bottom right shelf is called the Unknowns shelf. Click on the *Unknowns* label to reconfigure the stockroom to create a practice unknown. Click on the Co^{2+}, Cr^{3+}, and Cu^{2+} bottles and on the left side make the minimum = 0 and maximum = 3. Click on the *Save* arrow to return to the regular stockroom. An unknown test tube labeled *Practice* will be placed in the blue unknown rack. Drag the practice unknown from the blue rack to the metal stand and then return to the laboratory.

9. Test the *Practice* unknown and determine if it contains each of the ions Co^{2+}, Cr^{3+}, and Cu^{2+}. To check your results, click on the *Lab Book* and on the left page, click the *Report* button, select the ions you think are present in the unknown, click *Submit*, then *Ok*. If the ion button is green, you correctly determined whether the ion was present or not. If the ion button is red you did not make the correct analysis. Return to the laboratory and click the red disposal bucket to clear the lab. If you want to repeat with a new practice unknown, return to the stockroom and retrieve it from the blue rack. Continue until you obtain only green buttons when submitted.

10. After you have finished with your practice unknowns, you are now ready to accept your assigned unknown. Clear the laboratory of any test tubes by clicking on the red disposal bucket. Return to the stockroom and then click on the clipboard hanging below the green arrow. The clipboard contains a list of test tubes containing known and unknown solutions. The unknowns are labeled with a list of possible cations followed by the unknown number. Select Preset #6, which will give you an unknown that could contain any combination of Co^{2+}, Cr^{3+}, and Cu^{2+} or all of them or just water. Test your assigned unknown and report the cations found in your unknown in the space below. Don't forget to record your unknown number.

    Unknown _____   Cations found: **Answers for unknowns are listed in the back of this manual.**

8-5: Identification of Cations in Solution – Ba^{2+}, Sr^{2+}, Ca^{2+}, Mg^{2+}

The process of determining the composition of a sample by conducting chemical tests is called qualitative analysis. By using the appropriate tests and applying logic, the identities of the ions present in an unknown solution can be determined. A qualitative analysis scheme is typically made up of a systematic set of chemical reactions where a certain subset of the ions present in the solution are selectively precipitated and removed. The color of the precipitates and solutions provide the means to identify the ions present. Flame tests are also used to identify certain ions that are difficult to identify chemically. In this assignment, you will need to develop your own qualitative analysis scheme to separate and identify the Group II cations Ba^{2+}, Sr^{2+}, Ca^{2+}, and Mg^{2+}. As you complete this analysis, remember that careful observation and logical reasoning are the keys to a successful qualitative analysis.

1. Start *Virtual ChemLab* and select *Identification of Cations in Solution* from the list of assignments. The lab will open in the Inorganic laboratory.

2. Enter the stockroom by clicking inside the *Stockroom* window. Once inside the stockroom, drag a test tube from the box and place it on the metal test tube stand. Now click on the Ba^{2+}, Sr^{2+}, Ca^{2+}, and Mg^{2+} bottles to add these cations to the test tube and click **Done** to send the test tube out to the laboratory. Return to the laboratory and click on the TV monitor handle to pull it down. As you proceed with the chemical analysis watch the TV screen to see the chemistry involved in the chemical reactions. You may also want to make some copies of your original test tube by clicking on the **Divide** button in case you make a mistake and need to start over.

3. *What do the solubility rules tell you about the way to separate the second group of cations? How can you tell each of the ions in this group apart? Think about changing the temperature and the pH. Design your own qualitative scheme for identification of these four Group II ions and write it below. Experiment with each of the four ions alone and then in combinations. Test an unknown to see if you can really determine the presence or absence of each of the four ions in this group.*

   Add HNO_3 then Na_2SO_4. White precipitate means Ba is present.
   Make the solution pH4. White precipitate means Sr is present.
   Make the solution pH7 then heat. White precipitate means Ca is present.
   Add NaOH. White precipitate means Mg is present.

4. Return to the *Stockroom*. The bottom right shelf is called the Unknowns shelf. Click on the *Unknowns* label to reconfigure the stockroom to create a practice unknown. Click on the Ba^{2+}, Sr^{2+}, Ca^{2+}, and Mg^{2+} bottles and on the left side make the minimum = 0 and maximum = 4. Click on the **Save** arrow to return to the regular stockroom. An unknown test tube labeled *Practice* will be placed in the blue unknown rack. Drag the practice unknown from the blue rack to the metal stand and then return to the laboratory.

5. Test the *Practice* unknown and determine if it contains each of the ions Ba^{2+}, Sr^{2+}, Ca^{2+}, and Mg^{2+}. To check your results, click on the *Lab Book* and on the left page, click the **Report** button, select the ions you think are present in the unknown, click **Submit**, then **Ok**. If the ion button is green, you correctly determined whether the ion was present or not. If the ion button is red you did not make the correct analysis. Return to the laboratory and click the red disposal bucket to clear the lab. If you want to repeat with a new practice unknown, return to the stockroom and retrieve it from the blue rack. Continue until you obtain only green buttons when submitted.

6. After you have finished with your practice unknowns, you are now ready to accept your assigned unknown. Clear the laboratory of any test tubes by clicking on the red disposal bucket. Return to the stockroom and then click on the clipboard hanging below the green arrow. The clipboard contains a list of test tubes containing known and unknown solutions. The unknowns are labeled with a list of possible cations followed by the unknown number. Select Preset #8, which will give you an unknown that could contain any combination of Ba^{2+}, Sr^{2+}, Ca^{2+}, and Mg^{2+} or all of them or just water. Test your assigned unknown and report the cations found in your unknown in the space below. Don't forget to record your unknown number.

Unknown _____   Cations found: **Answers for unknowns are listed in the back of this manual.**

8-6: Identification of Cations in Solution – Co^{2+}, Cu^{2+}, Ni^{2+}

The process of determining the composition of a sample by conducting chemical tests is called qualitative analysis. By using the appropriate tests and applying logic, the identities of the ions present in an unknown solution can be determined. A qualitative analysis scheme is typically made up of a systematic set of chemical reactions where a certain subset of the ions present in the solution are selectively precipitated and removed. The color of the precipitates and solutions provide the means to identify the ions present. Flame tests are also used to identify certain ions that are difficult to identify chemically. In this assignment, you will need to develop your own qualitative analysis scheme to separate and identify the transition metal cations Co^{2+}, Cu^{2+}, and Ni^{2+}. As you complete this analysis, remember that careful observation and logical reasoning are the keys to a successful qualitative analysis.

1. Start *Virtual ChemLab* and select *Identification of Cations in Solution* from the list of assignments. The lab will open in the Inorganic laboratory.

2. Enter the stockroom by clicking inside the *Stockroom* window. Once inside the stockroom, drag a test tube from the box and place it on the metal test tube stand. Now click on the Co^{2+}, Cu^{2+}, and Ni^{2+} bottles to add these cations to the test tube and click **Done** to send the test tube out to the laboratory. Return to the laboratory and click on the TV monitor handle to pull it down. As you proceed with the chemical analysis watch the TV screen to see the chemistry involved in the chemical reactions. You may also want to make some copies of your original test tube by clicking on the **Divide** button in case you make a mistake and need to start over.

3. *What do the solubility rules tell you about the way to separate the second group of cations? How can you tell each of the ions in this group apart? Think about changing the temperature and the pH. Design your own qualitative scheme for identification of these three transition metal ions and write it below. Experiment with each of the three ions alone and then in combinations. Test an unknown to see if you can really determine the presence or absence of each of the three ions in this group.*

   Add NH_3 and then NaOH. The precipitate is Co and Ni: the deep blue is Cu. Centrifuge and decant. Heat, then add HNO_3 to the precipitate. Centrifuge and decant. The green solution is Ni. The black precipitate is Co. Heat the black precipitate and you get a pink solution, which is Co. The green Ni solution can go to pH 10 or 14 (NaOH) to get a green precipitate.

4. Return to the *Stockroom*. The bottom right shelf is called the Unknowns shelf. Click on the *Unknowns* label to reconfigure the stockroom to create a practice unknown. Click on the Co^{2+}, Cu^{2+}, and Ni^{2+} bottles and on the left side make the minimum = 0 and maximum = 3. Click on the **Save** arrow to return to the regular stockroom. An unknown test tube labeled *Practice* will be placed in the blue unknown rack. Drag the practice unknown from the blue rack to the metal stand and then return to the laboratory.

5. Test the *Practice* unknown and determine if it contains each of the ions Co^{2+}, Cu^{2+}, and Ni^{2+}. To check your results, click on the *Lab Book* and on the left page, click the **Report** button, select the ions you think are present in the unknown, click **Submit**, then **Ok**. If the ion button is green, you correctly determined whether the ion was present or not. If the ion button is red you did not make the correct analysis. Return to the laboratory and click the red disposal bucket to clear the lab. If you want to repeat with a new practice unknown, return to the stockroom and retrieve it from the blue rack. Continue until you obtain only green buttons when submitted.

6. After you have finished with your practice unknowns, you are now ready to accept your assigned unknown. Clear the laboratory of any test tubes by clicking on the red disposal bucket. Return to the stockroom and then click on the clipboard hanging below the green arrow. The clipboard contains a list of test tubes containing known and unknown solutions. The unknowns are labeled with a list of possible cations followed by the unknown number. Select Preset #10, which will give you an unknown that could contain any combination of Co^{2+}, Cu^{2+}, and Ni^{2+} or all of them or just water. Test your assigned unknown and report the cations found in your unknown in the space below. Don't forget to record your unknown number.

Unknown _____   Cations found: **<u>Answers for unknowns are listed in the back of this manual.</u>**

Additional Assignments

The following worksheets contain additional assignments that are more advanced, explore topics with more depth, or introduce you to the more detailed parts of the *Virtual ChemLab* simulations. Keep in mind that these assignments are *not* contained in the electronic workbook found in the virtual hallway. To perform these assignments, you must enter the general chemistry laboratory by clicking on the General Chemistry door and then select the appropriate laboratory workbench as indicated in the assignment. In general, there are fewer step-by-step directions in these assignments and it is assumed you are familiar with the laboratory interface.

Also included in this section in the Instructor's Manual, but not found in the student workbook, are schemes and reactions for a number of different inorganic qualitative analysis unknowns that can be performed and assigned with the inorganic simulation. These schemes are provided as a resource for the instructor and demonstrate the myriad number of reactions and separation schemes that are provided in the simulation. The worksheets in the student workbook provide students the most common and basic qualitative analysis unknowns, but with a network installation an instructor can assign unknowns that fit the level of the students and the topics covered in class.

Inert Salts

Na^+ and Cl^- are often referred to as spectator ions. This is because during a simple reaction like a titration of sodium hydroxide with hydrochloric acid, they do not affect the equivalence point or pH of the reaction. These ions are stable enough that they are not affected by the pH. They exist as separate salts. Although inert salts do not affect the pH of titrations, they do affect the conductivity of solutions. In this assignment you will look at how inert salts affect the conductivity of acid/base titrations.

1. Take out Preset Experiment 1. Run the titration and graph the pH and conductivity curves on the following graph. Label the axis.

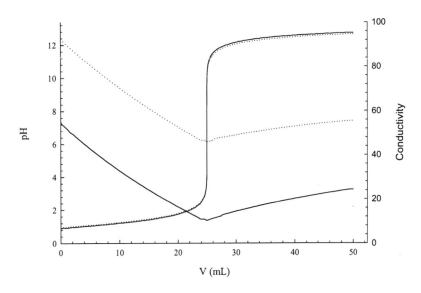

2. *Describe the shape of the conductivity curve. Why is it shaped the way it is?* **The conductivity**

   decreases until the equivalence point is reached and then it increases. As the equivalence point is

   reached, neutralization is occurring and there are increasingly less charged species. After the

   equivalence point, there are more charged species.

3. Take out Preset Experiment 1 again. Perform the same titration after adding approximately 3.0 g NaCl. In a different color draw the new pH and conductivity curves on the graph above.

4. *How did the conductivity of the titration change with the addition of NaCl? Why?*

   The pH titration curve itself did not change. The shape of the conductivity curve stayed the

   same but the conductivity was consistently higher with the addition of NaCl. This is because the

   more charged ions there are in solution, the more electricity it is capable of conducting.

Graphing Titration Data

There are many ways to determine the equivalence point of a titration. The most common way is to use the end point of the titration, found by using an indicator or noticing a color change in a redox titration, as an estimate for the equivalence point. If an appropriate indicator is used, its accuracy can be close. However, a more accurate way to determine the equivalence point is to use pH versus volume data to find the point at which the slope of the line of the titration is greatest. In this assignment, you will use a spreadsheet to accurately calculate the equivalence point of a titration.

Take out Preset Experiment 5. The calibrated pH meter is in the beaker, the graph window is open, and 0.9062 g of the $NaHCO_3$ solid is in the beaker. The conductivity meter is also turned on and in the beaker, but will not be used for this assignment. The indicator Methyl orange is in the analyte beaker. Calculate where you expect the equivalence point to be. Open your lab book and save the titration information as it nears and passes the expected equivalence point. With the titration of a weak base, it is best to save the data when the stopcock is on the slowest or second to slowest setting. Open the link in the lab book and copy the data to a spreadsheet. Create a graph showing the pH as a function of volume. It should look similar to the graph in the graph window.

In another column in your spreadsheet, calculate the slope between the individual titration points. This can be done by dividing the difference between the current and previous pHs by the difference between the current and previous volumes. Graph the line of these calculations on the same graph as the graph of the pH as a function of volume. The point at which this line reaches the highest point is the equivalence point of the titration. Include this graph with this assignment.

1. *Why does this method work to accurately determine the equivalence point?* **This method determines the equivalence point accurately by calculating when the pH changes the greatest amount in the smallest amount of titrant delivered.**

2. *What is the equivalence point of the titration?* **16.46 mL**

3. *What is the percentage difference between the equivalence point you calculated and the expected equivalence point from your preliminary calculation?*

4. *Why is this method more accurate than using an indicator to estimate the equivalence points?* **Indicators are only an estimate of an equivalence point because they change at a specific pH and this pH may not be near the actual equivalence point pH of the titration.**

5. *Is this technique more useful with titrations of a strong acid and base or titrations where either the acid or the base is weak? Why?* **This method is more useful with weak acid or weak base titrations since the titration curve at the equivalence point is not as steep and takes place over a smaller range of pH's.**

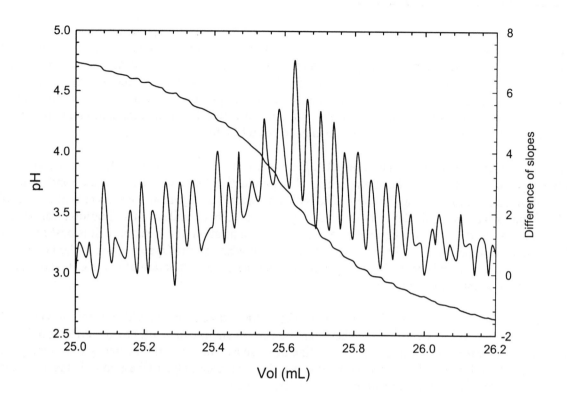

Activities

"Activity" is a term that helps us understand how a substance will react in circumstances different than that of a selected reference state. Activities are necessary for precise calculations of equilibrium solutions because the ionic strength of dissociated molecules has some effect on the equilibrium. In order to account for activities, a more accurate form of the equilibrium constant equation is needed. This equation is $K = \dfrac{[C]^c \gamma_C^c [D]^d \gamma_D^d}{[A]^a \gamma_A^a [B]^b \gamma_B^b}$. The activity coefficient γ equals one in the reference state, which is the ideal state. As the solutions deviates from the reference state, the activity coefficients also deviate from one. Thus, γ measures the deviation from the ideal state. You will not be using this equation to make calculations, but note that in the stockroom of the titration laboratory, there is a switch where you can decide whether or not activities affect your solution. In this assignment you will learn more about activities and in what circumstances they most affect a solution.

1. Take out Preset Experiment 1. This is a strong acid strong base titration. There are 25 mL of HCl in the beaker. Perform the titration with the activity coefficients on and off. Use data from these titrations to calculate the concentration of NaOH as though it were an unknown.

   How much of a difference do the activities make in these calculations? __**No difference**__

2. Design a titration using KHP and NaOH. Since KHP is a solid, you can determine the molarity of the solution when you mix it with water. Mix a solution where the concentration of the solution is 3.0 M or greater. Titrate this solution with NaOH when the activity coefficients are off. Calculate the concentration of NaOH as if it were an unknown. Repeat this procedure with the activity coefficients on. Show your calculations for the concentration of NaOH.

3. *What difference do the activities make when the KHP is in a more concentrated solution?*

   __**Activity coefficients will make a difference of approximately 0.01%.**__

Indicators

Indicators are chemical dyes that change color over a specific range of pH. For example, litmus changes from red to blue as the acid is converted to its conjugate base. The best indicators have intense colors so that only a few drops of dilute indicator will cause the color to change. Indicators provide a way to estimate the equivalence point of a titration, which is when the moles of analyte have been consumed by moles of titrant. The point at which the indicator changes color is called the end point. In this assignment, you will learn more about using indicators.

1. Take out Preset Experiment 1. This is a strong acid strong base titration. *Look at the indicator chart and list three indicators that would be appropriate for this titration.* If you are not sure where the equivalence point is, perform the titration with the pH meter.

   bromocresol green, cresol red, phenolphthalein

   (other answers: thymol blue, methyl orange, bromocresol purple)

2. *Graph a titration curve for this titration and show where each of the three indicators you chose change colors on the following graph.*

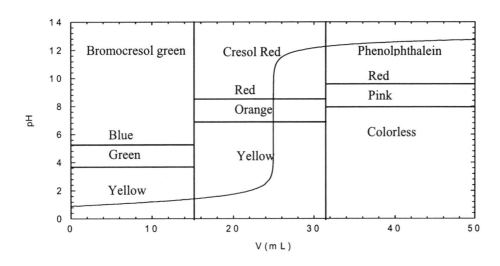

3. Now take out Preset Experiment 3. This is a weak acid strong base titration. *Which indicators would*

   be appropriate for this titration? **crescol red, thymol blue, bromocrescol purple, phenolphthalein**

4. The end points of indicators are only estimates of the equivalence point. *What characteristics of an indicator need to be considered to choose one that will give the most accurate estimate possible?*

   The indicator needs to change color at a pH as near to the pH of the equivalence point as

   possible.

Will indicator end points generally be more accurate with a strong acid strong base titration or one in which the acid or base is weak? Why? **Indicators are more accurate in a strong acid strong base titration. In titrations where the acid or base is weak, the titration line near the equivalence point is less steep. The greater the difference between the pH at which the indicator changes color and the pH at the equivalence point, the greater amount of error is introduced.**

Buoyancy

In a titration lab, there are many factors that can affect the accuracy of your measurements. Since small errors can make a difference in the results, it is important to eliminate all sources of error that you have control over. In this assignment, you will learn how to compensate for a buoyancy error that occurs when a substance is weighed on the balance.

The buoyancy equation is $m = m_{obs} \dfrac{\left(1 - \dfrac{d_a}{d_w}\right)}{\left(1 - \dfrac{d_a}{d}\right)}$ where m_{obs} is the observed mass from the balance, d_a is the density of air, d_w is the density of the standard weights, and d is the density of the substance being weighed. m is the corrected (actual) mass of the sample.

1. A buoyancy error occurs when the density of the substance being weighed is different than the density of the standard weights that were used to calibrate the balance. *Why is error introduced into the measurement if the density of the substance being weighed and the density of the substance used to calibrate the balance are not the same?* **The observed mass of the substance being weighed varies by the mass of the air it displaces. If the substance has a density different than that of the substance that was calibrated, it will displace a different amount of air.**

2. Take out KHP from the stockroom. Weigh out approximately 2.00 g of KHP. *Record the mass of KHP you measured out according to the balance.* **Answers will vary.**

3. The density of air is 0.0012 g/mL near 760 torr and 25° C and the density of the weights is 8.0 g/mL. The density of KHP is 1.64 g/mL. *Using the buoyancy equation, what is the corrected mass of the sample you measured out?*

   Answers will vary.

4. *What is the percentage difference in moles of KHP between the measured and corrected mass of the sample?* The molecular weight of KHP is 204.22 g/mol. **approximately 0.10 %**

5. *How will the calculation of an equivalence point in an acid base titration be affected if buoyancy corrections are not made?* **The calculation will be off by approximately 0.10 %.**

Glassware Calibration

The glassware you will use in the virtual chemistry laboratory is as individual to you as your own glassware in a real laboratory. There is an error in your glassware similar to the glassware error in a real laboratory. To have the most accurate calculations in your work, you must calibrate your pipet and buret to receive your tolerance level of your glassware. The error you calculate will be applicable each time you use that glassware.

The density of water at 25°C is 0.9970479g/ml. With this information, you can calculate the exact volume of water delivered if you know the mass of water delivered.

1. Open the buret window and lab book. Fill the buret with water. Tare a beaker by placing it on the balance and clicking on *Tare*. Place the tared beaker under the buret and deliver 10 mL of water into the beaker. Record the exact volume of water delivered below according to the buret reading to the nearest 0.02 mL. *Take the beaker to the balance and record the mass of water delivered. Do this four times, taring the beaker before each new addition of water from the buret.* When you have finished, you should have delivered approximately 40 mL from the buret.

   Volume #1: __**Answers will vary.**__   Mass #1: _____

   Volume #2: _____   Mass #2: _____

   Volume #3: _____   Mass #3: _____

   Volume #4: _____   Mass #4: _____

2. *Calculate the actual volume delivered each time using the density of water.*

   Volume #1: __**Answers will vary.**__   Volume #3: _____

   Volume #2: _____   Volume #4: _____

3. *Calculate the correction in mL at each volume delivered.* (The correction is the amount you have to add or subtract from the amount delivered according buret reading in order to know the correct volume delivered.)

   Volume #1: _____   Volume #3: _____

   Volume #2: _____   Volume #4: _____

4. *Plot the points for the total volume delivered from the buret versus on the x-axis versus the correction in mL at each volume on the y-axis. Connect the points to show the correction at each 10 mL interval.*

Example

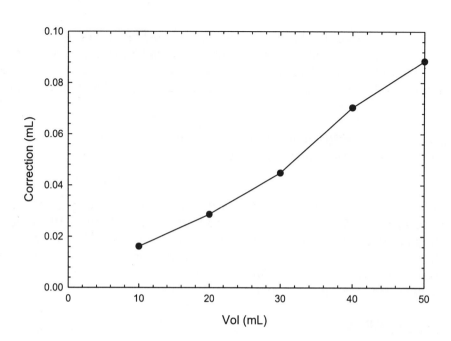

All glassware needs to be calibrated in order to be used accurately in the lab. Now you are going to calibrate the 25 mL pipet.

5. Open the pipet drawer. Double click on the 25 ml pipet. Take a beaker out and add some water. Fill the pipet and move the beaker of water. Tare a different beaker by placing it on the balance and clicking on *Tare*. Place the tared beaker under the pipet to empty the pipet into the beaker. *Take the beaker to the balance and record the mass of water. Do this three times.*

Mass #1: _____   Mass #2: _____   Mass #3: _____

6. *Calculate the actual volume delivered each time.*

Volume #1: _____   Volume #2: _____   Volume #3: _____

7. *What is the average correction required for your 25 mL pipet?* **Answers will vary.** _____

Boyle's Law: 1/Volume versus Pressure – 1

Robert Boyle, a philosopher and theologian, studied the properties of gases in the seventeenth century. He noticed that gases behave similarly to springs; when compressed or expanded, they tend to 'spring' back to their original volume. He published his findings in 1662 in a monograph entitled "The Spring of the Air and Its Effects." You will make observations similar to those of Robert Boyle.

The purpose of this experiment is to learn more about the relationship between the pressure and volume of an ideal gas. You will do this by graphing values of $1/V$ versus P. Graphing the inverse of the volume will make the relationship between P and V easier to see graphically. In order to obtain data to graph, you will be changing pressure as all other variables except for volume are kept constant.

Take out Preset Experiment 1. Open your lab book and save the data as you increase the pressure from 1 atm. Calculate $1/V$ for each of the corresponding volumes at each pressure. These are the values you will use to make your graph. Graph $1/V$ on the y-axis versus P on the x-axis on the chart below. Repeat the procedure with N_2 (Preset Experiment 2) and with a van der Waals gas with the a and b parameters set to N_2 (Preset Experiment 8). Your graph should at least cover the maximum pressure of N_2. Label the graph.

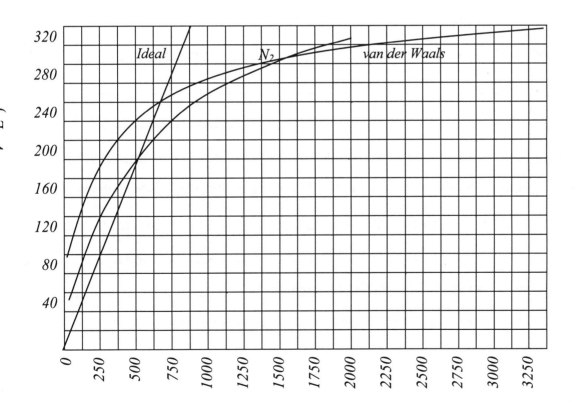

1. *Which line is straight?* **the ideal gas line**

2. *What is the relationship between P and V? Use the straight line to explain.* **Since a straight line means that the two variables are proportional, the values of P and 1/V are proportional. This means that P and V are inversely proportional.**

    What affects the slope of this line? **temperature and the number of moles of gas**

3. *Name some of the reasons that the other lines are not straight.* **N_2 is a real gas, which means that it has attractive and repulsive interactions. At high pressures, the intermolecular repulsive forces between the molecules of N_2 are dominant and make the volume bigger and the value of V^{-1} smaller than it is for an ideal gas. The van der Waals gas is not straight because it is modeled after a real gas and takes into account the attractive and repulsive interactions.**

4. The van der Waals parameters that were used for these data points are the ones for N_2. *Where is the van der Waals line closest to the N_2 line?* **It is closest at pressures below 300 atmospheres.**

5. *Where is the van der Waals line not close to the N_2 line? Why?* **The van der Waals line isn't close to the N_2 line at higher pressures because even though the van der Waals equation accounts for intermolecular interactions, it is still an oversimplification of what happens in real gases. At higher pressures, the van der Waals approximation becomes more inaccurate because the repulsive interactions in real gases are greater at higher pressures than the van der Waals equation can account for.**

6. *Where is the van der Waals approximation the most accurate?* **at low pressures**

Boyle's Law: 1/Volume versus Pressure – 2

Robert Boyle, a philosopher and theologian, studied the properties of gases in the seventeenth century. He noticed that gases behave similarly to springs; when compressed or expanded, they tend to 'spring' back to their original volume. He published his findings in 1662 in a monograph entitled "The Spring of the Air and Its Effects." You will make observations similar to those of Robert Boyle.

The purpose of this experiment is to learn more about the relationship between the pressure and volume of an ideal gas. You will do this by graphing values of $1/V$ versus P. Graphing the inverse of the volume will make the relationship between P and V easier to see in the form of a graph. In order to obtain data to graph, you will be changing pressure as all other variables except for volume are kept constant.

Choose an experiment where pressure or volume is dependent on the other and then save the data in your lab book as you increase or decrease the independent variable. Use this data to calculate $1/V$ for each data point. Complete this procedure for an ideal gas, CO_2, He, and N_2. Graph $1/V$ on the y-axis versus P on the x-axis for each gas on a spreadsheet. Include in your graph the maximum pressures of all of the real gases. Make sure that all parameters of the gases are the same when you save the data so the lines can be compared. Label your graph. *(An example of the required graph is included at the end of the assignment.)*

1. *Which line is straight?* __the ideal gas line.__

2. *What affects the slope of this line?* __temperature and number of moles__

3. *Why aren't the other lines straight?* __The other gases are real gases and have repulsive and__

    __attractive interactions which keeps their behavior from matching that of ideal gases.__

4. *Where are the lines most similar to the straight line?* __The real gases are most similar to an__

    __ideal gas at low pressures.__

5. *Where are they different?* __Above 50 atmospheres for CO_2 and above and two or three hundred__

    __atmospheres for the other gases.__

6. *From your graph, what can you say in general about real gases as the pressure increases?*

    __The ideal gas law is an accurate predictor of the behavior of real gases at low pressures.__

7. *Use your graph to describe the behavior of N_2 and helium.* Note that the *a* parameter of the van der Waals gas for Helium is 0.0341 and that of N_2 is 1.39 $L^2 \cdot atm \cdot mol^{-2}$.

    __The graph shows that at equal pressures, N_2 occupies less volume than Helium. This is due to__

    __the greater attractive interactions between the molecules of N_2 which decrease the__

    __pressure.__

8. *Why does the line for CO₂ slope above the ideal line and the lines for N₂ and Helium slope below the ideal line?* **The attractive interactions in N₂ and Helium dominate at high pressures while the repulsive interactions dominate for CO₂.**

9. *Explain why some real gases behave more like an ideal gas than other real gases.* **Helium is a real gas with behavior most similar to that of an ideal gas. This is because helium is smaller and has fewer intermolecular interactions. CO₂ is a larger and more complex molecule than helium and so its intermolecular attractions are stronger and its behavior is less ideal than that of helium.**

10. *What is another way to graph values derived from P and V so that the graph will be a straight line?* **P on the y-axis and V on the x-axis**

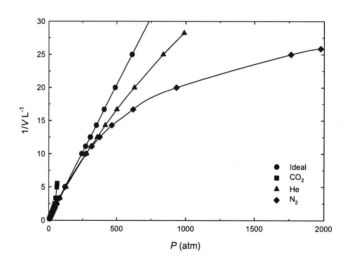

Compressibility

The compressibility of a gas, $z=PV/nRT$, is an effective method for comparing the behavior of real gases to that of an ideal gas. For an ideal gas z is always equal to one, therefore, deviations from one are a measure of the non-ideality of the gas. You will use this compressibility factor to make observations about the behavior of real gases.

Take out the experiment where volume is dependent on pressure and temperature. For this assignment you will be using N_2. Set the temperature to 150 K and adjust the pressures to those listed in the table below. For each pressure, calculate the compressibility and list it in the table. Calculate the compressibilities for the pressures listed at 250 K and 1000 K. *Using the data from the table, graph compressibility on the y-axis versus pressure for the data of each temperature on the graph below. Label your graph.*

150 K	
P (atm)	z
20	0.88
80	0.52
500	1.64
1000	2.87
1200	3.34

250 K	
P (atm)	z
20	0.99
200	1.12
500	1.41
1000	2.15
1200	2.44

1000 K	
P (atm)	z
20	1.01
200	1.07
500	1.18
1000	1.37
1200	1.44

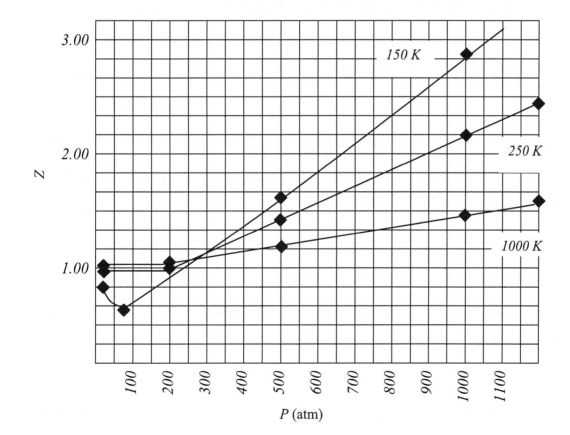

1. *What causes the ratio PV/nRT to go below one for a nonideal gas?* **Attractive interactions between the gas molecules cause the pressure of the gas to be less when it is in a volume of fixed size or cause the volume to be less when the volume is flexible. Decreased volume or pressure when all other variables are the same causes the ratio of z to be less than one.**

2. *What causes the ratio PV/nRT to go above one for a nonideal gas?* **Repulsive interactions cause the pressure or volume to be greater than they would be for an ideal gas with all other variables held fixed.**

3. *What is happening when the line's slope changes from negative to positive? Why does this happen?* **This is the point where the repulsive interactions begin to be stronger than the attractive interactions of the gas. Increasing pressure forces the gas molecules closer together and the percent of the volume that is taken up by the gas molecules increases. Since repulsive interactions are largely a measure of the volume that the gas molecules exclude, repulsive interactions increase as the distance between the gas molecules decreases.**

4. *At which point is the repulsive force the most dominant?* **The repulsive forces are most dominant at the highest pressure the gas reaches for each temperature.**

5. *What happens to the behavior of the gas as the pressure increases? Why does this happen?* **As pressure increases, the gas tends to become less ideal because the attractive forces become stronger. This happens because increased pressure forces the molecules together which also increases their interactions with each other.**

6. *What happens to the behavior of the gas as the temperature increases? Why does this happen?* **As the temperature rises, the gas becomes more ideal. This is because faster moving molecules do not interact with each other as much as slower moving molecules and since there are fewer interactions, the compressibility will be closer to one.**

7. *What can you say in general about where N_2 gas most behaves like an ideal gas?* **N_2 behaves most like an ideal gas at high temperatures and low pressures.**

8. *How would the compressibility be affected if you used m³ instead of L for volume? What if you used degrees Celsius for temperature?* <u>**Compressibility would not be affected by using m³ for volume. The compressibility could not be calculated using degrees Celsius because the Celsius scale is not an absolute scale.**</u>

Van der Waals Gases – 1

The van der Waals gas equation is a closer approximation to the behavior of real gases than the ideal gas equation because it accounts for attractive and repulsive forces. The equation for a van der Waals gas is $\left(P + a\dfrac{n^2}{V^2}\right)(V - nb) = nRT$. The term that includes the parameter a accounts for the attractive interactions of the gas and the b term accounts for repulsive interactions. These parameters are unique for every gas and are determined by fitting experimental PVT data of real gases. The purpose of this experiment is to learn more about the van der Waals equation and its relationship to real gases. You will do this by rearranging the van der Waals equation and then applying it to real gas conditions in order to observe specific properties of van der Waals gases as compared to real gases.

1. The compressibility of a gas, $z = PV/nRT$, is an effective method for comparing the behavior of real gases to that of an ideal gas. For an ideal gas z is always equal to one, therefore, deviations from one are a measure of the non-ideality of the gas. Solve for the compressibility of the van der Waals equation and then use the equation to answer the following two questions. It may be easier to first solve for the pressure of the van der Waals gas.

$$z = \frac{1}{1 - bn/V} - \frac{an}{RTV}$$

2. *Explain how the attractive interactions of a van der Waals gas affect its compressibility.*

   The a parameter decreases the compressibility of a van der Waals gas with the term - an/RTV.

3. *Explain how the repulsive forces of a van der Waals gas affect its compressibility.*

   The b parameter increases the compressibility of a van der Waals gas with the term

   1/ (1 – bn/V).

   Check how close van der Waals gases are to their real gas counterparts. Take out the experiment where pressure is dependent on volume and temperature. You will be using N_2 gas and the N_2 van der Waals gas with parameters $a = 1.390$ atm· $L^2 \cdot mol^{-2}$ and $b = 0.03913$ L·mol^{-1}. Set the variables to 1.000 mol and 100 K and calculate the compressibility at the volumes listed in the tables below.

Compare this to the compressibility of the van der Waals gas and calculate the percentage difference between the two values.

Volume (L)	$Z N_2$	$Z vdW$	% diff.
4.000	0.960	0.968	0.77
3.000	0.947	0.957	1.03
2.000	0.921	0.935	1.57

Calculate the following values at 500 K.

Volume (L)	$Z N_2$	$Z vdW$	% diff.
4.000	1.004	1.001	0.28
2.000	1.009	1.003	0.56
1.000	1.018	1.007	1.09

Calculate the following values at 1200 K.

Volume (L)	$Z N_2$	$Z vdW$	% diff.
4.000	1.007	1.006	0.11
2.000	1.015	1.013	0.22
1.000	1.031	1.027	0.42

4. *What is the general trend of the difference between the compressibility of the real gas and the compressibility of the van der Waal gas as the temperature increases? Why?*

Over most values, the percent difference between the two gases generally decreases as the temperature goes up. As the temperature increases, van der Waals gases are a better approximation.

5. *What is the general trend as the volume decreases? Why?* **The difference between the real and van der Waals gas grows as the volume decreases. Real gas behavior is closer to ideal gas behavior as the temperature increases and this allows the van der Waals gas to be a closer approximation to real gas behavior.**

6. *Under what conditions is the van der Waals equation the best approximation for the behavior of the real gas N_2?* **low pressure and high temperature**

Van der Waals Gases – 2

The van der Waals gas equation is a closer approximation to the behavior of real gases than the ideal gas equation because it accounts for attractive and repulsive forces. The equation for a van der Waals gas is $\left(P + a\dfrac{n^2}{V^2}\right)(V - nb) = nRT$. The term that includes the parameter a accounts for the attractive interactions of the gas and the b term accounts for repulsive interactions. These parameters are unique for every gas and are determined by fitting experimental PVT data of real gases. The purpose of this experiment is to learn more about the van der Waals equation and its relationship to real gases. You will do this by rearranging the van der Waals equation and then applying it to real gas conditions in order to observe specific properties of van der Waals gases as compared to real gases.

1. The compressibility of a gas, $z=PV/nRT$, is an effective method for comparing the behavior of real gases to that of an ideal gas. For an ideal gas z is always equal to one, therefore, deviations from one are a measure of the non-ideality of the gas. Solve for the compressibility of the van der Waals equation and then use the equation to answer the following two questions. It may be easier to first solve for the pressure of the van der Waals gas.

$$z = \frac{1}{1 - bn/V} - \frac{an}{RTV}$$

2. *Explain how the attractive interactions of a van der Waals gas affect its compressibility.*

    The a parameter decreases the compressibility of a van der Waals gas with the term - an/RTV.

3. *Explain how the repulsive interactions of a van der Waals gas affect its compressibility.*

    The b parameter increases the compressibility of a van der Waals gas with the term

    1/ (1 – bn/V).

Check how close van der Waals gases are to their real gas counterparts. Take out the experiment where pressure is dependent on volume and temperature. You will be using N_2 gas and the N_2 van der Waals gas with parameters $a = 1.390$ atm· L^2·mol^{-2} and $b = 0.03913$ L·mol^{-1}. Set the variables to 1.000 mol and 100 K and calculate the compressibility at the volumes listed in the tables below.

Compare this to the compressibility of the van der Waals gas and calculate the percentage difference between the two values.

Volume (L)	$Z\ N_2$	$Z\ vdW$	% diff.
4.000	0.960	0.968	0.77
3.000	0.947	0.957	1.03
2.000	0.921	0.935	1.57
1.000	0.843	0.871	3.33
0.880	0.822	0.854	3.85

Calculate the following values at 500 K.

Volume (L)	$Z\ N_2$	$Z\ vdW$	% diff.
4.000	1.004	1.001	0.28
2.000	1.009	1.003	0.56
1.000	1.018	1.007	1.09
0.100	1.321	1.303	1.36
0.049	2.323	4.575	96.94

Calculate the following values at 1200 K.

Volume (L)	$Z\ N_2$	$Z\ vdW$	% diff.
4.000	1.007	1.006	0.11
2.000	1.015	1.013	0.22
1.000	1.031	1.027	0.42
0.500	1.064	1.057	0.73
0.081	1.606	1.779	10.78

4. *What is the general trend of the difference between the compressibility of the real gas and the compressibility of the van der Waals gas as the temperature increases? Why?*

Over most values, the percent difference between the two gases generally decreases as the temperature goes up. Real gas behavior is closer to ideal gas behavior as the temperature increases and this allows the van der Waals gas to be a better approximation to real gas behavior.

5. *What is the general trend as the volume decreases? Why?* **The difference between the real and van der Waals gas grows as the volume decreases. Pressure increases the deviation of the real gas from behavior similar to an ideal gas, and the less ideal the behavior of the real gas is, the harder it is to fit to a single equation.**

6. *Under what conditions is the van der Waals equation the best approximation for the behavior of the*

   real gas N₂? <u>**low pressure and high temperature**</u>

7. At 100 K, 500 K, and 1200 K, the volumes 0.880 L, 0.049 L, and 0.081 L, respectively, are within 1 mL of the minimum volume of N_2 at each respective temperature. *What causes the wide disparity between the percent differences at 0.880 L, 0.049 L, and 0.081 L? Why are these differences significantly different from those at the other volumes?*

   <u>**The two smallest volumes are at the higher temperatures are near the upper limit of pressure**</u>

   <u>**for N_2. At these high pressures, repulsive interactions cause a large deviation from ideal**</u>

   <u>**behavior. In these extreme conditions, the van der Waals equation does not match real gas**</u>

   <u>**behavior closely. At higher temperatures, the van der Waals equation is closer to the behavior**</u>

   <u>**of the real gas. The percent difference at 100 K is smaller because at this temperature, the**</u>

   <u>**pressure limit of the real gas is also smaller because of the vapor pressure equilibrium line.**</u>

   <u>**Since the pressure is not very high, the gas behaves closer to an ideal gas.**</u>

Thomson

As scientists began to examine atoms, their first discovery was that they could extract negatively charged particles from atoms. They called these particles electrons. In order to understand the nature of these particles, they wanted to know how much they weighed and how much charge they carried. Thomson showed that if you could measure how much a beam of electrons were bent in an electric and magnetic field, you could figure out the ratio of mass to charge for the particles. You will repeat some of Thomson's experiments in this lab.

1. Set up the optics table for the Thomson experiment by placing the electron gun on the table, aimed at the phosphor screen, and placing the electric and magnetic fields between them right in front of the phosphor screen.

2. Turn on the phosphor screen, and push the grid button.

3. Set the electron gun energy to 100 eV with an intensity of 1 nA.

4. Increase the voltage of the electric field to 10 V.

   What happens to the spot from the electron gun? __It shifts to the left.__

   How is the electric field calculated from the applied voltage? __$E = V/d_{plates}$__

   Which direction is the electric field pointing? __out of the computer screen__

   What is the force produced by an electric field? __$F = qE$__

   What voltage do you have to apply to move the spot to the first line in the grid? __2.56 V__

   What voltage is necessary to move it just off the screen? __16.0 V__

5. Increase the electron gun energy to 500 eV.

   How does increasing the electron gun energy change the speed of the electrons? __The speed of the electrons increases__

   How does this increase change the deflection of the electrons? __They are deflected less.__

   Why does the deflection change? __As the speed of the electrons increases, the electrons are not in the electric field as long, so the electric force acts on the electrons for a shorter time.__

   What voltage do you need to deflect the electrons to the edge of the screen? __77.5 V__

   To the first grid line? __12.7 V__

6. Decrease the electron gun energy to 10 eV.

   How does this change the deflection of the electrons? __The electrons are deflected more.__

7. Choose at least five other electron energies, and find the voltages necessary to deflect the electron beam to the edge of the screen. Then plot a graph of electron energy versus voltage.

e^- Energy	Voltage
50 eV	7.73 V
100 eV	15.5 V
150 eV	23.3 V
200 eV	31.0 V
250 eV	38.7 V
300 eV	46.5 V
350 eV	54.3 V
400 eV	62.0 V
450 eV	69.8 V
500 eV	77.5 V

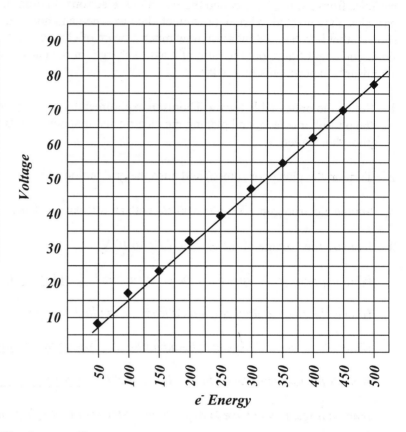

What is the trend of the data? __The data are linear.__

8. Using your graph, predict the voltage necessary to deflect a 235 eV electron beam to the edge of the screen, and then test to determine whether your prediction is right. Finally, predict the electron energy necessary to have the beam deflected to the edge of the screen by a voltage of 20 V, and test to determine whether your prediction is right.

(235 eV electron beam) Voltage prediction: __36 V__ *Measured voltage:* __36.4 V__

(20 V) Electron energy prediction: __135 eV__ *Measured electron energy:* __130 eV__

9. Turn off the electric field, and repeat the experiment with the magnetic field. Set the electron gun energy back to 100 eV, and turn the magnetic field on to 20 μT.

What happens to the spot from the electron gun? __It shifts to the right.__

Which direction is the magnetic field pointing? __into the optics table__

What is the force produced by a magnetic field? __$F = q \cdot v \times B$__

210

10. As before, choose several electron energies, and find the magnetic fields necessary to deflect the electron beam to the edge of the screen. Then, plot a graph of electron energy versus field.

e⁻ Energy	Magnetic field
50 eV	37.0 μT
100 eV	52.5 μT
150 eV	64.0 μT
200 eV	74.5 μT
250 eV	83.0 μT
300 eV	91.0 μT
350 eV	98.0 μT
400 eV	105 μT
450 eV	111 μT
500 eV	117 μT

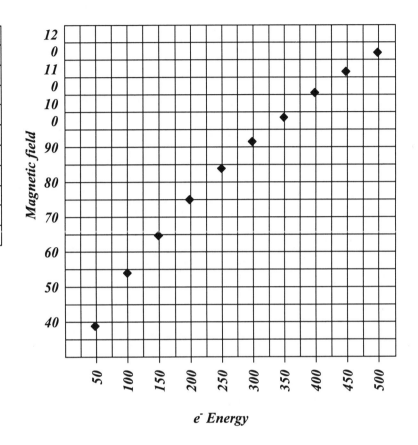

How does the magnetic field change the electron beam differently than the electric field? __**The**__

magnetic field does not have a linear relationship to electron energy, but the electric field does.

Rutherford Backscattering

A key experiment in understanding the nature of atomic structure was completed by Ernest Rutherford in 1911. He set up an experiment that directed a beam of alpha particles (helium nuclei) through a gold foil and then onto a detector screen. He observed that alpha particles were not only emerging in the direction that he expected, but that he could detect alpha particles at all angles, even straight backwards. He described this as ". . . almost as incredible as if you fired a 15-inch shell at a piece of tissue paper and it came back and hit you." He suggested that the experiment could be understood if almost all of the mass of an atom was concentrated in a small, positively charged central nucleus. In this experiment, you will make observations similar to those of Professor Rutherford.

1. Set up the Rutherford experiment by placing the alpha-particle source on the optics table, pointed at the foil holder with a gold foil, and placing the phosphor screen behind the gold foil to detect the alpha particles coming through the foil.

2. Turn on both the alpha source and the phosphor screen. Observe the screen with the alpha-particle beam shining directly through the foil and into the phosphor screen.

   What do the different signals on the screen mean? **The majority of the alpha particles pass directly through the gold foil, but some of them are deflected.**

3. Now change the detector to a different location. (If you don't see a signal for a position, you might have to turn on the persist button, and wait for a few minutes.)

   What differences do you see in the signal? **There is no large signal in the middle of the screen, and the other signals are not as frequent.**

   How many distinct locations can you put the detector in? **seven**

   How does the signal depend on the angle formed by the source/foil/detector combination? **The greater the angle, the greater the signal.**

4. Using the persist button, it is possible to estimate the number of particles that hit the screen as a function of angle. You can do this by counting the particles that hit the screen over a given length of time. Now graph this rate (in particle hits per second) as a function of angle.

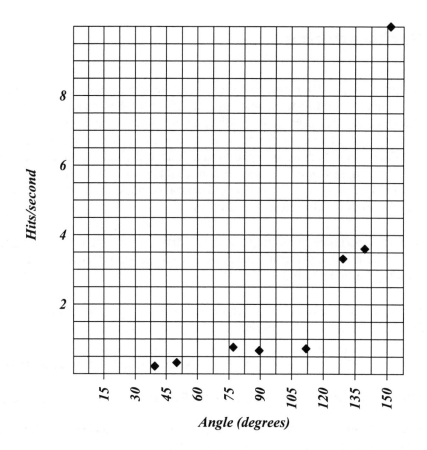

Angle (degrees)

<u>**The alpha-particle source produces 100,000 particles per second in a beam that is 1 mm**</u>

<u>**wide.**</u>

What percentage of the particles is being scattered backwards?

<u>**(0.06/100,000) × 100% = 0.00006%**</u>

5. Assuming that scattering backwards means that the alpha particle hits a nuclei head on, and that the metal foil is 0.001 cm thick, estimate the diameter of a gold nucleus.

   Note: The atomic diameter of a gold atom is about 2.88×10^{-10} m.
   Calculations:

   $$layers = \frac{0.00001}{2.88 \, x \, 10^{-10}} \, ;$$

   $$\frac{A_{nucleus}}{A_{atom}} = \frac{(\# \, scattered / \sec) / layers}{100,000} \, ;$$

   $$d_{nucleus} = d_{atom} \sqrt{\frac{\# \, scattered / \sec}{100,000 \, x \, layers}} \, .$$

Gold nucleus diameter: <u>**1.2×10^{-15} m**</u>

6. If R is the radius of an atomic nucleus, r_0 is the radius of a nucleon, and A is the atomic number, show how R can be approximated by $R = r_0 A^{1/3}$.

$$V_{nucleus} = \frac{4}{3}\pi R^3 \approx \left(\frac{4}{3}\pi r_0^{\,3}\right) A \; ;$$

$$R^3 \approx r_0^{\,3} A \; ;$$

$$R \approx r_0^{\,3} A^{\frac{1}{3}} \, .$$

7. Given that the value of r_0 is approximately 1.4 fm, calculate the size of the gold nucleus.

Expected size of gold nucleus: <u>**$R = r_0 A^{1/3} = 6.0 \times 10^{-15}$ m**</u>

How well does your previous calculation from your measurements agree with this expected value?

  <u>**The previous calculation is the same order of magnitude, but is about five times smaller.**</u>

Why is your measured value not the same as the expected value?   <u>**All the backwards**</u>

<u>**scattering is not taken into account since the measured value is less than the expected value.**</u>

Photoelectric Effect – 1

Though Einstein is most famous for his work in describing relativity in mechanics, his Nobel Prize was for understanding a very simple experiment. It was long understood that if you directed light of certain wavelength at a piece of metal, it would emit electrons. Several inconsistencies in the results were known, which led Einstein to suggest that we need to think of light as being composed of particles and not just as waves. You will have a chance to recreate some of the measurements that led to Einstein's theory.

1. Set up the photoelectric effect experiment by placing the laser, a Sodium (Na) foil, and the phosphor screen detector on the table. You need to place them so that the laser and the phosphor screen are each at about a 45-degree angle to the foil. Turn on the phosphor screen. Set the laser power to 1 nW and set the laser to the largest wavelength which still gives a signal.

    What wavelength (to within 1 nm) is the largest that still gives a signal?   **450 nm**

    What is the equation that relates the wavelength of a photon to the energy of a photon?   **$E = hc/\lambda$**

    We define the work function to be the minimum energy necessary to remove an electron from the metal.

    In nm what is the work function of Na?   **450 nm**

    What is it in eV?   **2.76 eV**

    Based on what you know about atoms, which would you predict has the smallest work function, Na,

    K, Rb, or Cs?   **Cs**

2. Measure the work functions for Na, K, Rb and Cs. Record the values in eV units.

    Na   **2.76 eV**   *K*   **2.30 eV**   *Rb*   **2.16 eV**   *Cs*   **2.14 eV**

    Do these values agree with your chemical intuition?   **Yes. It takes less energy to eject electrons**

    from the bigger atoms, since the electrons are farther from the nucleus.

3. *Predict the order of increasing work functions for Co, Ni, Cu and Zn, and then measure the work functions for these elements. Again, record the values in eV units.*

    Ranking prediction: **Co < Ni < Cu < Zn**

    Measured values for the work functions:

    Co   **5.03 eV**   *Ni*   **5.17 eV**   *Cu*   **4.67 eV**   *Zn*   **4.34 eV**

4. Make a graph of work function versus atomic number for every available metal foil.

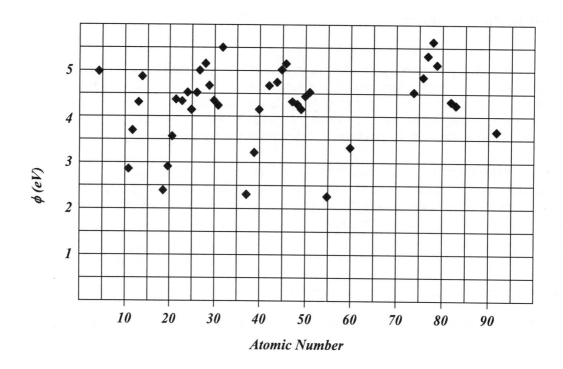

Describe the periodic trends in the results. __In general, the work function decreases going down__ __a group and increases across a period. However, the work function is less predictable for the__ __transition elements.__

Can you make any conclusions or generalizations about the trends you observed? __The atomic__ __radius increases going down a group and decreases across a period.__

Photoelectric Effect – 2

Though Einstein is most famous for his work in describing relativity in mechanics, his Nobel Prize was for understanding a very simple experiment. It was long understood that if you directed light of certain wavelength at a piece of metal, it would emit electrons. Several inconsistencies in the results were known, which led Einstein to suggest that we need to think of light as being composed of particles and not just as waves. You will have a chance to recreate some of the measurements that led to Einstein's theory.

1. Set up the photoelectric effect experiment by placing the laser, a Sodium (Na) foil, and the bolometer on the table. The laser and the bolometer need to each be at a 45-degree angle to the face of the metal foil. Turn on the laser, and set the power to 1 nW and the wavelength to 400 nm.

2. The bolometer measures the kinetic energy of electrons emitted from the metal. You should see a peak on the bolometer detector screen. Zoom in on the area of the peak so that you can accurately read the kinetic energy of the electrons. Record this value.

   Kinetic energy of electrons: __0.34 eV__

3. Einstein suggested that the energy of the emitted electrons was the energy of a photon of light minus the work function of the metal, or the energy that binds the electrons to the metal. Calculate the work function (in units of eV) by taking the difference of the energy of a photon from the laser minus the kinetic energy of an electron.

   Work function for Na: __2.76 eV__

4. Measure the electron kinetic energy at five different wavelengths of light (less than 450 nm), and calculate the work function (ϕ) in units of eV.

λ	100	200	250	300	350
Energy of photon	12.4 eV	6.2 eV	5.0 eV	4.1 eV	3.5 eV
Kinetic energy of electron	9.7 eV	3.4 eV	2.2 eV	1.4 eV	0.8 eV
ϕ	2.7 eV	2.8 eV	2.8 eV	2.7 eV	2.7 eV

   Is the work function independent of wavelength?   __Yes__

   Based on what you know about atoms, which would you predict would have the smallest work function, Na, K, Rb or Cs?   __Cs__

5. Measure the work functions for Na, K, Rb and Cs.

   Na __2.76 eV__   *K* __2.30 eV__   *Rb* __2.16 eV__   *Cs* __2.14 eV__

Do these values agree with your chemical intuition?   <u>**Yes. It takes less energy to eject electrons**</u>

<u>**from the bigger atoms, since the electrons are farther from the nucleus.**</u>

6. Predict the order of increasing work functions for Co, Ni, Cu and Zn, and then measure the work functions for these elements.

   Ranking prediction: <u>**Co < Ni < Cu < Zn**</u>

   Measured values for the work functions:

   Co <u>**5.03 eV**</u>   *Ni* <u>**5.17 eV**</u>   *Cu* <u>**4.67 eV**</u>   *Zn* <u>**4.34 eV**</u>

7. Make a graph of work function versus atomic number for every available metal foil.

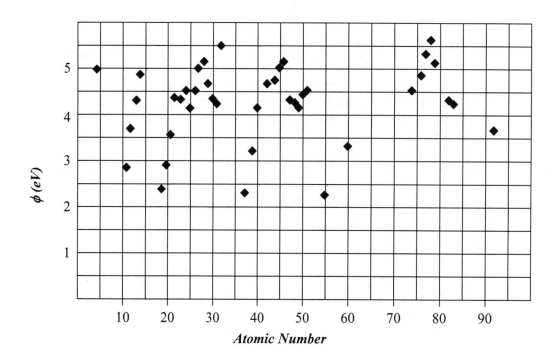

Describe the periodic trends in the results.   <u>**In general, the work function decreases going down**</u>

<u>**a group and increases across a period. However, the work function is less predictable for the**</u>

<u>**transition elements.**</u>

Can you make any conclusions or generalizations about the trends you observed?   <u>**The atomic**</u>

<u>**radius increases going down a group and decreases across a period.**</u>

de Broglie – 1

de Broglie was the first person to suggest that particles could be considered as having wave properties. Specifically, he suggested that $\lambda = constant / p$ (wavelength is inversely proportional to momentum). In this assignment, you will calculate the constant that relates λ to p.

1. Set up the optics table to measure the diffraction of electrons with an energy of 2 meV using the electron gun, the two-slit device, and the phosphor screen. Set the current (intensity) of the electron gun to at least 1 nA.

   What is the kinetic energy of the electrons in Joules? __**3.20 J**__

2. Adjust the slit spacing, and observe how the diffraction pattern changes accordingly.

   How does the diffraction pattern change when you increase the spacing between the slits? __**The**__ __**number of diffraction lines increases.**__

3. Find a slit spacing that gives 7 to 11 well-defined diffraction fringes.

   Draw a picture of the diffraction pattern.

   Slit spacing: __**130 nm**__

   What characteristic of the electron accounts for the diffraction pattern created by the two-slit

   experiment? __**Electrons have wave properties, which create the diffraction pattern.**__

4. Now, change the electron gun for the laser, and the phosphor screen for the camera. Set the intensity of the laser to at least 1 nW.

5. Keeping the slit spacing the same, find the wavelength of light that gives the same diffraction pattern.

   Wavelength: __**~ 27.2 nm**__

   How is this wavelength related to the wavelength of the electrons? __**It is approximately the same**__ __**as the wavelength of the electrons.**__

6. Given that $E_{kinetic} = p^2/2m$, solve for p and then calculate the constant that relates p with λ.

   Calculations:

   $p = \sqrt{2mE}$

   constant $= \lambda\sqrt{2mE}$

   Constant = __6.6×10^{-34} **J·s**_____

de Broglie – 2

de Broglie was the first person to suggest that particles could be considered as having wave properties. Specifically, he suggested that $\lambda = constant\,/\,p$ (wavelength is inversely proportional to momentum). In this assignment, you will calculate the constant that relates λ to p.

1. Set up the optics table to measure the diffraction of electrons using the electron gun, the two-slit device, and the phosphor screen. Set the current of the electron gun to at least 1 nA. Set the slit spacing to 100 nm.

2. Adjust the kinetic energy of the electrons.

   What happens to the diffraction pattern as you increase the energy of the electrons?   __The number__

   __of diffraction lines increases.__

   Does this support de Broglie's equation? If so, how?   __Yes. According to de Broglie's equation,__

   __the wavelength decreases as the momentum increases. The momentum increases as the energy__

   __increases, so the wavelength decreases, which results in more diffraction lines.__

   Express the constant in de Broglie's equation as a function of kinetic energy, mass, and wavelength.

   Since $E_{kinetic} = p^2/2m$ **, then constant** $= \lambda\sqrt{2mE}$

3. Set the electron gun energy between 1 and 4 meV. Find a slit spacing that gives 7 to 11 well-defined diffraction fringes. Then, by using the laser and video camera, find the wavelength that gives this same diffraction pattern for this particular slit spacing. Repeat this procedure for two different kinetic energies, and record the values in the following table. Then calculate the constant that relates p with λ.

Electron Kinetic Energy	Slit Spacing	Diffraction Pattern	Wavelength	Constant
1.5 meV	117 nm	7 fringes	31.9 nm	6.67×10^{-34}J·s
2.5 meV	115 nm	9 fringes	24.5 nm	6.62×10^{-34}J·s
3.5 meV	98 nm	9 fringes	21.3 nm	6.65×10^{-34}J·s

   Averaged value for constant: __6.65×10^{-34}J·s__

4. This constant that you have calculated is known as Planck's constant. Look up its actual value and compare it with your value.

   % deviation from Planck's constant: __$(6.65 \times 10^{-34} - 6.63 \times 10^{-34})/6.63 \times 10^{-34} \times 100\% = 0.3\%$__

HCl Gas Absorbance

HCl gas does not absorb visible light, but it does absorb infrared light. When it absorbs one photon of infrared light to go from the ground vibrational state to the first excited vibrational state, it can also change rotational states. These rotations are also quantized, meaning that molecules can only rotate at certain frequencies. In this lab, you will measure the rotational energy changes that accompany vibrational changes.

1. Go to the stockroom, and check out the super light bulb, the gas cell with HCl gas, and the spectrometer. Set up the experiment with the light shining through the gas and into the spectrometer. Turn on the spectrometer, and set the units to frequency.

   Draw a picture of what you see.

There are two large sets of peaks due to the hydrogen atoms. Hydrogen has two different isotopes (different nuclear weights). We label these H (for hydrogen), which has a mass of 1 amu (atomic mass unit), and D (for deuterium), which has a mass of 2 amu.

Which one would you expect to absorb at the lower frequency and why? **Hydrogen, since it has a larger reduced mass and the energy spacing between absorption peaks is smaller for the lower frequency peaks. (Energy spacing is inversely proportional to reduced mass.) In addition, hydrogen is more abundant than deuterium, and the lower frequency peaks are more intense.**

Which isotope is more abundant? **hydrogen**

Do the relative intensities of the two sets of peaks correlate to their natural abundances? Why or why not? **No. The intensities of the two sets of peaks are too similar. The natural abundance of deuterium is less than 0.02% of all hydrogen atoms. DCl must have been added to the sample.**

2. Zoom in on the lower frequency peaks.

Draw a picture of what you see.

Chlorine atoms also come in two isotopes with masses of 35 and 37 amu. By zooming in sufficiently, you will notice that each main peak is a doublet.

Predict which peaks of the doublets belong to ^{35}Cl and which to ^{37}Cl. <u>**The smaller peaks belong to**</u>

<u>**^{37}Cl and the larger peaks belong to ^{35}Cl.**</u>

Which is more abundant? <u>**^{35}Cl**</u>

Does this agree with the mass for chlorine that you see on a periodic table (which is an average mass

based on natural abundances)? <u>**Yes. The periodic table gives chlorine a mass of 35.45 amu,**</u>

<u>**which is in between the two isotopic masses, yet closer to the mass of the more abundant**</u>

<u>**isotope.**</u>

Both large sets of peaks have two branches of peaks. The branch of lower frequency peaks have a change from a higher rotational state in the ground vibrational state to a lower one in the first excited vibrational state, and the higher frequency peaks have a change from a lower rotational state in the ground vibrational state to a higher one in the first excited vibrational.

Which branch of peaks is more intense? <u>**the higher frequency peaks**</u>

Why? <u>**The intensity of the peaks depends on the number of molecules in the various**</u>

<u>**vibrational and rotational states. Since the majority of atoms are in the ground rotational**</u>

<u>**state, the higher branch will be more intense. (The transitions causing the lower frequency**</u>

<u>**branch of peaks start from above the ground rotational state.)**</u>

I$_2$ Gas Absorbance

I$_2$ gas is interesting because it absorbs visible light, which causes an electron to move between two electronic energy levels. At the same time, the molecule can change vibrational energy. Because the vibrations are quantized (the molecule can only vibrate at certain frequencies), the spectrum is not continuous, but instead has peaks where the vibrations change from one energy level to another.

1. Go to the stockroom and bring out the super light bulb, the gas cell with I$_2$ gas, and the spectrometer. Set up the experiment with the light shining through the gas and into the spectrometer.

2. Carefully zoom in on the spectrum.

   Draw the basic structure that you see.

3. Increase the power of the super light bulb.

   Does the spectrum change? Why or why not?   **No. Although there are more photons, the same**

   ratio of different types of electronic and vibrational energy transitions will occur, which results

   in the same spectrum.

4. Change into frequency units, and zoom in on the area of the spectrum near where it absorbs the most light (where the transmittance is the lowest). You should see a series of peaks. Using the cursor and the *x-y* scale, measure the difference in frequency between neighboring peaks for the first 10 well-resolved peaks (highest energy peaks). Numbering the peaks from 1 to 10, plot the differences in frequency against peak number.

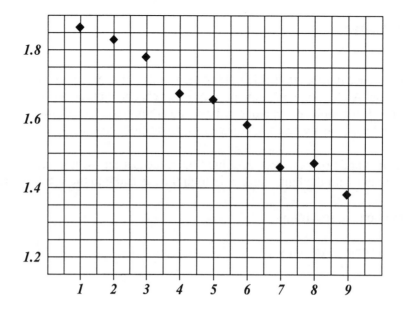

What does the function look like? __linear__

What happens to the difference in frequency between neighboring peaks at higher frequency peaks?

The difference decreases.

What happens to the energy difference between neighboring peaks at higher frequency peaks? __It__
decreases.

What does this tell you about vibrational modes within an electronic state? **Successive vibrational energy levels are closer together at higher energies, and they will eventually become continuous (at the dissociation energy).**

Water Absorption

Water absorbs light in the infrared region of the electromagnetic spectrum. Absorption spectroscopy in the infrared region is called infrared (IR) spectroscopy. Infrared radiation causes the bonds within molecules to vibrate. For this reason, IR spectroscopy is sometimes called vibrational spectroscopy. The atoms within molecules are always moving. The bonds between atoms will absorb light if the light is at the same frequency as the frequency of the vibration of the bond. Thus, bonds act like springs, and just the right amount of energy must be added to make them vibrate. The absorption of this energy makes the vibration have greater amplitude, yet the vibration remains at the same frequency and wavelength. A certain functional group will always absorb within the same general region of the spectrum. For example, the O—H group gives a strong absorption peak around 2778 nm to 3125 nm.

1. Set up the optics table for this experiment by selecting *Absorption in Liquids – Water* on the clipboard of preset experiments.

    What source is used in this experiment? __the super light bulb__

    How is the light produced by this source different than the light produced by the laser? __The super__ __light bulb emits light at all wavelengths from 20 nm to 20,000 nm, whereas the laser produces__ __light at only one wavelength.__

    Which liquid sample is being used in this experiment? __water__

    What detector is used in this experiment and what does it measure? __The spectrometer measures__ __the intensity of light over many wavelengths.__

    Draw a rough sketch of the spectrum.

    Between what wavelengths is the first wide absorption peak? __2600 nm – 3700 nm__

    What causes this absorption peak? __the O—H bond__

2. On the spectrometer screen, switch the toggle from *FULL* to *VISIBLE*.

    What do you observe? __There is no absorption in this region.__

Would you expect water to absorb light in the visible region? Why or why not? <u>**No. Water is**</u>

<u>**transparent and should not absorb nor reflect light in the visible region.**</u>

Raman Scattering

The vibrational modes of a molecule are quantized, which means that molecules can only vibrate at certain frequencies. In normal light absorbance spectroscopy, absorbance peaks are observed at frequencies of light that have the correct amount of energy to make molecules vibrate one step faster. C. V. Raman, a scientist from India, was the first person to demonstrate another type of spectroscopy, and so it is named after him. In this measurement, you send laser light in the visible region through a sample. Most of the photons in the beam travel through the sample, but a small number interact with the sample and are scattered in different directions. An even smaller number (less than one in a million) interact with the sample and during the process either absorb one vibrational energy quantum from a molecule (leading to photons with a bit more energy) or give one quantum of energy to a molecule (leading to photons with a bit less energy). In the Raman spectra, make sure to zoom in to the spectra in the wings around the central peak to see the other peaks. These satellite peaks are very small.

1. Go to the stockroom; bring out the laser, the gas cell filled with HCl, and the spectrometer; and arrange them on the table with the laser directed into the gas cell, and the laser and spectrometer at a 90-degree angle from each other.

2. Set the laser power to 1 nW and the wavelength to 620 nm. Turn on the spectrometer.

   Draw a picture of what you see.

   What causes each peak? **Photons that have given a vibrational energy quantum to an HCl molecule cause the peak to the right. Photons that have absorbed a vibrational energy quantum cause the peak to the left. The main peak is formed by photons that are scattered by the sample, but have not given or absorbed a vibrational quantum energy.**

3. Increase the power of the laser.

   Does this change the spectrum? Why or why not? **No. Although there are more photons, the same proportion is still absorbing or giving a vibrational quantum energy as before.**

4. Now change the wavelength of the laser.

   Does this change the spectrum? If so, how? **Yes. All peaks shift to higher wavelengths as you**

   increase the wavelength of the laser and to the left as you decrease the wavelength of the laser.

5. With the spectrometer set for wavelength, measure the difference between the main peak and the satellite peaks using laser wavelengths of 620, 570, 520, 470 and 420 nm. Only measure the satellite peak to the left.

Laser Wavelength	620	570	520	470	420
Difference (in λ)	**94.1 nm**	**80.5 nm**	**67.9 nm**	**56.1 nm**	**45.4 nm**

   Is the difference the same at different laser wavelengths? **No**

6. Make a plot of wavelength versus the difference.

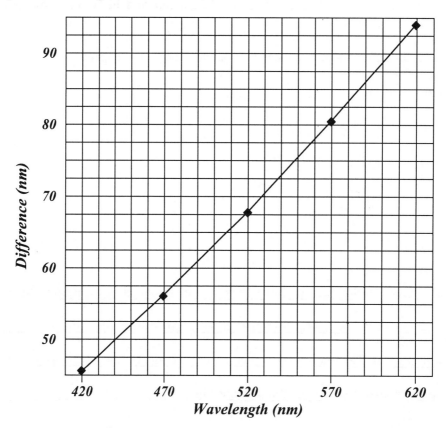

   Is the function linear? **No**

   How is wavelength related to energy? **Wavelength is inversely proportional to energy: E = hc/ν.**

7. With the spectrometer set for frequency, measure the difference between the main peak and the satellite peaks in terahertz (THz) using the same laser wavelengths as before (620, 570, 520, 470, and 420 nm). Again, only measure the satellite peak to the left.

Laser Wavelength	620	570	520	470	420
Difference (in ν)	86.6 THz	86.6 THz	86.6 THz	86.6 THz	86.6 THz

Is this difference constant? Why should this be expected? **Yes. Whatever the starting wavelength and frequency, the photons absorb or give the same amount of energy.**

What is the difference in the Raman spectrum in THz? **86.6 THz**

What wavelength of light has this frequency? **3462 nm**

8. Exchange the laser with the super light bulb, and measure the absorbance spectrum by placing the spectrometer in line with the super light bulb and the sample.

Do you see an absorbance peak at the wavelength that you specified earlier? **No**

Why or why not? **The selection rules for Raman absorption allow for the transition from one vibrational state to the next without a change in the rotational state. However, this transition is not allowed in infrared spectroscopy, as the vibrational transition must be accompanied by a rotational transition.**

9. Switch the super light bulb for the laser again. Set the wavelength of the laser 100 nm below that of your specified wavelength. Set the intensity of the laser to at least 1 nW. Then exchange the spectrometer for the photodiode. Turn on the photodiode, and keep it in line with the laser and sample.

What is the function of the photodiode? **The photodiode measures the integrated intensity of light over many wavelengths and plots this intensity as a function of time.**

10. Slowly increase the wavelength of the laser 200 nm.

What do you observe? **The intensity drops and rises.**

What causes the differences in intensity? **Absorption peaks in the infrared region cause the differences in intensity. Vibrational transitions accompanied by rotational transitions cause the absorption peaks.**

Now we will do some measurements with liquids.

11. Return the gas cell and photodiode to the stockroom, and replace it with the liquid cell and spectrometer, respectively. Fill the cell with Benzene (C_6H_6), and return both to the laboratory. Set up the experiment again for a Raman experiment using a laser wavelength of 620 nm.

Draw a picture of the spectrum.

12. Measure the difference in frequency between each satellite peak in the spectrum and the main peak (the frequency of the laser beam).

Main peak frequency: ___ **483.5 THz**

Satellite peak number	v	v of symmetrical peak	Difference between main and satellite v's
1	**465.7 THz**	**502.1 THz**	**18.2 THz**
2	**458.4 THz**	**509.4 THz**	**25.5 THz**
3	**454.1 THz**	**513.6 THz**	**29.8 THz**
4	**448.6 THz**	**519.2 THz**	**35.3 THz**
5	**436.3 THz**	**531.4 THz**	**47.6 THz**
6	**435.7 THz**	**532.1 THz**	**48.2 THz**
7	**415 THz**	**552.7 THz**	**68.9 THz**
8	**410.1 THz**	**557.6 THz**	**73.8 THz**
9	**407.5 THz**	**560.2 THz**	**76.4 THz**
10	**395.4 THz**	**572.3 THz**	**88.5 THz**
11	**392 THz**	**575.7 THz**	**91.9 THz**

13. Look at the spectrum of each of the liquids, and count the number of satellite peaks for each one.

Which has the most peaks? __**C_6H_{10} – cyclohexene**__

Which has the least? __**H_2O – water**__

What are the differences between liquids and gases in a Raman spectrum?

Besides water, these liquids have many more satellite peaks than the gases.

Why? **These liquids have more atoms in each molecule than the gases, so**

they have more vibrational modes. However, all of the vibrational mode

in water are IR active, so they are inactive in Raman spectroscopy.

	# of satellite peaks
C_6H_6	11
H_2O	0
CCl_4	7
C_6H_{12}	14
THF	23
MeOH	17
CH_3CN	15
C_6H_{10}	29

Additional Inorganic Qualitative Analysis Unknowns

Included in the following section, but not found in the student workbook, are schemes and reactions for a number of different inorganic qualitative analysis unknowns that can be performed and assigned with the inorganic simulation. These schemes are provided as a resource for the instructor and demonstrate the myriad number of reactions and separation schemes that are provided in the simulation. The qualitative analysis worksheets in the student workbook provide students the most common and basic qualitative analysis unknowns, but with a network installation an instructor can assign unknowns that fit the level of the students and the topics covered in class.

Assignment 1 – Full Cation Set

Difficulty level: 10

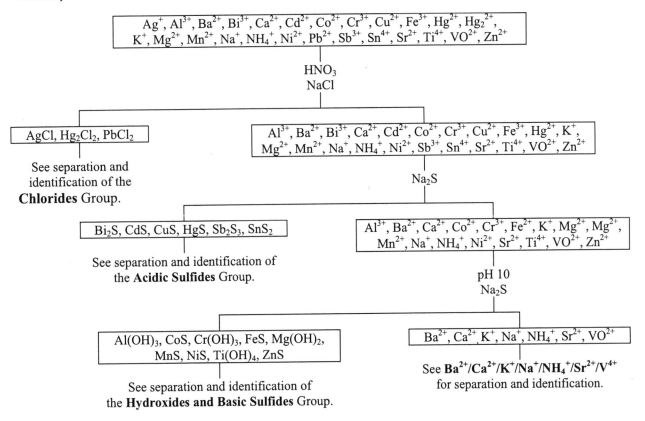

The Full Cation Set can be separated into four major groups: the **Chlorides**, the **Acidic Sulfides**, the **Hydroxides and Basic Sulfides**, and a fourth group that forms few precipitates. From these four groups, each cation can then be separated and/or identified. See each group for separation, identification, reactions, and chemistry discussion.

Assignment 2 – $Ag^+/Hg_2^{2+}/Pb^{2+}$ (The Chlorides)

Difficulty level: 3

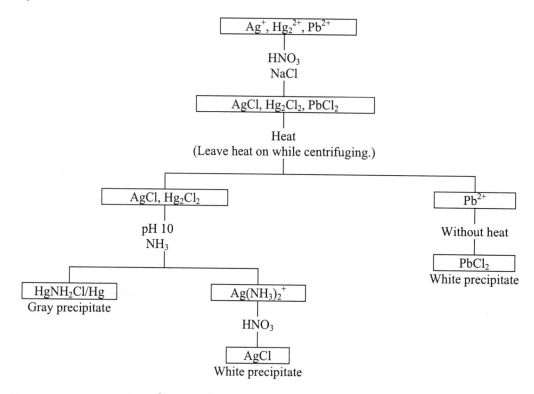

Chloride precipitates out Ag^+, Hg_2^{2+}, and Pb^{2+}, the first group in the full scheme. Lead chloride is somewhat soluble and is more soluble in hot water. Silver forms a complex with ammonia strong enough to dissolve the silver chloride precipitate. Mercury (I) chloride reacts with ammonia to form mercury and mercury (II) amidochloride. This type of reaction in which an element is both reduced and oxidized is called a disproportionation reaction.

Reactions:

$Ag^+(aq) + Cl^-(aq) \rightarrow AgCl(s)$ (white)
$AgCl(s)$ (white) $+ 2NH_3(aq) \rightarrow Ag(NH_3)_2^+(aq) + Cl^-(aq)$

$Hg_2^{2+}(aq) + 2Cl^-(aq) \rightarrow Hg_2Cl_2(s)$ (white)
$Hg_2Cl_2(s)$ (white) $+ 2NH_3(aq) \rightarrow HgNH_2Cl(s)$ (white) $+ Hg(s)$ (white) $+ NH_4^+(aq) + Cl^-(aq)$

$Pb^{2+}(aq) + 2Cl^-(aq) \rightarrow PbCl_2(s)$ (white)
$PbCl_2(s)$ (white) $+ Heat \rightarrow Pb^{2+}(aq) + 2Cl^-(aq)$

Assignment 3 – Bi^{3+}/Cd^{2+}/Cu^{2+}/Hg^{2+}/$Sb3^+$/Sn^{4+}
(The Acidic Sulfides)

Difficulty level: 7

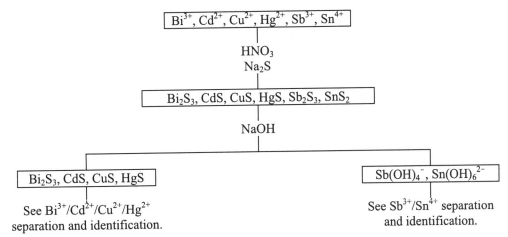

The high insolubility of these sulfide precipitates lets these cations precipitate even in acidic conditions. Upon addition of sodium hydroxide, both tin (IV) and antimony (III) sulfides dissolve to form hydroxide complexes.

Reactions:

$2Bi^{3+}(aq) + 3S^{2-}(aq) \rightarrow Bi_2S_3(s)$ (dark brown)

$Cd^{2+}(aq) + S^{2-}(aq) \rightarrow CdS(s)$ (orange)

$Cu^{2+}(aq)$ (light blue) $+ S^{2-}(aq) \rightarrow CuS(s)$ (dark brown)

$Hg^{2+}(aq) + S^{2-}(aq) \rightarrow HgS(s)$ (black)

$2Sb^{3+}(aq) + 3S^{2-}(aq) + H^+(aq) \rightarrow Sb_2S_3(s)$ (orange) $+ H^+(aq)$
$Sb_2S_3(s)$ (orange) $+ 4OH^-(aq) \rightarrow 2Sb(OH)_4^-(aq) + 3S^{2-}(aq)$

$Sn^{4+}(aq) + 2S^{2-}(aq) + H^+(aq) \rightarrow SnS_2(s)$ (yellow) $+ H^+(aq)$
$SnS_2(s)$ (yellow) $+ 6OH^-(aq) \rightarrow Sb(OH)_6^{2-}(aq) + 2S^{2-}(aq)$

Assignment 4 – $Bi^{3+}/Cd^{2+}/Cu^{2+}/Hg^{2+}$

Difficulty level: 6

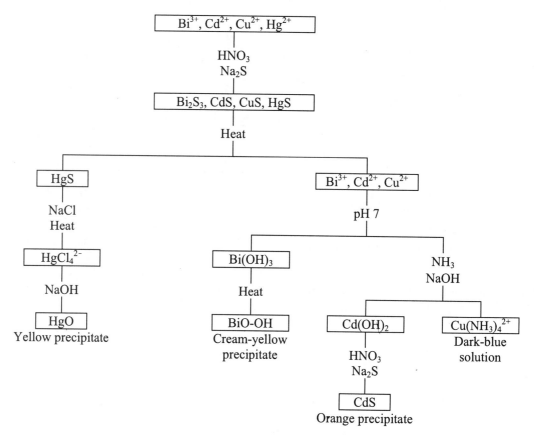

Mercury (II) sulfide is the most insoluble sulfide. It only dissolves in **aqua regia** (a combination of nitric acid and hydrochloric acid) with heat. Bismuth, cadmium, and copper cations dissolve more readily.

Reactions:

$2Bi^{3+}(aq) + 3S^{2-}(aq) \rightarrow Bi_2S_3(s)$ (dark brown)
$Bi_2S_3(s)$ (dark brown) $+ H^+(aq) + Heat \rightarrow 2Bi^{3+}(aq) + 3S(s) + 2NO(g) + 4H_2O$
$Bi^{3+}(aq) + 3OH^-(aq) \rightarrow Bi(OH)_3(s)$ (white)
$Bi(OH)_3(s)$ (white) $+ Heat \rightarrow BiO\text{-}OH(s)$ (cream yellow) $+ H_2O$

$Cd^{2+}(aq) + S^{2-}(aq) \rightarrow CdS(s)$ (orange)
$CdS(s)$ (orange) $+ 2H^+(aq) + Heat \rightarrow Cd^{2+}(aq) + H_2S(g)$
$Cd^{2+}(aq) + 2OH^-(aq) \rightarrow Cd(OH)_2(s)$ (white)

$Cu^{2+}(aq)$ (light blue) $+ S^{2-}(aq) \rightarrow CuS(s)$ (dark brown)
$3CuS(s)$ (dark brown) $+ 8H^+(aq) + 2NO_3^-(aq) + Heat \rightarrow 3Cu^{2+}(aq) + 3S(s) + 2NO(g) + 4 H_2O$
$Cu^{2+}(aq)$ (light blue) $+ 2OH^-(aq) \rightarrow Cu(OH)_2(s)$ (blue)
$Cu(OH)_2(s)$ (blue) $+ 4NH_3(aq) \rightarrow Cu(NH_3)_4^{2+}(aq)$ (dark blue) $+ 2OH^-(aq)$

$Hg^{2+}(aq) + S^{2-}(aq) \rightarrow HgS(s)$ (black)
$3HgS(s)$ (black) $+ 8H^+(aq) + 2NO_3^-(aq) + 12Cl^-(aq) + Heat \rightarrow 3HgCl_4^{2-}(aq) + 3S(s) + 2NO(g) + 4H_2O$
$HgCl_4^{2-}(aq) + 2OH^-(aq) \rightarrow HgO(s)$ (yellow) $+ H_2O + 4Cl^-(aq)$

240

Assignment 5 – Sb^{3+}/Sn^{4+}

Difficulty level: 4

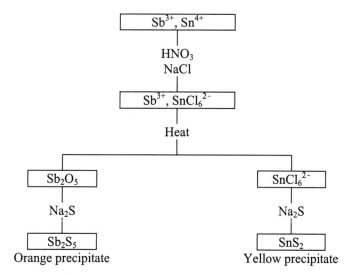

Antimony and tin behave very similarly, which is expected due to their juxtaposition in the periodic table. Both antimony (III) and tin (IV) are soluble in acidic solution with chloride ion; however, upon addition of heat, antimony is oxidized and forms an insoluble oxide precipitate.

Reactions:

$2Sb^{3+}(aq) + 5H_2O + Heat \rightarrow Sb_2O_5(s)$ (white) $+ 6H^+(aq) + 2H_2(g)$
$Sb_2O_5(s)$ (white) $+ 5S^{2-}(aq) + H^+(aq) \rightarrow Sb_2S_5(s)$ (orange) $+ H^+(aq)$

$Sn^{4+}(aq) + H^+(aq) + 6Cl^-(aq) \rightarrow SnCl_6^{2-}(aq) + H^+(aq)$
$SnCl_6^{2-}(aq) + 2S^{2-}(aq) + H^+(aq) \rightarrow SnS_2(s)$ (yellow) $+ 6Cl^-(aq) + H^+(aq)$

Assignment 6 – $Al^{3+}/Co^{2+}/Cr^{3+}/Fe^{2+}/Fe^{3+}/Mg^{2+}/Mn^{2+}/Ni^{2+}/Ti^{4+}/Zn^{2+}$ (The Hydroxides and Basic Sulfides)

Difficulty level: 8

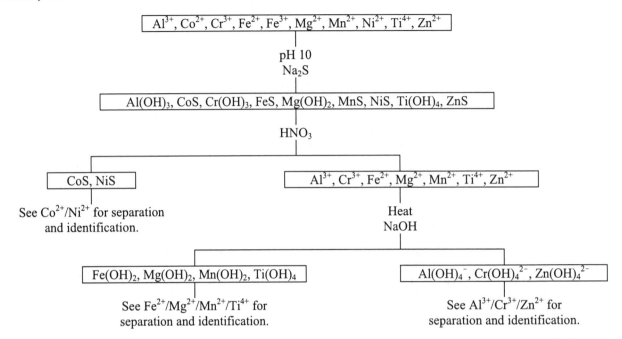

The sulfides in this group (the basic sulfides) are more soluble than the sulfides precipitated out in acid. Cobalt sulfide and nickel sulfide are more insoluble than the other basic sulfides. Even though cobalt sulfide and nickel sulfide cannot be formed in acidic conditions, these sulfides do not dissolve in acid due to their high insolubility. The aluminum (III), chromium (III), and zinc (II) hydroxides are all amphoteric meaning that they dissolve in both acid and base.

Reactions:

$Al^{3+}(aq) + 3OH^-(aq)$ (pH 10) $\rightarrow Al(OH)_3(s)$ (white)
$Al(OH)_3(s)$ (white) $+ OH^-(aq) \rightarrow Al(OH)_4^-(aq)$

$Co^{2+}(aq)$ (pink) $+ S^{2-}(aq) \rightarrow CoS(s)$ (black)

$Cr^{3+}(aq)$ (purple) $+ 3OH^-(aq)$ (pH 10) $\rightarrow Cr(OH)_3(s)$ (gray)
$Cr(OH)_3(s)$ (gray) $+ OH^-(aq) \rightarrow Cr(OH)_4^-(aq)$ (green)

$Fe^{2+}(aq) + S^{2-}(aq) \rightarrow FeS(s)$ (black)
$2Fe^{3+}(aq)$ (yellow) $+ 3S^{2-}(aq) \rightarrow 2FeS(s)$ (black) $+ S(s)$
$FeS(s)$ (black) $+ 2H^+(aq) \rightarrow Fe^{2+}(aq) + H_2S(g)$
$Fe^{2+}(aq) + 2OH^-(aq) \rightarrow Fe(OH)_2(s)$ (pea green)

$Mg^{2+}(aq) + 2OH^-(aq) \rightarrow Mg(OH)_2(s)$ (white gel)
$Mn^{2+}(aq) + S^{2-}(aq) \rightarrow MnS(s)$ (cream yellow)
$MnS(s)$ (cream yellow) $+ 2H^+(aq) \rightarrow Mn^{2+}(aq) + H_2S(g)$
$Mn^{2+}(aq) + 2OH^-(aq) \rightarrow Mn(OH)_2(s)$ (brown/orange)

$Ni^{2+}(aq)$ (green) $+ S^{2-}(aq) \rightarrow NiS(s)$ (black)

$Ti^{4+}(aq) + 4OH^-(aq) \rightarrow Ti(OH)_4(s)$ (white)

$Zn^{2+}(aq) + S^{2-}(aq) \rightarrow ZnS(s)$ (white)
$ZnS(s)$ (white) $+ 2H^+(aq) \rightarrow Zn^{2+}(aq) + H_2S(g)$
$Zn^{2+}(aq) + 4OH^-(aq) \rightarrow Zn(OH)_4^{2-}(aq)$

Assignment 7 - Assignment 7 – Co^{2+}/Ni^{2+}

Difficulty level: 4

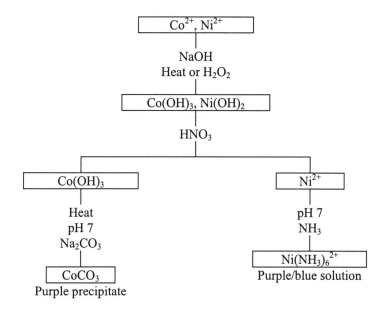

Cobalt and nickel are next to each other in the periodic table, and as expected, they behave very similarly. However, in a basic solution with either heat or hydrogen peroxide, cobalt (II) is oxidized and forms a very insoluble hydroxide. Nickel cannot be oxidized, but it forms nickel (II) hydroxide that dissolves readily in acid.

Reactions:

$Co^{2+}(aq)$ (pink) + $2OH^-(aq) \rightarrow Co(OH)_2(s)$ (pink/tan)
$4Co(OH)_2(s)$ (pink/tan) + $2H_2O + O_2(g) + OH^-(aq) + Heat \rightarrow 4Co(OH)_3(s)$ (dark brown) + $OH^-(aq)$
$2Co(OH)_2(s)$ (pink/tan) + $H_2O_2(aq) + OH^-(aq) \rightarrow 2Co(OH)_3(s)$ (dark brown) + $OH^-(aq)$

$Ni^{2+}(aq)$ (green) + $2OH^-(aq) \rightarrow Ni(OH)_2(s)$ (light green)
$Ni^{2+}(aq)$ (green) + $6NH_3(aq) \rightarrow Ni(NH_3)_6^{2+}(aq)$ (purple/blue)

Assignment 8 – Fe^{2+}/Mg^{2+}/Mn^{2+}/Ti^{4+}

Difficulty level: 6

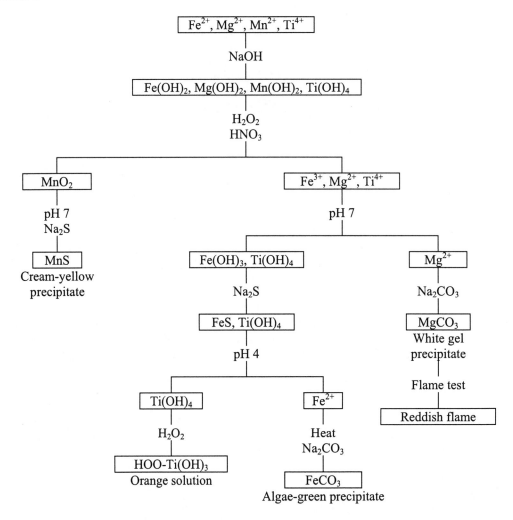

Manganese is oxidized by hydrogen peroxide in basic solution. Iron, magnesium, and titanium are separated according to their solubility in water. Both iron (III) and titanium form insoluble hydroxides at pH 4, but iron (II) does not. Thus, sulfide ion is used to reduce iron (III) to iron (II).

Reactions:

$Fe^{2+}(aq) + 2OH^-(aq) \rightarrow Fe(OH)_2(s)$ (pea green)

$2Fe(OH)_2(s)$ (pea green) $+ H_2O_2(aq) + OH^-(aq)$
$\quad \rightarrow 2Fe(OH)_3(s)$ (red/orange) $+ OH^-(aq)$

$2Fe^{3+}(aq) + 3S^{2-}(aq) \rightarrow 2FeS(s)$ (black) $+ S(s)$

$Fe^{2+}(aq) + CO_3^{2-}(aq) \rightarrow FeCO_3(s)$ (algae green)

$Mg^{2+}(aq) + 2OH^-(aq) \rightarrow Mg(OH)_2(s)$ (white gel)

$Mg^{2+}(aq) + CO_3^{2-}(aq) \rightarrow MgCO_3(s)$ (white gel)

$Mn^{2+}(aq) + 2OH^-(aq) \rightarrow Mn(OH)_2(s)$ (brown/orange)

$Mn(OH)_2(s)$ (brown/orange) $+ H_2O_2(aq) + OH^-(aq)$
$\quad \rightarrow MnO_2(s)$ (dark brown) $+ 2H_2O + OH^-(aq)$

$MnO_2(s)$ (dark brown) $+ 4H^+(aq) + 2S^{2-}(aq)$
$\quad \rightarrow MnS(s)$ (cream yellow) $+ S(s) + 2H_2O$

$Ti^{4+}(aq) + 4OH^-(aq) \rightarrow Ti(OH)_4(s)$ (white)

$Ti(OH)_4(s)$ (white) $+ H_2O_2$ (pH 4)
$\quad \rightarrow HOO\text{-}Ti(OH)_3(s)$ (orange) $+ H_2O$

244

Assignment 9 – Al³⁺/Cr³⁺/Zn²⁺

Difficulty level: 4

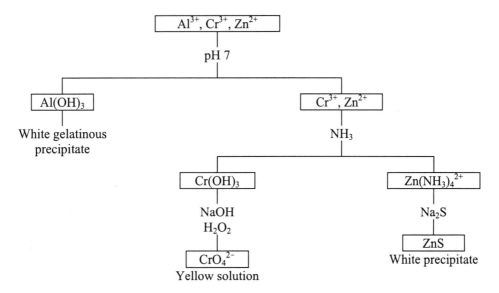

The aluminum (III), chromium (III), and zinc (II) all form amphoteric hydroxides, meaning that they dissolve in both acid and base. Aluminum forms a very insoluble hydroxide that does not dissolve in solution at pH 7. Oxidation of chromium to chromate is a simple way to confirm the presence of chromium. Zinc forms an ammonia complex, which allows separation from the other amphoteric hydroxides.

Reactions:

$Al^{3+}(aq) + 3OH^-(aq) \rightarrow Al(OH)_3(s)$ (white)

$Cr^{3+}(aq)$ (purple) $+ 3NH_3(aq) + 3H_2O \rightarrow Cr(OH)_3(s)$ (gray) $+ 3NH_4^+(aq)$
$Cr(OH)_3(s)$ (gray) $+ OH^-(aq) \rightarrow Cr(OH)_4^-(aq)$ (green)
$2Cr(OH)_4^-(aq)$ (green) $+ 3H_2O_2(aq) + 2OH^-(aq) \rightarrow 2CrO_4^{2-}(aq)$ (yellow) $+ 8H_2O$

$Zn^{2+}(aq) + 4NH_3(aq) \rightarrow Zn(NH_3)_4^{2+}(aq)$

Assignment 10 – $Ba^{2+}/Ca^{2+}/K^+/Na^+/NH_4^+/Sr^{2+}/V^{4+}$

Difficulty level: 5

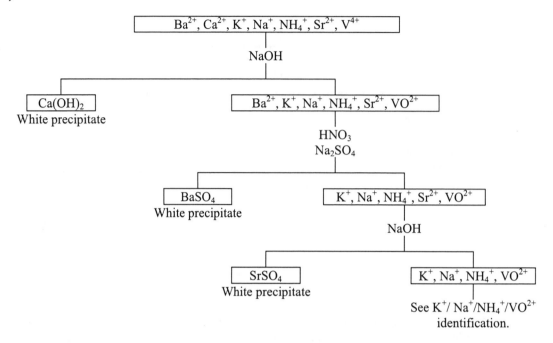

Calcium ion precipitates out in very basic solution. Barium and strontium have very similar chemistry. Both cations precipitate out with sulfate, but strontium sulfate is more soluble. In acidic solution, there is not as much free sulfate due to the formation of bisulfate: $H^+ + SO_4^{2-} \rightarrow HSO_4$. Thus, in acidic solution, strontium will not precipitate out with sulfate, but barium sulfate will precipitate due to its greater insolubility.

Reactions:

$Ba^{2+}(aq) + SO_4^{2-}(aq) \rightarrow BaSO_4(s)$ (white)

$Ca^{2+}(aq) + 2OH^-(aq) \rightarrow Ca(OH)_2(s)$ (white)

$Sr^{2+}(aq) + SO_4^{2-}(aq) \rightarrow SrSO_4(s)$ (white)

Assignment 11 – K^+/Na^+/NH_4^+/V^{4+}

Difficulty level: 2

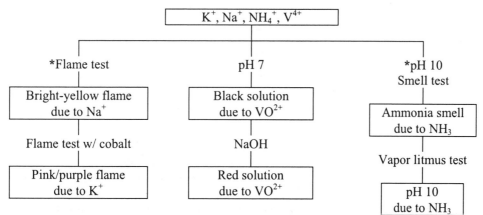

*Use original solution when testing for Na^+ or NH_4^+. If Ti^{4+} or Bi^{3+} are in the solution, make solution pH 7 and centrifuge. Use supernatant only for flame tests.

The original solution should be used for testing sodium and ammonia since these cations can be added in the laboratory room. However, since Ti^{4+} and Bi^{3+} both have bright flame tests like Na^+, these cations must be removed from the solution to not confuse them for Na^+. Although none of the cations in this group can be precipitated, they can be identified by flame tests, pH tests, and solution color.

Assignment 12 – Fe^{2+}/Fe^{3+}

Difficulty level: 1

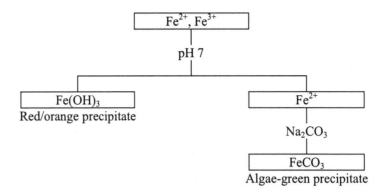

The +2 and +3 oxidation states of iron significantly change the solution chemistry of iron. Iron (III) forms a red/orange hydroxide precipitate in water. Iron (II) forms a green hydroxide, but only in basic solution. In addition, iron (III) does not form a carbonate precipitate, but iron (II) does form a carbonate precipitate.

Reactions:

$Fe^{2+}(aq) + CO_3^{2-}(aq) \rightarrow FeCO_3(s)$ (algae green)

Fe^{3+}(yellow) + $3H_2O \rightarrow Fe(OH)_3(s)$ (red/orange) + $3H^+(aq)$

Assignment 13 – Hg_2^{2+}/Hg^{2+}

Difficulty level: 1

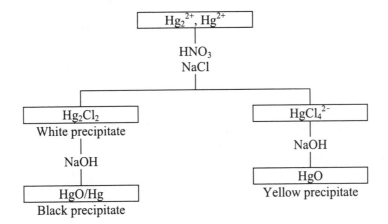

Mercury (I) forms a white chloride precipitate in acidic condition, while mercury (II) forms a soluble complex with chloride. Upon addition of sodium hydroxide, mercury (II) forms mercuric oxide, a yellow precipitate.

Reactions:

$Hg_2^{2+}(aq) + 2Cl^-(aq) \rightarrow Hg_2Cl_2(s)$ (white)

$Hg^{2+}(aq) + 4Cl^-(aq) \rightarrow HgCl_4^-(aq)$
$HgCl_4^{2-}(aq) + 2OH^-(aq) \rightarrow HgO(s)$ (yellow) $+ H_2O + 4Cl^-(aq)$

Assignment 14 – K⁺/Na⁺

Difficulty level: 1

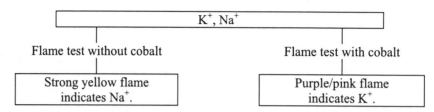

Sodium and potassium can only be detected by their flame tests. Sodium gives a strong yellow flame. Potassium gives a purple/pink flame. The bright sodium flame can mask out the potassium flame, but cobalt glass can be used, which absorbs most of the bright color from the sodium.

Assignment 15 – K$^+$/Na$^+$/V^{4+}

Difficulty level: 1

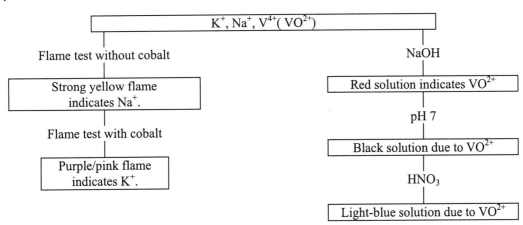

Although these cations do not form precipitates, they can be identified by flame tests and by solution color. Sodium gives a strong yellow flame, and potassium gives a purple/pink flame behind cobalt glass. Vanadium (IV) exists as VO2+ in solution, and this complex changes color according to pH.

Assignment 16 – Ag⁺/Cu²⁺/NH₄⁺

Difficulty level: 2

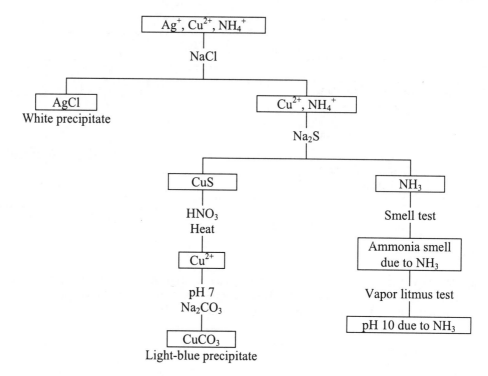

Silver (I) is one of the few cations that forms a chloride precipitate, allowing for an easy separation from many other cations. Copper (II) can be detected in various ways; it will precipitate out with several of the reagents while ammonia stays in solution.

Reactions:

$Ag^+(aq) + Cl^-(aq) \rightarrow AgCl(s)$ (white)

$Cu^{2+}(aq)$ (light blue) $+ S^{2-}(aq) \rightarrow CuS(s)$ (dark brown)
$3CuS(s)$ (dark brown) $+ 8H^+(aq) + 2NO_3^-(aq) + Heat \rightarrow 3Cu^{2+}(aq) + 3S(s) + 2NO(g) + 4 H_2O$
$Cu^{2+}(aq)$ (light blue) $+ CO_3^{2-}(aq) \rightarrow CuCO_3(s)$ (light blue)

Assignment 17 – Al^{3+}/Mg^{2+}/Na^{+}

Difficulty level: 2

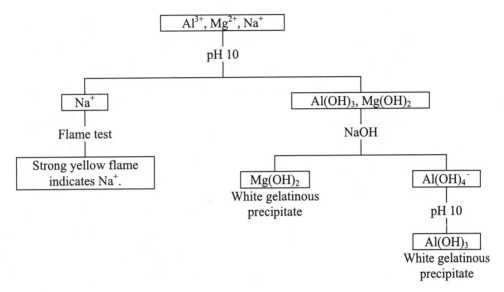

Aluminum (III) and magnesium (II) both form hydroxide precipitates, but aluminum (III) hydroxide dissolves in excess base. The characteristic bright-yellow flame indicates sodium is present.

Reactions:

Al^{3+}(aq) + 3OH^{-}(aq) (pH 10) → Al(OH)$_3$(s) (white gel)
Al^{3+}(aq) + 4OH^{-}(aq) → Al(OH)$_4$$^{-}$(aq)

Mg^{2+}(aq) + 2OH^{-}(aq) → Mg(OH)$_2$(s) (white gel)

Assignment 18 – $Ba^{2+}/Co^{2+}/Hg_2^{2+}$

Difficulty level: 2

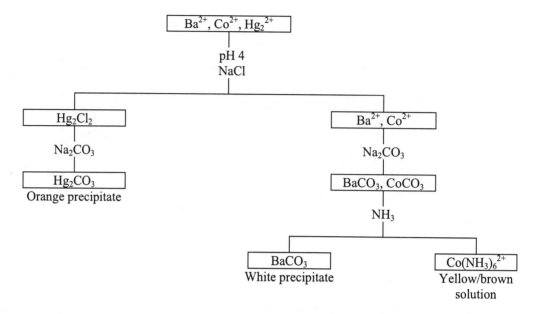

Mercury (I) is one of the few cations that forms a chloride precipitate. Barium (II) and cobalt (II) form carbonate precipitates. Cobalt (II) forms a complex with ammonia that dissolves the carbonate precipitate.

Reactions:

$Ba^{2+}(aq) + CO_3^{2-}(aq) \rightarrow BaCO_3(s)$

$Co^{2+}(aq) + CO_3^{2-}(aq) \rightarrow CoCO_3(s)$ (purple)
$CoCO_3(s)$ (purple) $+ 6NH_3(aq) \rightarrow Co(NH_3)_6^{2+}(aq)$ (yellow/brown) $+ CO_3^{2-}(aq)$

$Hg_2^{2+}(aq) + 2Cl^-(aq) \rightarrow Hg_2Cl_2(s)$ (white)
$Hg_2Cl_2(s)$ (white) $+ CO_3^{2-}(aq) \rightarrow Hg_2CO_3(s)$ (orange)

Assignment 19 – Ca^{2+}/Cu^{2+}/Sn^{4+}

Difficulty level: 2

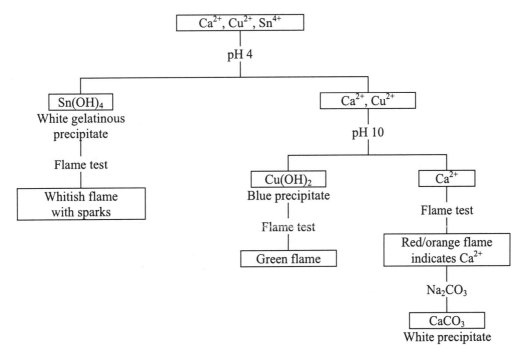

Calcium, copper, and tin are spread out over the periodic table, and their chemistry is appreciably different. Tin (IV) is very acidic and forms a hydroxide precipitate even in acidic solution. Copper (II) forms a hydroxide precipitate at pH 10, but calcium (II) will not form a hydroxide precipitate except under very basic conditions. Calcium (II) will also form a carbonate precipitate. Flame tests of each cation can further identify the cations, since each has a unique flame.

Reactions:

$Ca^{2+}(aq) + CO_3^{2-}(aq) \rightarrow CaCO_3(s)$ (white)

$Cu^{2+}(aq) + 2OH^-(aq) \rightarrow Cu(OH)_2(s)$ (white)

$Sn^{4+}(aq) + 4H_2O \rightarrow Sn(OH)_4(s)$ (white) $+ 4H^+(aq)$

Assignment 20 – $Cr^{3+}/Ti^{4+}/V^{4+}$

Difficulty level: 2

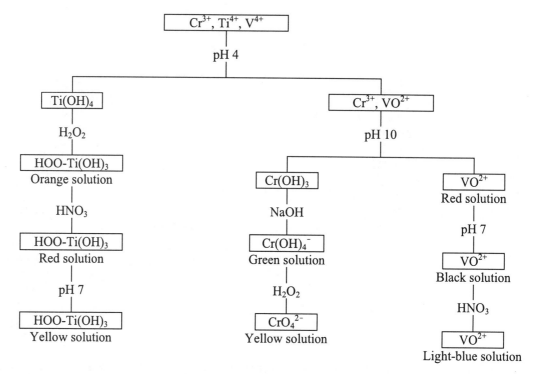

Chromium, titanium, and vanadium lay next to each other in the periodic table. The chemistry of these cations is quite different, but they all have bright-colored solutions. Titanium (IV) is more acidic than chromium (III) and vanadium (IV), and its hydroxide forms even in acidic conditions. Chromium (III) also forms a hydroxide precipitate, but only at pH 10. Upon addition of hydrogen peroxide, titanium (IV) forms a complex that changes color according to pH. Vanadium (IV) exists as VO^{2+} in solution, and this complex also changes color according to pH. Chromium also has several colors of solution. The chromium (III) cation gives a purple solution. Upon addition of excess base, a green chromium hydroxide complex is formed. Hydrogen peroxide oxidizes chromium (III) forming chromate, which gives a yellow solution.

Reactions:

$Cr^{3+}(aq)$ (purple) $+ 3OH^-(aq) \rightarrow Cr(OH)_3(s)$ (gray)
$Cr(OH)_3(s)$ (gray) $+ OH^-(aq) \rightarrow Cr(OH)_4^-(aq)$ (green)
$2Cr(OH)_4^-(aq)$ (green) $+ 3H_2O_2(aq) + 2OH^-(aq) \rightarrow 2CrO_4^{2-}(aq)$ (yellow) $+ 8H_2O$

$Ti^{4+}(aq) + 4OH^-(aq) \rightarrow Ti(OH)_4(s)$ (white)
$Ti(OH)_4(s)$ (white) $+ H_2O_2$ (pH 4) $\rightarrow HOO\text{-}Ti(OH)_3(s)$ (orange) $+ H_2O$

$V^{4+}(aq) + H_2O \rightarrow VO^{2+}(aq)$ (green) $+ 2H^+(aq)$

Assignment 21 – $Cu^{2+}/K^+/Ti^{4+}$

Difficulty level: 2

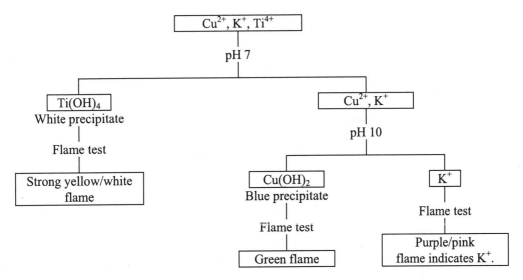

Titanium (IV) forms a hydroxide precipitate in water. Copper (II) forms a hydroxide precipitate in basic solution. The distinctive flame tests of copper, potassium, and titanium cations indicate the presence of these cations. Copper gives a green flame. Titanium gives a strong yellow/white flame. Potassium gives a purple/pink flame.

Reactions:

Cu^{2+}(aq) (light blue) + $2OH^-$(aq) → $Cu(OH)_2$(s) (blue)

Ti^{4+}(aq) + $4H_2O$ → $Ti(OH)_4$(s) (white) + $4H^+$(aq)

Assignment 22 – Fe^{2+}/NH$_4^+$/Sr^{2+}

Difficulty level: 2

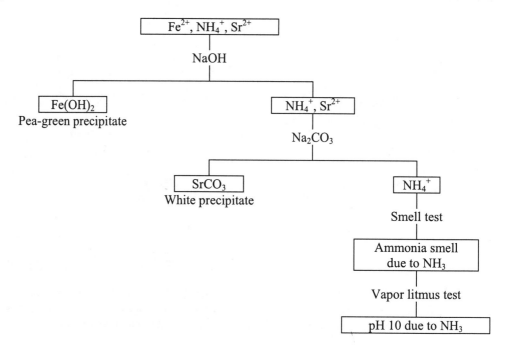

The chemistry of these cations is very different making their separation simple. Iron (II) forms a pea-green hydroxide precipitate in basic solution. Strontium (II) forms a white carbonate precipitate upon addition of carbonate. Ammonia does not precipitate out, but it can be identified by its characteristic smell or its basic vapor.

Reactions:

$Fe^{2+}(aq) + 2OH^-(aq) \rightarrow Fe(OH)_2(s)$ (pea green)

$Sr^{2+}(aq) + CO_3^{2-}(aq) \rightarrow SrCO_3(s)$ (white)

Assignment 23 – $Ag^+/Ni^{2+}/Sr^{2+}$

Difficulty level: 3

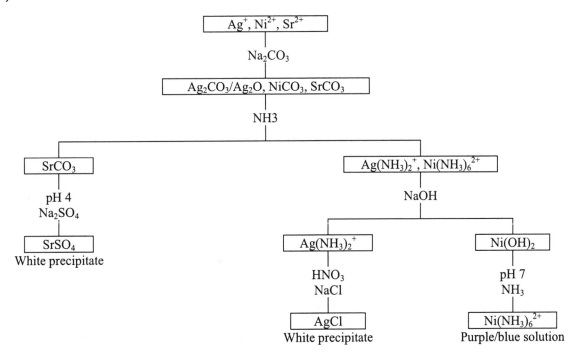

All three cations form insoluble carbonates. However, nickel (II) and silver (I) dissolve in ammonia and strontium (II) does not. The chemistry of these cations is appreciably different, so these cations may be separated and identified in various ways.

Reactions:

$2Ag^+(aq) + 2OH^-(aq) \rightarrow Ag_2O(s) \text{ (brown)} + H_2O$
$Ag_2O(s) \text{ (brown)} + 4NH_3(aq) + H_2O \rightarrow 2Ag(NH_3)_2^+(aq) + 2OH^-(aq)$
$2Ag^+(aq) + CO_3^{2-}(aq) \text{ (pH 10)} \rightarrow Ag_2CO_3(s) \text{ (cream yellow)}$
$Ag_2CO_3(s) \text{ (cream yellow)} + 4NH_3(aq) \rightarrow 2Ag(NH_3)_2^+(aq) + CO_3^{2-}(aq)$
$Ag(NH_3)_2^+(aq) + 2H^+(aq) \rightarrow Ag^+(aq) + 2NH_4^+(aq)$
$Ag^+(aq) + Cl^-(aq) \rightarrow AgCl(s) \text{ (white)}$

$Ni^{2+}(aq) \text{ (green)} + CO_3^{2-}(aq) \rightarrow NiCO_3(s) \text{ (light green)}$
$NiCO_3(s) \text{ (light green)} + NH_3(aq) \rightarrow Ni(NH_3)_6^{2+}(aq) \text{ (purple/blue)}$
$Ni(NH_3)_6^{2+}(aq) \text{ (purple/blue)} + OH^-(aq) \rightarrow Ni(OH)_2(s) \text{ (light green)}$

$Sr^{2+}(aq) + CO_3^{2-}(aq) \rightarrow SrCO_3(s) \text{ (white)}$
$SrCO_3(s) \text{ (white)} + 2H^+(aq) \rightarrow Sr^{2+}(aq) + H_2O + CO_2(g)$
$Sr^{2+}(aq) + SO_4^{2-}(aq) \rightarrow SrSO_4(s) \text{ (white)}$

Assignment 24 – $Al^{3+}/Cr^{3+}/Zn^{2+}$

Difficulty level: 3

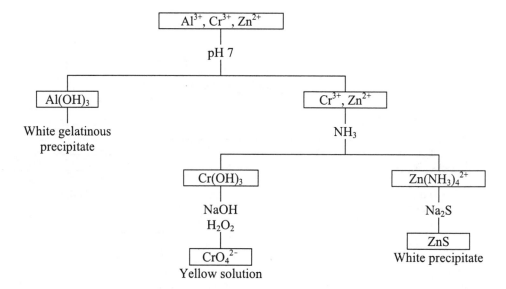

All three cations form hydroxide precipitates and dissolve in excess base. Zinc (II) dissolves in ammonia, but aluminum (III) and chromium (III) do not. The sulfide anion precipitates out the zinc cation, forming zinc sulfide. Chromium is separated from aluminum by oxidizing it to the chromate anion, which is soluble and yellow.

Reactions:

$Al^{3+}(aq) + 3OH^-(aq)$ (pH 10) $\rightarrow Al(OH)_3(s)$ (white gel)

$Cr^{3+}(aq) + 3OH^-(aq)$ (pH 10) $\rightarrow Cr(OH)_3(s)$ (gray)
$Cr^{3+}(aq) + 4OH^-(aq) \rightarrow Cr(OH)_4^-(aq)$ (green)
$2Cr(OH)_4^-(aq)$ (green) $+ 3H_2O_2(aq) + 2OH^-(aq) \rightarrow 2CrO_4^{2-}(aq)$ (yellow) $+ 8H_2O$

$Zn^{2+}(aq) + 4NH_3(aq) \rightarrow Zn(NH_3)_4^{2+}(aq)$
$Zn(NH_3)_4^{2+}(aq) + S^{2-}(aq) \rightarrow ZnS(s)$ (white) $+ 4NH_3(aq)$

Assignment 25 – Ba²⁺/Sr²⁺

Difficulty level: 3

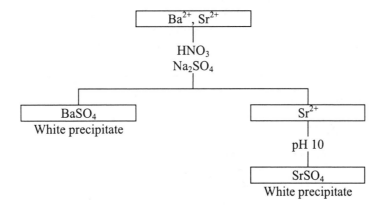

Barium and strontium have similar chemistry. They both form carbonate and sulfate precipitates. The relative solubilities of barium (II) sulfate and strontium (II) sulfate allow for their separation. Barium (II) sulfate forms even in acidic solution, when there is not as much free sulfate. In acidic solution, some of the sulfate anions form bisulfate anions according to the reaction $H^+ + SO_4^{2-} \rightarrow HSO_4^-$. Strontium (II) sulfate, which is more soluble than barium sulfate, does not precipitate out in acidic solution.

Reactions:

$Ba^{2+}(aq) + SO_4^{2-}(aq) \rightarrow BaSO_4(s)$ (white)

$Sr^{2+}(aq) + SO_4^{2-}(aq) \rightarrow SrSO_4(s)$ (white)

Assignment 26 – $Bi^{3+}/Hg^{2+}/Pb^{2+}$

Difficulty level: 3

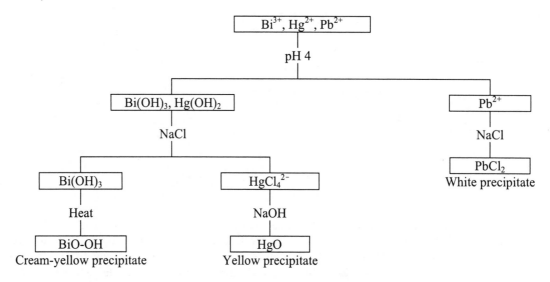

All three cations form hydroxide precipitates, but the bismuth (III) and mercury (II) hydroxides are very insoluble as they form even under acidic conditions. The lead (II) chloride precipitate identifies lead (II), as lead (II) is one of the few cations that forms a chloride precipitate. Mercury (II) forms a complex with chloride, allowing for its separation from white bismuth (III) hydroxide. In basic conditions, yellow mercuric oxide identifies the presence of mercury (II).

Reactions:

$Bi^{3+}(aq) + 3H_2O \rightarrow Bi(OH)_3(s)$ (white) $+ 3H^+(aq)$
$Bi(OH)_3(s)$ (white) $+ Heat \rightarrow BiO\text{-}OH(s)$ (cream yellow) $+ H_2O$

$Hg^{2+}(aq) + H_2O \rightarrow Hg(OH)_2(s)$ (cream yellow)
$Hg(OH)_2(s)$ (cream yellow) $+ 4Cl^-(aq) \rightarrow HgCl_4^{2-}(aq) + 2OH^-(aq)$
$HgCl_4^{2-}(aq) + 2OH^-(aq) \rightarrow HgO(s)$ (yellow) $+ H_2O + 4Cl^-(aq)$

$Pb^{2+}(aq) + 2Cl^-(aq) \rightarrow PbCl_2(s)$ (white)

Assignment 27 – Ca²⁺/K⁺/Mg²⁺/Na⁺

Difficulty level: 3

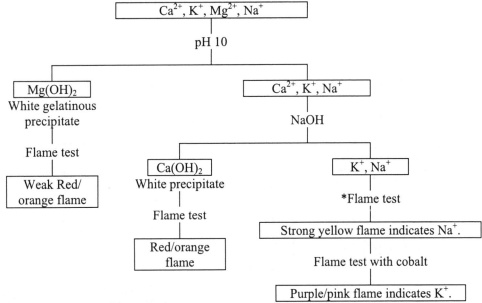

*Use original solution when testing for Na^+.

Calcium (II) and magnesium (II) both form hydroxide precipitates. Magnesium (II) hydroxide is less soluble and thus forms at a lower pH than calcium (II). Potassium and sodium cations can be identified by their distinctive flame tests. However, the original solution must be used for the sodium flame test, since sodium hydroxide was added as a reagent.

Reactions:

$$Ca^{2+}(aq) + 2OH^-(aq) \rightarrow Ca(OH)_2(s) \text{ (white)}$$

$$Mg^{2+}(aq) + 2OH^-(aq) \rightarrow Mg(OH)_2(s) \text{ (white gel)}$$

Assignment 28 – $Ca^{2+}/K^+/Ti^{4+}/V^{4+}$

Difficulty level: 3

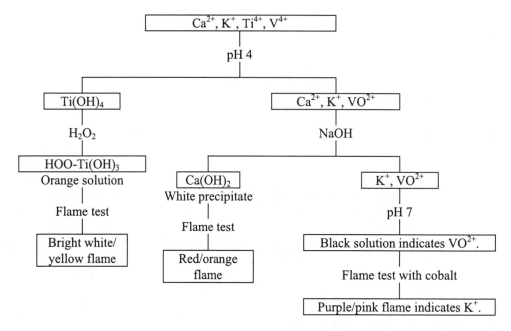

Potassium, calcium, titanium, and vanadium are all within the same row in the periodic table. Titanium (IV) and calcium (II) both form hydroxide precipitates, but calcium (II) will only form a hydroxide precipitate in very basic conditions. Vanadium (IV) always exists as VO^{2+} in solution, and this complex changes according to pH, making vanadium (IV) identifiable. A purple/pink flame behind cobalt glass identifies the presence of potassium.

Reactions:

$Ca^{2+}(aq) + 2OH^-(aq) \rightarrow Ca(OH)_2(s)$ (white)

$Ti^{4+}(aq) + 4H_2O \rightarrow Ti(OH)_4(s)$ (white) $+ 4H^+(aq)$
$Ti(OH)_4(s)$ (white) $+ H_2O_2$ (pH 4) $\rightarrow HOO\text{-}Ti(OH)_3(s)$ (orange) $+ H_2O$

$V^{4+}(aq) + 2OH^-(aq) \rightarrow VO^{2+}(aq)$ (green) $+ H_2O$

Assignment 29 – $Cd^{2+}/Co^{2+}/Cu^{2+}$

Difficulty level: 3

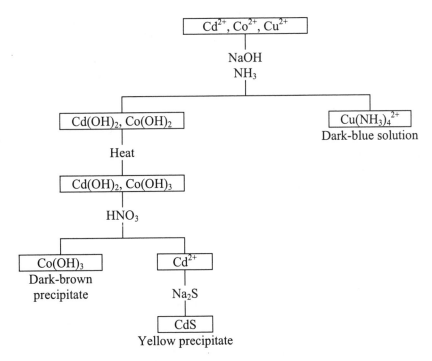

These cations form soluble complexes with ammonia at pH 10. However, cadmium (II) and cobalt (II) form hydroxide precipitates at high pH, while copper (II) remains dissolved in solution. Heat oxidizes cobalt (II) hydroxide to cobalt (III) hydroxide, which is very insoluble. Cobalt (III) hydroxide does not dissolve in acid, unless heated. Cadmium (II) hydroxide dissolves readily in acid and is identified by its yellow sulfide precipitate.

Reactions:

$Cd^{2+}(aq) + 2OH^-(aq) \rightarrow Cd(OH)_2(s)$ (white)
$Cd^{2+}(aq) + S^{2-}(aq) \rightarrow CdS(s)$ (yellow)

$Co^{2+}(aq)$ (pink) $+ 2OH^-(aq) \rightarrow Co(OH)_2(s)$ (pink/tan)
$Co(OH)_2(s)$ (pink/tan) $+ 6NH_3(aq)$ (pH 10) $\rightarrow Co(NH_3)_6^{2+}(aq) + 2OH^-(aq)$
$Co(NH_3)_6^{2+}(aq) + 2OH^-(aq) \rightarrow Co(OH)_2(s)$ (pink/tan) $+ 6NH_3(aq)$
$4Co(OH)_2(s)$ (pink/tan) $+ 2H_2O + O_2(g) + OH^-(aq) + Heat \rightarrow 4Co(OH)_3(s)$ (dark brown) $+ OH^-(aq)$

$Cu^{2+}(aq)$ (light blue) $+ 2OH^-(aq) \rightarrow Cu(OH)_2(s)$ (blue)
$Cu(OH)_2(s)$ (blue) $+ 4NH_3(aq) \rightarrow Cu(NH_3)_4^{2+}(aq)$ (dark blue) $+ 2OH^-(aq)$

265

Assignment 30 – $Cd^{2+}/Hg^{2+}/Zn^{2+}$

Difficulty level: 3

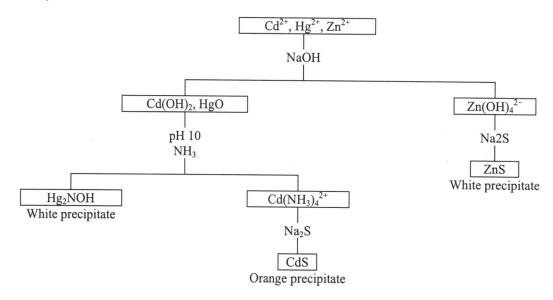

Cadmium, mercury, and zinc lie within the same period of the periodic table, but the chemistry of their cations is very different. Cadmium (II), mercury (II), and zinc (II) hydroxides all precipitate out at pH 10, but zinc (II) hydroxide dissolves in excess base. Formation of a white zinc (II) sulfide precipitate identifies the presence of zinc. Cadmium (II) complexes with ammonia dissolving the cadmium (II) hydroxide precipitate at pH 10. The cadmium (II) sulfide precipitate is stronger than the cadmium (II) ammonia complex, so formation of an orange precipitate upon addition of sulfide identifies the presence of cadmium. Mercuric oxide (HgO) does not dissolve in ammonia, but it forms a white precipitate.

Reactions:

$Cd^{2+}(aq) + 2OH^-(aq) \rightarrow Cd(OH)_2(s)$ (white)
$Cd(OH)_2(s)$ (white) $+ 4NH_3(aq) \rightarrow Cd(NH_3)_4^{2+}(aq) + 2OH^-(aq)$
$Cd(NH_3)_4^{2+}(aq) + S^{2-}(aq) \rightarrow CdS(s)$ (orange) $+ 4NH_3(aq)$

$Hg^{2+}(aq) + 2OH^-(aq) \rightarrow HgO(s)$ (yellow) $+ H_2O$
$2HgO(s)$ (yellow) $+ NH_3(aq)$ (pH 10)$\rightarrow Hg_2NOH(s)$ (white) $+ H_2O$

$Zn^{2+}(aq) + 4OH^-(aq) \rightarrow Zn(OH)_4^{2-}(aq)$
$Zn(OH)_4^{2-}(aq) + S^{2-}(aq) \rightarrow ZnS(s)$ (white) $+ 4OH^-(aq)$

Assignment 31 – $Co^{2+}/Cr^{3+}/Cu^{2+}$

Difficulty level: 3

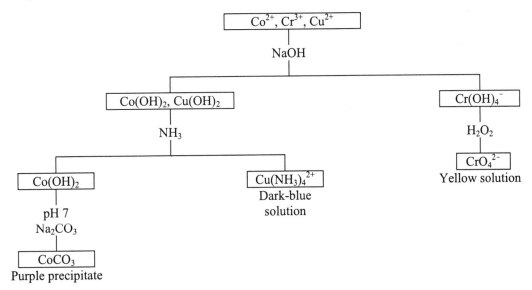

Cobalt (II), chromium (III), and copper all form hydroxide precipitates at pH 10, but chromium (III) dissolves in excess base. The chromium (III) hydroxide complex is green, but further detection of chromium is made by oxidizing chromium (III) to the yellow chromate anion. Cobalt (II) and copper (II) both form complexes with ammonia, but only the copper (II) ammonia complex forms in excess base. The dark-blue copper ammonia complex identifies the presence of copper. The cobalt (II) hydroxide precipitate is tan, but by lowering the pH and adding carbonate, a purple precipitate is formed.

Reactions:

Co^{2+}(aq) (pink) + $2OH^-$(aq) → $Co(OH)_2$(s) (pink/tan)
Co^{2+}(aq) (pink) + CO_3^{2-}(aq) → $CoCO_3$(s) (purple)

Cu^{2+}(aq) (light blue) + $2OH^-$(aq) → $Cu(OH)_2$(s) (blue)
$Cu(OH)_2$(s) (blue) + $4NH_3$(aq) → $Cu(NH_3)_4^{2+}$(aq) (dark blue) + $2OH^-$(aq)

Cr^{3+}(aq) (purple) + $4OH^-$(aq) → $Cr(OH)_4^-$(aq) (green)
$2Cr(OH)_4^-$(aq) (green) + $3H_2O_2$(aq) + $2OH^-$(aq) → $2CrO_4^{2-}$(aq) (yellow) + $8H_2O$

Assignment 32 – $Cr^{3+}/Fe^{3+}/Ni^{2+}$

Difficulty level: 3

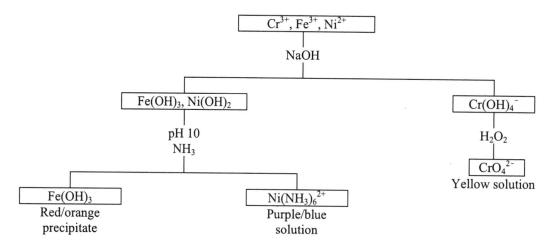

Chromium (III), iron (III), and nickel (II) form hydroxides in basic solutions, but chromium (III) dissolves in excess base. Hydrogen peroxide oxidizes chromium (III) to chromium (VI), which forms the yellow chromate anion. Iron (II) and nickel (II) hydroxides are separated upon the addition of ammonia at pH 10, since nickel (II) hydroxide dissolves as it forms a purple/blue complex with ammonia. A remaining red/orange precipitate is iron (III) hydroxide.

Reactions:

Cr^{3+}(aq) (purple) + $4OH^-$(aq) → $Cr(OH)_4^-$(aq) (green)
$2Cr(OH)_4^-$(aq) (green) + $3H_2O_2$(aq) + $2OH^-$(aq) → $2CrO_4^{2-}$(aq) (yellow) + $8H_2O$

Fe^{3+}(aq) (yellow) + $3OH^-$(aq) → $Fe(OH)_3$(s) (red/orange)

Ni^{2+}(aq) (green) + $2OH^-$(aq) → $Ni(OH)_2$(s) (light green)
Ni^{2+}(aq) (green) + $6NH_3$(aq) → $Ni(NH_3)_6^{2+}$(aq) (purple/blue)

Assignment 33 – $Cr^{3+}/Mg^{2+}/Mn^{2+}$

Difficulty level: 3

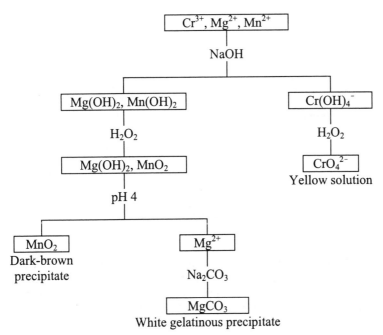

At pH 10, all three cations for hydroxide precipitate, but chromium (III) hydroxide dissolves in excess base while magnesium (II) hydroxide and manganese (II) hydroxide do not. The chromium (III) hydroxide complex is green, and further detection of chromium is made by oxidizing chromium (III) to the yellow chromate anion. Magnesium and manganese can be separated by oxidizing manganese (II) to manganese (IV), which forms a very insoluble oxide. Manganese (IV) oxide does not dissolve in acid, but magnesium (II) hydroxide dissolves in acid. Upon the addition of carbonate, white magnesium (II) carbonate identifies the presence of magnesium.

Reactions:

$Cr^{3+}(aq)$ (purple) $+ 4OH^-(aq) \rightarrow Cr(OH)_4^-(aq)$ (green)
$2Cr(OH)_4^-(aq)$ (green) $+ 3H_2O_2(aq) + 2OH^-(aq) \rightarrow 2CrO_4^{2-}(aq)$ (yellow) $+ 8H_2O$

$Mg^{2+}(aq) + 2OH^-(aq) \rightarrow Mg(OH)_2(s)$ (white gel)
$Mg^{2+}(aq) + CO_3^{2-}(aq) \rightarrow MgCO_3(s)$ (white gel)

$Mn^{2+}(aq) + 2OH^-(aq) + 2H_2O \rightarrow Mn(OH)_2(s)$ (brown/orange) $+ 2NH_4^+(aq)$
$Mn(OH)_2(s)$ (brown/orange) $+ H_2O_2(aq) + OH^-(aq) \rightarrow MnO_2(s)$ (dark brown) $+ 2H_2O + OH^-(aq)$

Assignment 34 – $Cu^{2+}/Fe^{3+}/Ni^{2+}$

Difficulty level: 3

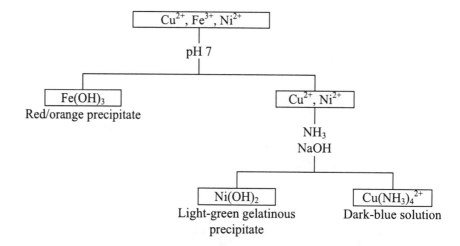

Iron (III) forms a red/orange hydroxide precipitate in water, but copper (II) and nickel (II) only form hydroxide precipitates in basic solution. Copper (II) and nickel (II) both form complexes with ammonia, but nickel (II) favors the hydroxide precipitate in excess base, while copper (II) remains in solution in the ammonia complex. Nickel (II) hydroxide is a light-green gelatinous precipitate, and the copper ammonia complex gives a dark-blue solution.

Reactions:

Cu^{2+}(aq) (light blue) + $4NH_3$(aq) → $Cu(NH_3)_4^{2+}$(aq) (dark blue)

Fe^{3+}(yellow) + $3H_2O$ → $Fe(OH)_3$(s) (red/orange) + $3H^+$(aq)

Ni^{2+}(aq) (green) + $2OH^-$(aq) → $Ni(OH)_2$(s) (light-green gel)

Assignment 35 – Al³⁺/Bi³⁺/Cr³⁺/Sb³⁺

Difficulty level: 4

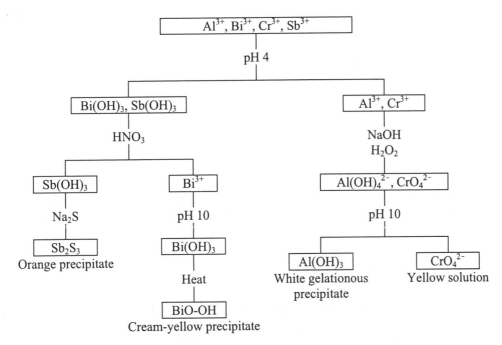

All four cations form hydroxide precipitates. Antimony (III) will form hydroxide precipitates readily, even at low pH. The other three cations are not as acidic, but they will form hydroxide precipitates in basic solutions. Chromium (III) can be separated and identified by oxidizing it to the bright-yellow chromate anion.

Reactions:

Al^{3+}(aq) + 3OH⁻(aq) (pH 10) → $Al(OH)_3$(s) (white gel)
Al^{3+}(aq) + 4OH⁻(aq) → $Al(OH)_4^-$(aq)

Bi^{3+}(aq) + $3H_2O$ → $Bi(OH)_3$(s) (white) + $3H^+$(aq)
$Bi(OH)_3$ + heat → BiO-OH(s) (cream yellow) + H_2O

Cr^{3+}(aq) + 4OH⁻(aq) → $Cr(OH)_4^-$(aq) (green)
$2Cr(OH)_4^-$(aq) (green) + $3H_2O_2$(aq) + 2OH⁻(aq) → $2CrO_4^{2-}$(aq) (yellow) + $8H_2O$

Sb^{3+}(aq) + $3H_2O$ → $Sb(OH)_3$(s) (white) + $3H^+$(aq)
$2Sb(OH)_3$(s) (white) + $6H^+$(aq) + $3S^{2-}$(aq) → Sb_2S_3(s) (orange) + $6H_2O$

Assignment 36 – Al^{3+}/Cr^{3+}/Mg^{2+}/Ti^{4+}

Difficulty level: 4

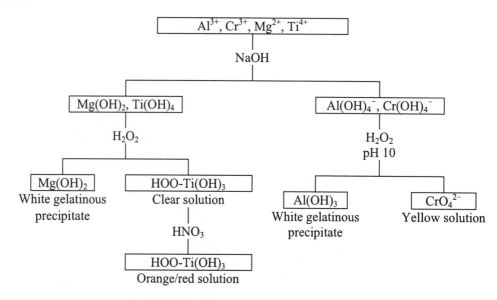

Aluminum (III) and chromium (III) cations are both amphoteric. (Their hydroxide precipitates will dissolve in both acid and base.) Titanium (IV) can be separated from many hydroxides since it forms a soluble complex with hydrogen peroxide. The pH-dependent color of the complex identifies the presence of the titanium cation. Chromium (III) can be oxidized to the soluble chromate anion, which can be separated from the aluminum hydroxide precipitate at pH 10.

Reactions:

Al^{3+}(aq) + 3OH⁻(aq) (pH 10) → $Al(OH)_3$(s) (white gel)
Al^{3+}(aq) + 4OH⁻(aq) → $Al(OH)_4^-$(aq)

Cr^{3+}(aq) + 4OH⁻(aq) → $Cr(OH)_4^-$(aq) (green)
$2Cr(OH)_4^-$(aq) (green) + $3H_2O_2$(aq) + 2OH⁻(aq) → $2CrO_4^{2-}$(aq) (yellow) + $8H_2O$

Mg^{2+}(aq) + 2OH⁻(aq) → $Mg(OH)_2$(s) (white gel)

Ti^{4+}(aq) + 4OH⁻(aq) → $Ti(OH)_4$(s) (white)
$Ti(OH)_4$(s) (white) + H_2O_2(aq) → $HOO-Ti(OH)_3$(aq) + H_2O

Assignment 37 − Al³⁺/Cr³⁺/Fe³⁺/NH₄⁺

Difficulty level: 4

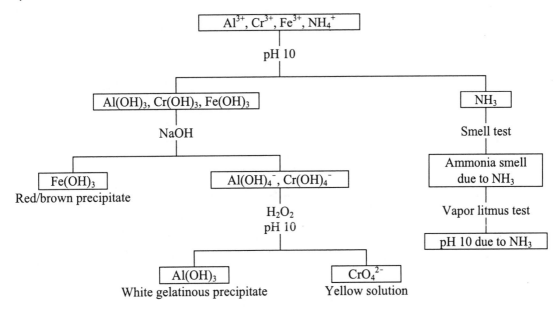

Aluminum (III), chromium (III), and iron (III) cations all form hydroxide precipitates, but aluminum (III) and chromium (III) both dissolve in excess base. Base and hydrogen peroxide oxidize chromium (III) to chromium (VI), which forms the soluble chromate anion. Ammonia does not precipitate out, but it is identified by its smell or basic vapor.

Reactions:

$Al^{3+}(aq) + 3OH^-(aq) \rightarrow Al(OH)_3(s)$ (white)
$Al(OH)_3(s)$ (white) $+ OH^-(aq) \rightarrow Al(OH)_4^-(aq)$

$Fe^{3+}(aq) + 3OH^-(aq) \rightarrow Fe(OH)_3(s)$ (red/brown)

$Cr^{3+}(aq) + 3OH^-(aq)$ (pH 10) $\rightarrow Cr(OH)_3(s)$ (gray)
$Cr(OH)_3(s)$ (gray) $+ OH^-(aq) \rightarrow Cr(OH)_4^-(aq)$ (green)
$2Cr(OH)_4^-(aq)$ (green) $+ 3H_2O_2(aq) + 2OH^-(aq) \rightarrow 2CrO_4^{2-}(aq)$ (yellow) $+ 8H_2O$

$NH_4^+(aq) + OH^-(aq) \rightarrow NH_3(aq) + H_2O$

Assignment 38 – Al^{3+}/Cr^{3+}/Pb^{2+}/Zn^{2+}

Difficulty level: 4

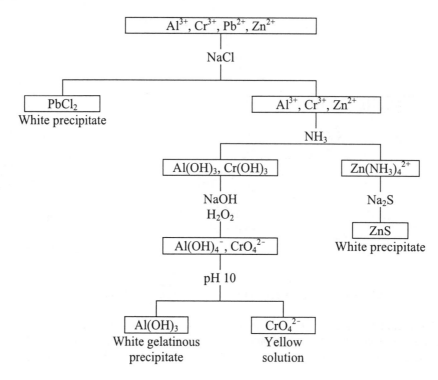

All four cations form hydroxide precipitates and dissolve in excess base. Lead (II) is one of the few cations that forms a chloride precipitate. Zinc (II) dissolves in ammonia, but aluminum (III) and chromium (III) do not. Sulfide precipitates out zinc (II), forming zinc sulfide. Chromium (III) is separated from aluminum (III) by oxidizing it to the chromate anion, which is soluble and yellow.

Reactions:

$Al^{3+}(aq) + 3OH^-(aq)$ (pH 10) $\rightarrow Al(OH)_3(s)$ (white gel)
$Al^{3+}(aq) + 4OH^-(aq) \rightarrow Al(OH)_4^-(aq)$

$Cr^{3+}(aq) + 3OH^-(aq)$ (pH 10) $\rightarrow Cr(OH)_3(s)$ (gray)
$Cr^{3+}(aq) + 4OH^-(aq) \rightarrow Cr(OH)_4^-(aq)$ (green)
$2Cr(OH)_4^-(aq)$ (green) $+ 3H_2O_2(aq) + 2OH^-(aq) \rightarrow 2CrO_4^{2-}(aq)$ (yellow) $+ 8H_2O$

$Pb^{2+}(aq) + 2Cl^-(aq) \rightarrow PbCl_2(s)$ (white)

$Zn^{2+}(aq) + 4NH_3(aq) \rightarrow Zn(NH_3)_4^{2+}(aq)$
$Zn(NH_3)_4^{2+}(aq) + S^{2-}(aq) \rightarrow ZnS(s)$ (white) $+ 4NH_3(aq)$

Assignment 39 – Ba²⁺/Bi³⁺/Hg²⁺/Pb²⁺

Difficulty level: 4

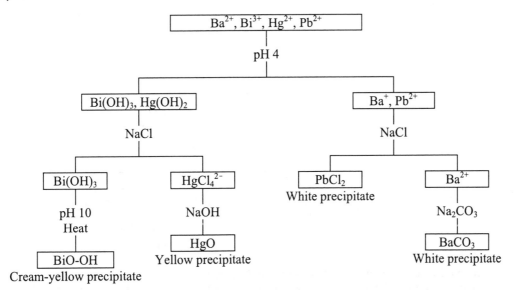

Bismuth (III) and mercury (II) both form hydroxide precipitates readily, even in acidic solution. Mercury (II) forms a complex with chloride in acidic solution. Lead (II) is one of the few cations that forms a chloride precipitate. The barium (II) carbonate precipitate indicates the presence of barium.

Reactions:

$Ba^{2+}(aq) + CO_3^{2-}(aq) \rightarrow BaCO_3(s)$ (white)

$Bi^{3+}(aq) + 3H_2O \rightarrow Bi(OH)_3(s)$ (white) $+ 3H^+(aq)$
$Bi(OH)_3 + Heat \rightarrow BiO\text{-}OH(s)$ (cream yellow) $+ H_2O$

$Hg^{2+}(aq) + H_2O \rightarrow Hg(OH)_2(s)$ (white) $+ 2H^+(aq)$
$Hg(OH)_2(s)$ (white) $+ 4Cl^-(aq) \rightarrow HgCl_4^{2-}(aq) + 2OH^-(aq)$
$HgCl_4^{2-}(aq) + 2OH^-(aq) \rightarrow HgO(s)$ (yellow) $+ H_2O + 4Cl^-(aq)$

$Pb^{2+}(aq) + 2Cl^-(aq) \rightarrow PbCl_2(s)$ (white)

Assignment 40 – $Ba^{2+}/K^+/Na^+/Sr^{2+}/V^{4+}$

Difficulty level: 4

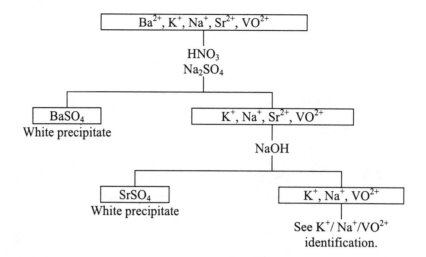

Barium and strontium have very similar chemistry. Both cations precipitate out with sulfate, but strontium (II) sulfate is more soluble. In acidic solution, there is not as much free sulfate due to the formation of bisulfate: $H^+ + SO_4^{2-} \rightarrow HSO_4$. Thus, in acidic solution, strontium (II) will not precipitate out with sulfate, but barium (II) sulfate will precipitate due to its greater insolubility. Potassium, sodium, and vanadium cations do not ever precipitate out with the available reagents, but they can be identified.

Reactions:

$Ba^{2+}(aq) + SO_4^{2-}(aq) \rightarrow BaSO_4(s)$ (white)

$Sr^{2+}(aq) + SO_4^{2-}(aq) \rightarrow SrSO_4(s)$ (white)

Assignment 41 – $Bi^{3+}/Fe^{3+}/Hg^{2+}$

Difficulty level: 4

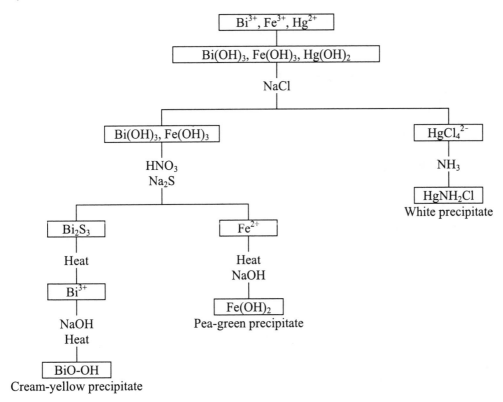

All three cations are acidic and form hydroxide precipitates in water. Mercury (II) forms a complex with chloride, allowing for its separation. Bismuth (III) forms a sulfide precipitate in acidic sulfide solution, but iron only precipitates out with sulfide in basic solution. However, sulfide reduces iron (III) to iron (II). Iron (II) is detected by its pea-green hydroxide.

Reactions:

$Bi^{3+}(aq) + 3H_2O \rightarrow Bi(OH)_3(s)$ (white) $+ 3H^+(aq)$
$2Bi^{3+}(aq) + 3S^{2-}(aq) \rightarrow Bi_2S_3(s)$ (dark brown)
$Bi_2S_3(s)$ (dark brown) $+ H^+(aq) + Heat \rightarrow 2Bi^{3+}(aq) + 3S(s) + 2NO(g) + 4H_2O$
$Bi(OH)_3(s)$ (white) $+ Heat \rightarrow BiO\text{-}OH(s)$ (cream yellow) $+ H_2O$

$Fe^{3+}(aq) + 3H_2O \rightarrow Fe(OH)_3(s)$ (red/brown) $+ 3H^+(aq)$
$2Fe^{3+}(aq)$ (yellow) $+ H_2S(aq) \rightarrow 2Fe^{2+}(aq) + 2H^+(aq) + S(s)$
$Fe^{2+}(aq) + 2OH^-(aq) \rightarrow Fe(OH)_2(s)$ (pea green)

$Hg^{2+}(aq) + H_2O \rightarrow Hg(OH)_2(s)$ (cream yellow)
$Hg(OH)_2(s)$ (cream yellow) $+ 4Cl^-(aq) \rightarrow HgCl_4^{2-}(aq) + 2OH^-(aq)$
$HgCl_4^{2-}(aq) + NH_3(aq) \rightarrow HgNH_2Cl(s)$ (white) $+ H^+(aq) + 3Cl^-(aq)$

Assignment 42 – $Cd^{2+}/Mn^{2+}/Pb^{2+}$

Difficulty level: 4

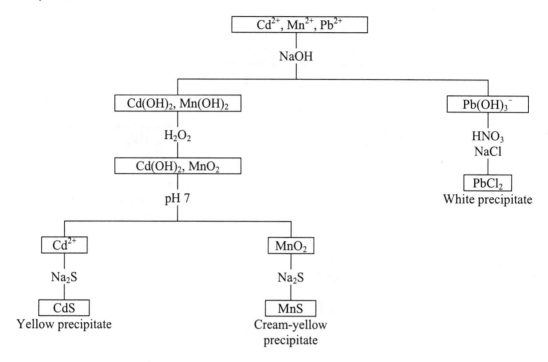

Cadmium (II), manganese (II), and lead (II) all form hydroxide precipitates at pH 10, but lead (II) is amphoteric and therefore dissolves in excess base. The white lead (II) chloride precipitate identifies the presence of lead. Cadmium (II) hydroxide dissolves in ammonia at pH 10 since cadmium (II) forms a complex with ammonia. A brown/orange precipitate after addition of ammonia is manganese (II) hydroxide. Addition of sulfide to the cadmium (II) ammonia complex will cause orange cadmium (II) sulfide to precipitate.

Reactions:

$Cd^{2+}(aq) + 2OH^-(aq) \rightarrow Cd(OH)_2(s)$ (white)
$Cd^{2+}(aq) + S^{2-}(aq) \rightarrow CdS(s)$ (orange)

$Mn^{2+}(aq) + 2OH^-(aq) \rightarrow Mn(OH)_2(s)$ (brown/orange)
$Mn(OH)_2(s) + H_2O_2(aq) + OH^-(aq) \rightarrow MnO_2(s)$ (dark brown) $+ 2H_2O + OH^-(aq)$
$MnO_2(s)$ (dark brown) $+ 4H^+(aq) + 2S^{2-}(aq) \rightarrow MnS(s)$ (cream yellow) $+ S(s) + 2H_2O$

$Pb^{2+}(aq) + 3OH^-(aq) \rightarrow Pb(OH)_3^-(aq)$
$Pb^{2+}(aq) + 2Cl^-(aq) \rightarrow PbCl_2(s)$ (white)

Assignment 43 – $Cd^{2+}/Sb^{3+}/Sn^{4+}$

Difficulty level: 4

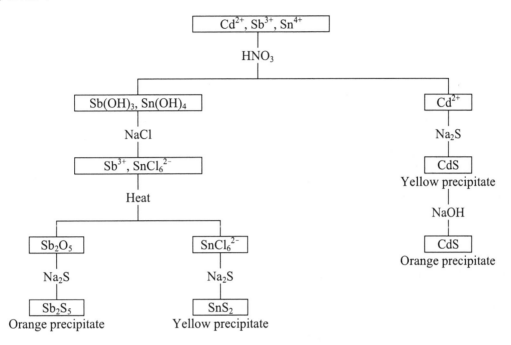

Cadmium, antimony, and tin are found in the same row in the periodic table. Antimony (III) and tin (IV) are more acidic than cadmium (II), and their hydroxide precipitates do not readily dissolve in acidic solution. Cadmium (II) precipitates out in acidic conditions with sulfide, forming a yellow precipitate. Antimony (III) and tin (IV) hydroxides dissolve in strong acidic solution in the presence of chloride. Heat oxidizes antimony (III) to antimony (V), which forms an insoluble oxide precipitate. The insoluble antimony (V) oxide can then be separated from the tin (IV) chloride complex. Both cations can be identified by their bright sulfide precipitates in acidic solution.

Reactions:

$Cd^{2+}(aq) + H^+(aq) + S^{2-}(aq) \rightarrow CdS(s) \text{ (yellow)} + H^+(aq)$
$CdS(s) \text{ (yellow)} + OH^-(aq) \rightarrow CdS(s) \text{ (orange)} + OH^-(aq)$

$Sb^{3+}(aq) + 3H_2O \rightarrow Sb(OH)_3(s) \text{ (white)} + 3H^+(aq)$
$Sb(OH)_3(s) \text{ (white)} + 3H^+(aq) + Cl^-(aq) \rightarrow Sb^{3+}(aq) + 3H_2O + Cl^-(aq)$
$2Sb^{3+}(aq) + 5H_2O + Heat \rightarrow Sb_2O_5(s) \text{ (white)} + 6H^+(aq) + 2H_2(g)$
$Sb_2O_5(s) \text{ (white)} + 5S^{2-}(aq) + H^+(aq) \rightarrow Sb_2S_5(s) \text{ (orange)} + H^+(aq)$

$Sn^{4+}(aq) + H_2O \rightarrow Sn(OH)_4(s) \text{ (white gel)} + 4H^+(aq)$
$Sn(OH)_4(s) + 4H^+(aq) + 6Cl^-(aq) \rightarrow SnCl_6^{2-}(aq) + 4H_2O$
$SnCl_6^{2-}(aq) + 2S^{2-}(aq) + H^+(aq) \rightarrow SnS_2(s) \text{ (yellow)} + 6Cl^-(aq) + H^+(aq)$

Assignment 44 – Co²⁺/Cu²⁺/Ni²⁺

Difficulty level: 4

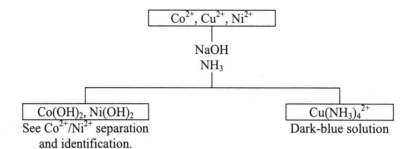

The blue copper (II) ammonia complex stays in solution in very basic solution, but cobalt (II) and nickel (II) hydroxides precipitate out. Cobalt and nickel have similar chemistry, but they can be separated by oxidizing cobalt (II) to cobalt (III), which forms an insoluble hydroxide.

Reactions:

Co^{2+}(aq) (pink) + $6NH_3$(aq) → $Co(NH_3)_6^{2+}$(aq) (yellow/brown)

Cu^{2+}(aq) (light blue) + $4NH_3$(aq) → $Cu(NH_3)_4^{2+}$(aq) (dark blue)

Ni^{2+}(aq) (green) + $6NH_3$(aq) → $Ni(NH_3)_6^{2+}$(aq) (purple/blue)

Assignment 45 – $Co^{2+}/Fe^{2+}/Hg_2^{2+}/Pb^{2+}$

Difficulty level: 4

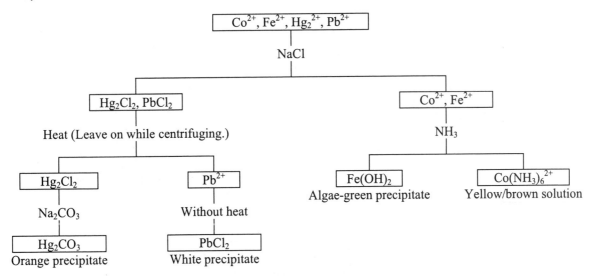

Mercury (I) and lead (II) both form chloride precipitates. As lead (II) chloride is much more soluble than mercury (I) chloride, it will dissolve upon addition of heat while mercury (I) chloride remains insoluble. When heat is taken away, lead (II) chloride will form again. Mercury (I) will form an orange carbonate precipitate upon the addition of carbonate. Cobalt (I) and iron (II) both form hydroxides in basic solution, but cobalt (II) forms a complex with ammonia if the solution is not too basic. An algae-green precipitate indicates iron (II) hyrdoxide, and a yellow/brown solution indicates cobalt is present.

Reactions:

$Co^{2+}(aq)$ (pink) $+ 6NH_3(aq) \rightarrow Co(NH_3)_6^{2+}(aq)$ (yellow/brown)

$Fe^{2+}(aq) + 2NH_3(aq) + 2H_2O \rightarrow Fe(OH)_2(s)$ (algae green) $+ 2NH_4^+(aq)$

$Hg_2^{2+}(aq) + 2Cl^-(aq) \rightarrow Hg_2Cl_2(s)$ (white)
$Hg_2Cl_2(s)$ (white) $+ CO_3^{2-}(aq) \rightarrow Hg_2CO_3(s)$ (orange) $+ 2Cl^-(aq)$

$Pb^{2+}(aq) + 2Cl^-(aq) \rightarrow PbCl_2(s)$ (white)
$PbCl_2(s)$ (white) $+ Heat \rightarrow Pb^{2+}(aq) + 2Cl^-(aq)$

Assignment 46 – $Co^{2+}/Fe^{2+}/Hg_2^{2+}/Pb^{2+}$

Difficulty level: 4

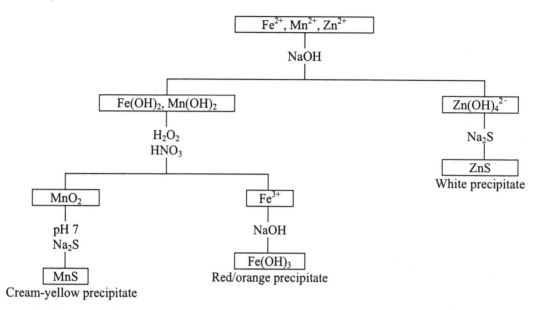

Zinc (II) hydroxide dissolves in excess base, but it will precipitate out with sulfide. In basic solution, hydrogen peroxide oxides iron (II) hydroxide and manganese (II) hydroxide to iron (III) hydroxide and manganese (IV) oxide respectively. Iron (III) hydroxide is more soluble than manganese (IV) oxide; it will dissolve in acid, while manganese (IV) oxide will not. Sulfide reduces manganese (IV) back to manganese (II), and manganese (II) sulfide is formed. Iron (III) forms a red/orange hydroxide.

Reactions:

$Fe^{2+}(aq) + 2OH^-(aq) \rightarrow Fe(OH)_2(s)$ (pea green)
$2Fe(OH)_2(s)$ (pea green) $+ H_2O_2(aq) + OH^-(aq) \rightarrow 2Fe(OH)_3(s)$ (red/orange) $+ OH^-(aq)$

$Mn^{2+}(aq) + 2OH^-(aq) \rightarrow Mn(OH)_2(s)$ (brown/orange)
$Mn(OH)_2(s)$ (brown/orange) $+ H_2O_2(aq) + OH^-(aq) \rightarrow MnO_2(s)$ (dark brown) $+ 2H_2O + OH^-(aq)$
$MnO_2(s)$ (dark brown) $+ 4H^+(aq) + 2S^{2-}(aq) \rightarrow MnS(s)$ (cream yellow) $+ S(s) + 2H_2O$

$Zn^{2+}(aq) + 4OH^-(aq) \rightarrow Zn(OH)_4^{2-}(aq)$
$Zn(OH)_4^{2-}(aq) + S^{2-}(aq) \rightarrow ZnS(s)$ (white) $+ 4OH^-(aq)$

Assignment 47 – $Mn^{2+}/NH_4^+/Pb^{2+}/Zn^{2+}$

Difficulty level: 4

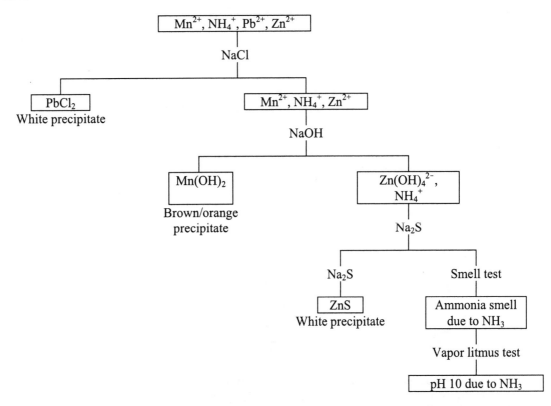

Lead (II) forms a white chloride precipitate. Manganese (II) forms a brown/orange hydroxide in excess base. Zinc (II) also forms a hydroxide in basic solution, but it forms a hydroxide complex in excess base. Zinc (II) forms white zinc (II) sulfide upon addition of sulfide even in excess base. Ammonia does not precipitate out, but it can be identified by its characteristic smell or its basic vapor.

Reactions:

$Pb^{2+}(aq) + 2Cl^-(aq) \rightarrow PbCl_2(s)$ (white)

$Mn^{2+}(aq) + 2OH^-(aq) \rightarrow Mn(OH)_2(s)$ (brown/orange)

$Zn^{2+}(aq) + 4OH^-(aq) \rightarrow Zn(OH)_4^{2-}(aq)$
$Zn(OH)_4^{2-}(aq) + S^{2-}(aq) \rightarrow ZnS(s)$ (white) $+ 4OH^-(aq)$

Assignment 48 – Co²⁺/Fe²⁺/Mn²⁺

Difficulty level: 4

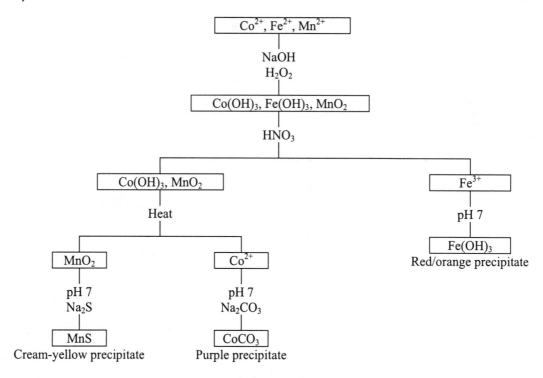

In basic solution, hydrogen peroxide oxidizes cobalt (II), iron (II), and manganese (II). The oxidized forms can be separated according to their relative solubilities. Iron (III) hydroxide readily dissolves in acid. Cobalt (III) hydroxide only dissolves in acid with heat. Even with heat and acid, manganese (IV) oxide will not dissolve, but manganese (IV) can be reduced back to manganese (II) by sulfide in basic conditions.

Reactions:

$2Co(OH)_2(s)$ (pink/tan) $+ H_2O_2(aq) + OH^-(aq) \rightarrow 2Co(OH)_3(s)$ (dark brown) $+ OH^-(aq)$
$4Co(OH)_3(s)$ (dark brown) $+ 8H^+(aq) + Heat \rightarrow 4Co^{2+}(aq)$ (pink) $+ 10H_2O + O_2(g)$
$Co^{2+}(aq)$ (pink) $+ CO_3^{2-}(aq) \rightarrow CoCO_3(s)$ (purple)

$2Fe^{2+}(aq) + H_2O_2(aq) + 4OH^-(aq) \rightarrow 2Fe(OH)_3(s)$ (red/orange)

$Mn^{2+}(aq) + H_2O_2(aq) + 2OH^-(aq) \rightarrow MnO_2(s)$ (dark brown) $+ 2H_2O$
$MnO_2(s)$ (dark brown) $+ 4H^+(aq) + 2S^{2-}(aq) \rightarrow MnS(s)$ (cream yellow) $+ S(s) + 2H_2O$

Assignment 49 – Ag⁺/Cd²⁺/Sb³⁺/Sn⁴⁺

Difficulty level: 5

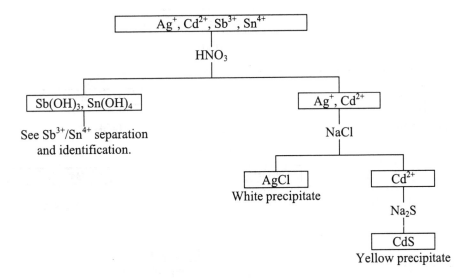

Antimony (III) and tin (IV) cations can be separated from most other cations because of their insoluble hydroxides (even at low pH). Silver (I) is one of the three cations that form a precipitate with chloride. Although cadmium (II) forms a bright-yellow sulfide in acidic conditions, it forms an orange precipitate with sulfide in basic conditions.

Reactions:

$Ag^+(aq) + Cl^-(aq) \rightarrow AgCl(s)$ (white)

$Cd^{2+}(aq) + S^{2-}(aq) \rightarrow CdS(s)$ (orange)

$Sb^{3+}(aq) + 3H_2O \rightarrow Sb(OH)_3(s)$ (white) $+ 3H^+(aq)$

$Sn^{4+}(aq) + 4H_2O \rightarrow Sn(OH)_4(s)$ (white) $+ 4H^+(aq)$

Assignment 50 – Ba²⁺/Ca²⁺/Mg²⁺/Sr²⁺

Difficulty level: 5

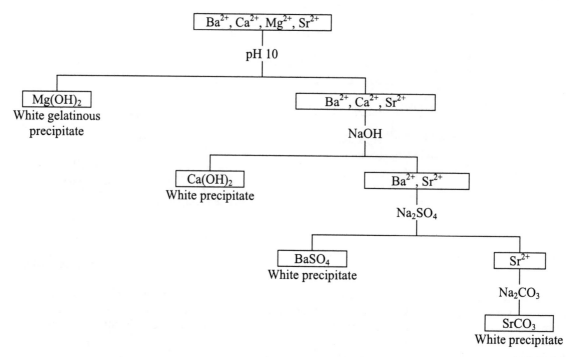

Barium, calcium, magnesium, and strontium are all Group II elements in the periodic table. Going down the periodic table, the hydroxides become more and more soluble. Barium and strontium have very similar chemistry. Both cations precipitate out with sulfate, but strontium (II) does not precipitate in very basic sulfate solution.

Reactions:

$Ba^{2+}(aq) + SO_4^{2-}(aq) \rightarrow BaSO_4(s)$ (white)

$Ca^{2+}(aq) + 2OH^-(aq) \rightarrow Ca(OH)_2(s)$ (white)

$Mg^{2+}(aq) + 2OH^-(aq) \rightarrow Mg(OH)_2(s)$ (white gel)

$Sr^{2+}(aq) + CO_3^{2-}(aq) \rightarrow SrCO_3(s)$ (white)

Assignment 51 – $Ba^{2+}/Hg^{2+}/Pb^{2+}/Sr^{2+}$

Difficulty level: 5

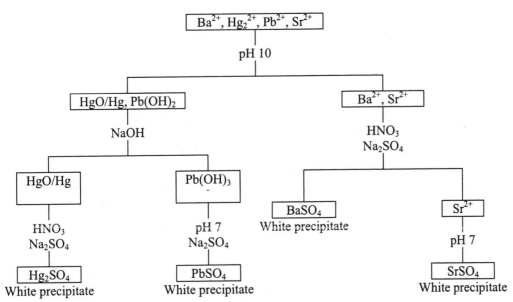

Both lead (II) and mercury (I) are insoluble at pH 10. Mercury (I) disproportionates in basic solution to form mercury (Hg) and mercuric oxide (HgO). Lead (II) forms a hydroxide precipitate at pH 10, but it dissolves in excess base. Barium and strontium have similar chemistry, but strontium (II) sulfate is more soluble than barium (II) sulfate. Thus, strontium sulfate will not precipitate out under acidic conditions, while the more insoluble barium sulfate will precipitate.

Reactions:

$Ba^{2+}(aq) + SO_4^{2-}(aq) \rightarrow BaSO_4(s)$ (white)

$Hg_2^{2+}(aq) + 2OH^-(aq) \rightarrow HgO/Hg(s)$ (black) $+ H_2O$
$HgO/Hg(s)$ (black) $+ 2H^+(aq) + SO_4^{2-}(aq) \rightarrow Hg_2SO_4(s)$ (white) $+ H_2O$

$Sr^{2+}(aq) + SO_4^{2-}(aq) \rightarrow SrSO_4(s)$ (white)

$Pb^{2+}(aq) + 2OH^-(aq)$ (pH 10) $\rightarrow Pb(OH)_2(s)$ (white)
$Pb(OH)_2(s) + OH^-(aq) \rightarrow Pb(OH)_3^-(s)$ (white)
$Pb^{2+}(aq) + SO_4^{2-}(aq) \rightarrow PbSO_4(s)$ (white)

287

Assignment 52 – $Ba^{2+}/K^+/Na^+/NH_4^+/Sr^{2+}/V^{4+}$

Difficulty level: 5

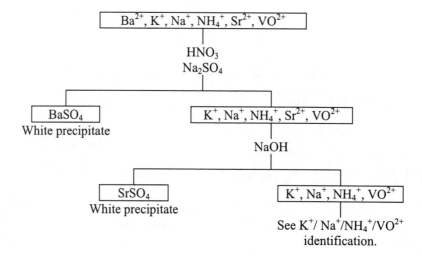

Barium and strontium have very similar chemistry. Both cations precipitate out with sulfate, but strontium (II) sulfate is more soluble. In acidic solution, there is not as much free sulfate due to the formation of bisulfate: $H^+ + SO_4^{2-} \rightarrow HSO_4$. Thus, in acidic solution, strontium (II) will not precipitate out with sulfate, but barium (II) sulfate will precipitate due to its greater insolubility. Potassium, sodium, ammonium, and vanadium cations do not ever precipitate out with the available reagents, but they can be identified.

Reactions:

$Ba^{2+}(aq) + SO_4^{2-}(aq) \rightarrow BaSO_4(s)$ (white)

$Sr^{2+}(aq) + SO_4^{2-}(aq) \rightarrow SrSO_4(s)$ (white)

Assignment 53 – $Ba^{2+}/K^+/Na^+/Sr^{2+}/V^{4+}$

Difficulty level: 5

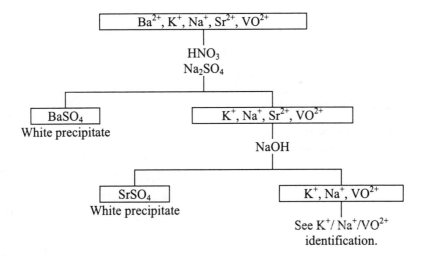

Barium and strontium have very similar chemistry. Both cations precipitate out with sulfate, but strontium (II) sulfate is more soluble. In acidic solution, there is not as much free sulfate due to the formation of bisulfate: $H^+ + SO_4^{2-} \rightarrow HSO_4$. Thus, in acidic solution, strontium (II) will not precipitate out with sulfate, but barium (II) sulfate will precipitate due to its greater insolubility. Potassium, sodium, and vanadium cations do not ever precipitate out with the available reagents, but they can be identified.

Reactions:

$Ba^{2+}(aq) + SO_4^{2-}(aq) \rightarrow BaSO_4(s)$ (white)

$Sr^{2+}(aq) + SO_4^{2-}(aq) \rightarrow SrSO_4(s)$ (white)

Assignment 54 – $Bi^{3+}/Pb^{2+}/Sb^{3+}/Sn^{4+}$

Difficulty level: 5

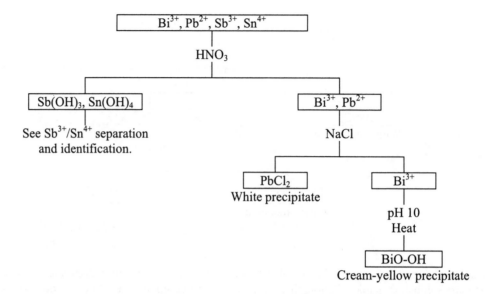

These cations are all close together in the periodic table and have similar chemistry. All four cations form hydroxide precipitates, but antimony (III) and tin (IV) are the most acidic as they form hydroxide precipitates even at very low pH. Addition of chloride will precipitate out lead (II) in acid. The formation of bismuth (III) hydroxide in basic solution identifies the presence of the bismuth cation.

Reactions:

$Bi^{3+}(aq) + 3OH^{-}(aq) \rightarrow Bi(OH)_3(s)$ (white)
$Bi(OH)_3(s)$ (white) $+ Heat \rightarrow BiO\text{-}OH(s)$ (cream yellow) $+ H_2O$

$Pb^{2+}(aq) + 2Cl^{-}(aq) \rightarrow PbCl_2(s)$ (white)

Assignment 55 – $Co^{2+}/Cu^{2+}/Fe^{3+}/Ni^{2+}$

Difficulty level: 5

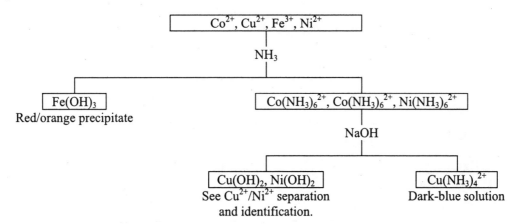

Cobalt (II), copper (II), iron (III), and nickel (II) all form hydroxide precipitates at pH 10, but cobalt (II), copper (II), and nickel (II) hydroxides dissolve in ammonia since these cations form complexes with ammonia. A red/orange precipitate after the addition on ammonia indicates the presence of iron (III). The blue copper (II) ammonia complex stays in solution in very basic solution, but cobalt (II) and nickel (II) hydroxides precipitate out. Cobalt and nickel have similar chemistry, but they can be separated by oxidizing cobalt (II) to cobalt (III), which forms an insoluble hydroxide.

Reactions:

$Co^{2+}(aq)$ (pink) $+ 6NH_3(aq) \rightarrow Co(NH_3)_6^{2+}(aq)$ (yellow/brown)

$Cu^{2+}(aq)$ (light blue) $+ 4NH_3(aq) \rightarrow Cu(NH_3)_4^{2+}(aq)$ (dark blue)

$Fe^{3+}(aq)$ (yellow) $+ 3NH_3(aq) + 3H_2O \rightarrow Fe(OH)_3(s)$ (red/orange) $+ 3NH_4^+(aq)$

$Ni^{2+}(aq)$ (green) $+ 6NH_3(aq) \rightarrow Ni(NH_3)_6^{2+}(aq)$ (purple/blue)

Assignment 56 – $Cu^{2+}/Fe^{2+}/Hg_2^{2+}/Ni^{2+}$

Difficulty level: 5

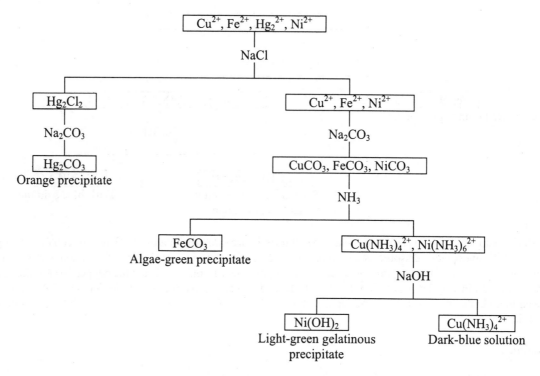

Mercury (I) precipitates out with chloride. The formation of mercurous carbonate, an orange precipitate, confirms the presence of mercury (I), when carbonate is added to the white mercurous chloride precipitate. Copper (II), iron (II), and nickel (II) also form carbonates. The copper (II) and nickel (II) carbonates dissolve in ammonia, since these cations form ammonia complexes. An algae-green precipitate formed after the addition of ammonia is iron (II) carbonate. In excess base, nickel (II) hydroxide precipitates out, but copper (II) remains in solution in the ammonia complex. Nickel (II) hydroxide is a light-green gelatinous precipitate, and the copper ammonia complex gives a dark-blue solution.

Reactions:

$Cu^{2+}(aq) + CO_3^{2-}(aq) \rightarrow CuCO_3(s)$ (pale blue)
$CuCO_3(s)$ (pale blue) $+ 4NH_3(aq) \rightarrow Cu(NH_3)_4^{2+}(aq)$ (dark blue) $+ CO_3^{2-}(aq)$

$Fe^{2+}(aq) + CO_3^{2-}(aq) \rightarrow FeCO_3(s)$ (algae green)

$Hg_2^{2+}(aq) + 2Cl^-(aq) \rightarrow Hg_2Cl_2(s)$ (white)
$Hg_2Cl_2(s)$ (white) $+ CO_3^{2-}(aq) \rightarrow Hg_2CO_3(s)$ (white) $+ 2Cl^-(aq)$

$Ni^{2+}(aq)$ (green) $+ CO_3^{2-}(aq) \rightarrow NiCO_3(s)$ (light-green gel)
$NiCO_3(s)$ (light-green gel) $\rightarrow Ni(NH_3)_6^{2+}(aq)$ (purple/blue)
$Ni(NH_3)_6^{2+}(aq)$ (purple/blue) $+ 2OH^-(aq) \rightarrow Ni(OH)_2(s)$ (light-green gel) $+ 6NH_3(aq)$

Assignment 57 – $Co^{2+}/Fe^{2+}/Mn^{2+}/Ni^{2+}/Zn^{2+}$

Difficulty level: 6

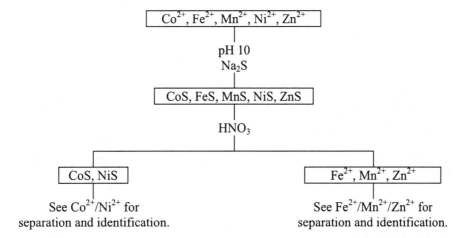

The sulfides of iron (II), manganese (II), and zinc (II) are more soluble than cobalt (II) and nickel (II) sulfides. Although, cobalt (II) and nickel (II) do not form sulfide precipitates in acidic solution, these sulfide precipitates do not readily dissolve once formed.

Reactions:

$Co^{2+}(aq)$ (pink) $+ S^{2-}(aq) \rightarrow CoS(s)$ (black)

$Fe^{2+}(aq) + S^{2-}(aq) \rightarrow FeS(s)$ (black)
$FeS(s)$ (black) $+ 2H^{+}(aq) \rightarrow Fe^{2+}(aq) + H_2S(g)$

$Mn^{2+}(aq) + S^{2-}(aq) \rightarrow MnS(s)$ (cream yellow)
$MnS(s)$ (cream yellow) $+ 2H^{+}(aq) \rightarrow Mn^{2+}(aq) + H_2S(g)$

$Ni^{2+}(aq)$ (green) $+ S^{2-}(aq) \rightarrow NiS(s)$ (black)

$Zn^{2+}(aq) + S^{2-}(aq) \rightarrow ZnS(s)$ (white)
$ZnS(s)$ (white) $+ 2H^{+}(aq) \rightarrow Zn^{2+}(aq) + H_2S(g)$

Assignment 58 – $Ag^+/Co^{2+}/Cr^{3+}/Cu^{2+}/Hg_2^{2+}/Pb^{2+}$

Difficulty level: 6

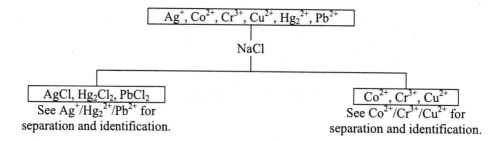

Silver (I), mercury (I) and lead (II) are the few cations that form chloride precipitates, and this allows for an easy separation of these cations from other cations.

Reactions:

$Ag^+(aq) + Cl^-(aq) \rightarrow AgCl(s)$ (white)

$Hg_2^{2+}(aq) + 2Cl^-(aq) \rightarrow Hg_2Cl_2(s)$ (white)

$Pb^{2+}(aq) + 2Cl^-(aq) \rightarrow PbCl_2(s)$ (white)

Assignment 59 – $Al^{3+}/Ba^{2+}/Co^{2+}/Cr^{3+}/Hg_2^{2+}/Pb^{2+}/Zn^{2+}$

Difficulty level: 6

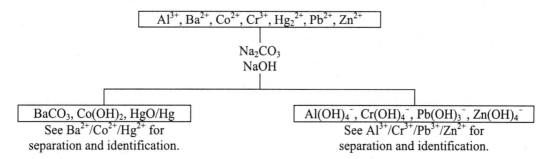

Aluminum (III), chromium (III), lead (II), and zinc (II) are amphoteric, meaning that their hydroxide precipitates dissolve in both acid and base. Barium (II), cobalt (II), and mercury (I) form carbonate precipitates. However, at high pH, barium (II) cobalt favors the hydroxide precipitate and mercury (I) disproportionates to form mercury and mercuric oxide.

Reactions:

$Al^{3+}(aq) + 3CO_3^{2-}(aq) + 3H_2O \rightarrow Al(OH)_3(s)$ (white gel) $+ HCO_3^-(aq)$
$Al(OH)_3(s)$ (white gel) $+ OH^-(aq) \rightarrow Al(OH)_4^-(aq)$

$Ba^{2+}(aq) + CO_3^{2-}(aq) \rightarrow BaCO_3(s)$ (white)

$Co^{2+}(aq) + CO_3^{2-}(aq) \rightarrow CoCO_3(s)$ (purple)
$CoCO_3(s)$ (purple) $+ 2OH^-(aq) \rightarrow Co(OH)_2(s)$ (tan) $+ CO_3^{2-}(aq)$

$Cr^{3+}(aq)$ (purple) $+ 3CO_3^{2-}(aq) + 3H_2O \rightarrow Cr(OH)_3(s)$ (gray) $+ HCO_3^-(aq)$
$Cr(OH)_3(s)$ (gray) $+ OH^-(aq) \rightarrow Cr(OH)_4^-(aq)$ (green)

$Hg_2^{2+}(aq) + CO_3^{2-}(aq) \rightarrow Hg_2CO_3(s)$ (orange)
$2Hg_2CO_3(s)$ (orange) $+ 2OH^-(aq) \rightarrow HgO/Hg(s)$ (black) $+ 2CO_3^{2-}(aq) + H_2O$

$Pb^{2+}(aq) + CO_3^{2-}(aq) \rightarrow PbCO_3(s)$ (white)
$PbCO_3(s)$ (white) $+ 3OH^-(aq) \rightarrow Pb(OH)_3^-(aq) + CO_3^{2-}(aq)$

$Zn^{2+}(aq) + CO_3^{2-}(aq) \rightarrow ZnCO_3(s)$ (white)
$ZnCO_3(s)$ (white) $+ 4OH^-(aq) \rightarrow Zn(OH)_4^{2-}(aq) + CO_3^{2}(aq)$

Assignment 60 – $Al^{3+}/Co^{2+}/Cr^{3+}/Fe^{3+}/Ni^{2+}/Zn^{2+}$

Difficulty level: 6

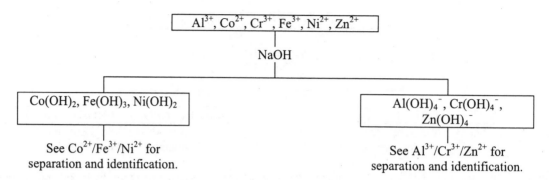

Aluminum (III), chromium (III), and zinc (II) are amphoteric, meaning that their hydroxide precipitates dissolve in both acid and base. The hydroxides of cobalt (II), iron (III), and nickel (II) will dissolve in acid, but not in base.

Reactions:

$Al^{3+}(aq) + 4OH^-(aq) \rightarrow Al(OH)_4^-(aq)$

$Co^{2+}(pink) + 2OH^-(aq) \rightarrow Co(OH)_2(s) \ (tan)$

$Cr^{3+}(aq) \ (purple) + 4OH^-(aq) \rightarrow Cr(OH)_4^-(aq) \ (green)$

$Fe^{3+}(aq) \ (yellow) + 3OH^-(aq) \rightarrow Fe(OH)_3(s) \ (red/orange)$

$Ni^{2+}(aq) \ (green) + 2OH^-(aq) \rightarrow Ni(OH)_2(s) \ (light \ green)$

$Zn^{2+}(aq) + 4OH^-(aq) \rightarrow Zn(OH)_4^-(aq)$

Assignment 61 – $Cd^{2+}/Co^{2+}/Cu^{2+}/Ni^{2+}/Zn^{2+}$

Difficulty level: 6

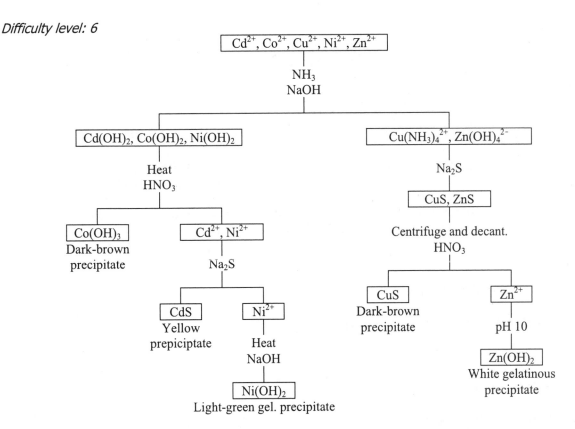

All five cations form ammonia complexes but only copper (II) and zinc (II) stay in solution at high pH. Copper and zinc can be separated based on their relative sulfide precipitate solubilties. As copper (II) sulfide is much less soluble than zinc (II) sulfide, it does not dissolve in acid while zinc (II) sulfide does dissolve in acid. A white precipitate at pH 10 identifies the presence of zinc. Heat oxidizes cobalt (II) hydroxide to cobalt (III) hydroxide, which is very insoluble. Cobalt (III) hydroxide can be separated from cadmium (II) hydroxide and nickel (II) hydroxide since these hydroxides dissolve in acid, but cobalt (III) hydroxide does not. Cadmium and nickel can be separated by adding sulfide, since cadmium (II) sulfide precipitates in acidic solution, but nickel (II) sulfide only precipitates out in basic solution.

Reactions:

$Cd^{2+}(aq) + 4NH_3(aq) \rightarrow Cd(NH_3)_4^{2+}(aq)$
$Cd(NH_3)_4^{2+}(aq) + 2OH^-(aq)$
$\qquad \rightarrow Cd(OH)_2(s)$ (white) $+ 4NH_3(aq)$
$Cd^{2+}(aq) + S^{2-}(aq) \rightarrow CdS(s)$ (orange)
$Co^{2+}(aq)$ (pink) $+ 4NH_3(aq)$
$\qquad \rightarrow Co(NH_3)_4^{2+}(aq)$ (yellow/brown)
$Co(NH_3)_4^{2+}(aq)$ (yellow/brown) $+ 2OH^-(aq)$
$\qquad \rightarrow Co(OH)_2(s)$ (pink/tan) $+ 4NH_3(aq)$
$4Co(OH)_2(s)$ (pink/tan) $+ 2H_2O + O_2(g) + OH^-(aq) +$
$\qquad$ Heat $\rightarrow 4Co(OH)_3(s)$ (dark brown) $+ OH^-(aq)$
$Cu^{2+}(aq)$ (light blue) $+ 4NH_3(aq)$
$\qquad \rightarrow Cu(NH_3)_4^{2+}(aq)$ (dark blue)
$Cu(NH_3)_4^{2+}(aq)$ (dark blue) $+ S^{2-}(aq)$
$\qquad \rightarrow CuS(s)$ (dark brown) $+ 4NH_3(aq)$

$Ni^{2+}(aq)$ (green) $+ 6NH_3(aq)$
$\qquad \rightarrow Ni(NH_3)_6^{2+}(aq)$ (purple/blue)
$Ni(NH_3)_6^{2+}(aq)$ (purple/blue) $+ 2OH-(aq)$
$\qquad \rightarrow Ni(OH)_2(s)$ (light green) $+ 6NH_3(aq)$
$Ni^{2+}(aq)$ (green) $+ 2OH^-(aq) \rightarrow Ni(OH)_2(s)$ (light green)
$Zn^{2+}(aq) + 4NH_3(aq) \rightarrow Zn(NH_3)_4^{2+}(aq)$
$Zn(NH_3)_4^{2+}(aq) + 4OH^-(aq)$
$\qquad \rightarrow Zn(OH)_4^{2-}(aq) + 4NH_3(aq)$
$Zn(OH)_4^{2-}(aq) + S^{2-}(aq) \rightarrow ZnS(s)$ (white) $+ 4OH^-(aq)$
$ZnS(s)$ (white) $+ 2H^+(aq) +$ Heat $\rightarrow Zn^{2+}(aq) + H_2S(g)$
$Zn^{2+}(aq) + 2OH^-(aq)$ (pH 10) $\rightarrow Zn(OH)_2(s)$ (white gel)

297

Assignment 62 – $Cd^{2+}/Mn^{2+}/Pb^{2+}/Sb^{3+}/Sn^{4+}$

Difficulty level: 6

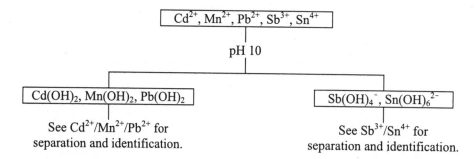

All six cations form hydroxide precipitates, but the hydroxides of antimony (III) and tin (IV) dissolve readily in basic solution. Lead (II) also forms a hydroxide complex in basic solution, but at a higher pH.

Reactions:

$Cd^{2+}(aq) + 2OH^-(aq) \rightarrow Cd(OH)_2(s)$ (white)

$Mn^{2+}(aq) + 2OH^-(aq) \rightarrow Mn(OH)_2(s)$ (brown/orange)

$Pb^{2+}(aq) + 2OH^-(aq)$ (pH 10) $\rightarrow Pb(OH)_2(s)$ (white)

$Sb^{3+}(aq) + 4OH^-(aq) \rightarrow Sb(OH)_4^-(aq)$

$Sn^{4+}(aq) + 6OH^-(aq) \rightarrow Sn(OH)_6^{2-}(aq)$

Assignment 63 – $Cd^{2+}/Co^{2+}/Cr^{3+}/Cu^{2+}/Fe^{3+}/Pb^{2+}/Zn^{2+}$

Difficulty level: 7

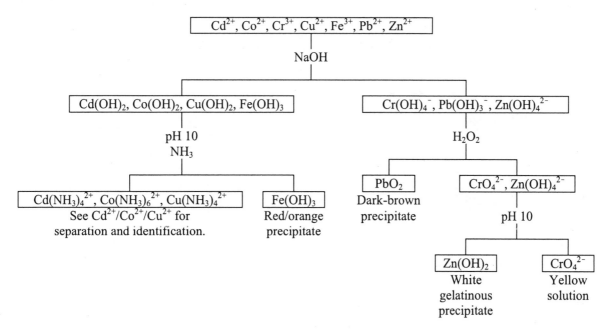

All of these cations form hydroxide precipitates at pH 10. However, chromium (III), lead (II), and zinc (II) are amphoteric and therefore dissolve in excess base. Hydrogen peroxide in basic solution oxidizes lead (II) to the insoluble lead (IV). Hydrogen peroxide in basic solution also oxidizes chromium (III) to chromium (VI), which exists as the soluble chromate anion. Cadmium (II), cobalt (II) and copper (II) can be separated from red iron (III) hydroxide since these cations all form soluble complexes with ammonia at pH 10.

Reactions:
$Cd^{2+}(aq) + 2OH^-(aq) \rightarrow Cd(OH)_2(s)$ (white)
$Cd(OH)_2(s)$ (white) $+ 4NH_3(aq)$ (pH 10) $\rightarrow Cd(NH_3)_4^{2+}(aq) + 2OH^-(aq)$

$Co^{2+}(aq)$ (pink) $+ 2OH^-(aq) \rightarrow Co(OH)_2(s)$ (pink/tan)
$Co(OH)_2(s)$ (pink/tan) $+ 6NH_3(aq)$ (pH 10) $\rightarrow Co(NH_3)_6^{2+}(aq) + 2OH^-(aq)$
$Co(NH_3)_6^{2+}(aq) + 2OH^-(aq) \rightarrow Co(OH)_2(s)$ (pink/tan) $+ 6NH_3(aq)$
$4Co(OH)_2(s)$ (pink/tan) $+ 2H_2O + O_2(g) + OH^-(aq) + Heat \rightarrow 4Co(OH)_3(s)$ (dark brown) $+ OH^-(aq)$

$Cr^{3+}(aq)$ (purple) $+ 3OH^-(aq)$ (pH 10) $\rightarrow Cr(OH)_3(s)$ (gray)
$Cr(OH)_3(s)$ (gray) $+ OH^-(aq) \rightarrow Cr(OH)_4^-(aq)$ (green)
$2Cr(OH)_4^-(aq)$ (green) $+ 3H_2O_2(aq) + 2OH^-(aq) \rightarrow 2CrO_4^{2-}(aq)$ (yellow) $+ 8H_2O$

$Cu^{2+}(aq)$ (light blue) $+ 2OH^-(aq) \rightarrow Cu(OH)_2(s)$ (blue)
$Cu(OH)_2(s)$ (blue) $+ 4NH_3(aq) \rightarrow Cu(NH_3)_4^{2+}(aq)$ (dark blue) $+ 2OH^-(aq)$

$Fe^{3+}(aq)$ (yellow) $+ 3OH^-(aq) \rightarrow Fe(OH)_3(s)$ (red/brown)

$Pb^{2+}(aq) + 3OH^-(aq) \rightarrow Pb(OH)_3^-(aq)$
$Pb(OH)_3^-(aq) + H_2O_2(aq) \rightarrow PbO_2(s)$ (dark brown) $+ 2H_2O + OH^-(aq)$

$Zn^{2+}(aq) + 4OH^-(aq) \rightarrow Zn(OH)_4^{2-}(aq)$
$Zn(OH)_4^{2}(aq)$ (pH 10) $\rightarrow Zn(OH)_2(s)$ (white) $+ 2OH^-(aq)$

Assignment 64 – $Co^{2+}/Cr^{3+}/Cu^{2+}/Fe^{3+}/Ni^{2+}/V^{4+}$

Difficulty level: 7

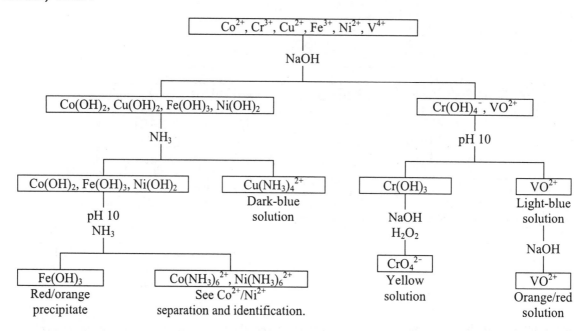

In excess base, cobalt(II), copper (II), iron (III), and nickel (II) form hydroxide precipitates, and chromium (III) and vanadium (IV) form soluble complexes. Vanadium (IV) exists as VO^{2+} in solution, and this complex changes color according to pH, making vanadium identifiable. Chromium (III) forms a gray hydroxide precipitate at pH, but it can also be identified by oxidizing it to the yellow chromate anion. Cobalt (II), copper (II), and nickel (II) can be separated from copper by adding ammonia, which forms a blue complex with copper even in very basic conditions. Cobalt (II) and nickel (II) also form complexes with ammonia, but only at pH 10. A red/orange precipitate indicates iron (III) is present. Cobalt and nickel have similar chemistry, but they can be separated by oxidizing cobalt (II) to cobalt (III), which forms an insoluble hydroxide.

Reactions:

$Co^{2+}(aq)$ (pink) $+ 2OH^-(aq) \rightarrow Co(OH)_2(s)$ (pink/tan)
$Co(OH)_2(s)$ (pink/tan) $+ 6NH_3(aq)$ (pH 10) $\rightarrow Co(NH_3)_6^{2+}(aq)$ (yellow/brown) $+ 2OH^-(aq)$

$Cr^{3+}(aq)$ (purple) $+ 4OH^-(aq) \rightarrow Cr(OH)_4^-(aq)$ (green)
$Cr(OH)_4^-(aq)$ (green) (pH 10) $\rightarrow Cr(OH)_3(s)$ (gray) $+ OH^-(aq)$
$2Cr(OH)_4^-(aq)$ (green) $+ 3H_2O_2(aq) + 2OH^-(aq) \rightarrow 2CrO_4^{2-}(aq)$ (yellow) $+ 8H_2O$

$Cu^{2+}(aq)$ (light blue) $+ 2OH^-(aq) \rightarrow Cu(OH)_2(s)$ (blue)
$Cu(OH)_2(s)$ (blue) $+ 4NH_3(aq) \rightarrow Cu(NH_3)_4^{2+}(aq)$ (dark blue) $+ 2OH^-(aq)$

$Fe^{3+}(aq)$ (yellow) $+ 3OH^-(aq) \rightarrow Fe(OH)_3(s)$ (red/orange)

$Ni^{2+}(aq)$ (green) $+ 2OH^-(aq) \rightarrow Ni(OH)_2(s)$ (light green)
$Ni(OH)_2(s)$ (light green) $+ 6NH_3(aq)$ (pH 10) $\rightarrow Ni(NH_3)_6^{2+}(aq)$ (purple/blue) $+ 2OH^-(aq)$

$V^{4+}(aq)$ (green) $+ 2OH^-(aq) \rightarrow VO^{2+}(aq)$ (orange/red)
$VO^{2+}(aq)$ (orange/red) (pH 10) $\rightarrow VO^{2+}(aq)$ (light blue)

Assignment 65 – $Co^{2+}/Fe^{2+}/Mn^{2+}/Ni^{2+}/Zn^{2+}$

Difficulty level: 7

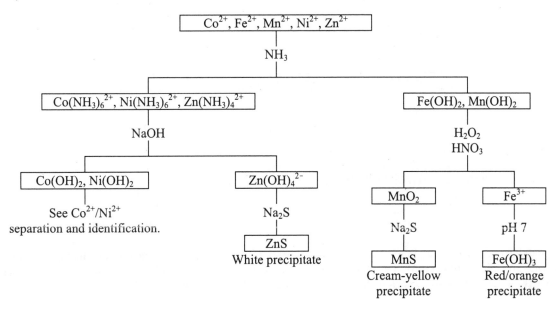

Cobalt (II), nickel (II), and zinc (II) form complexes with ammonia, while iron (II) and manganese (II) form hyrdoxide precipitates upon the addition of ammonia. In excess base, zinc (II) forms a hydroxide complex and cobalt and nickel form hydroxide precipitates. Addition of sulfide to the supernatant tests for zinc, since zinc (II) precipitates out with sulfide even in very basic conditions. Cobalt and nickel have similar chemistry, but they can be separated by oxidizing cobalt (II) to cobalt (III), which forms a very insoluble hydroxide. In basic solution, hydrogen peroxide oxidizes both iron (II) and manganese (II). Manganese (IV) oxide and iron (III) hyrdoxide can be separated according to their relative slubilities. Iron (III) hyrdoxide is more soluble and dissolves in acid, but manganese (IV) oxide does not dissolve in acid.

Reactions:

Co^{2+}(aq) (pink) + $6NH_3$(aq) → $Co(NH_3)_6^{2+}$(aq) (yellow/brown)
$Co(NH_3)_6^{2+}$(aq) (yellow/brown) + $2OH^-$(aq) → $Co(OH)_2$(s) (pink/tan) + $6NH_3$(aq)

Fe^{2+}(aq) + $2NH_3$(aq) + $2H_2O$ → $Fe(OH)_2$(s) (algae green) + $2NH_4^+$(aq)
$2Fe(OH)_2$(s) (pea green) + H_2O_2(aq) + OH^-(aq) → $2Fe(OH)_3$(s) (red/orange) + OH^-(aq)

Mn^{2+}(aq) + $2NH_3$(aq) + $2H_2O$ → $Mn(OH)_2$(s) (brown/orange) + $2NH_4^+$(aq)
$Mn(OH)_2$(s) (brown/orange) + H_2O_2(aq) + OH^-(aq) → MnO_2(s) (dark brown) + $2H_2O$ + OH^-(aq)
MnO_2(s) (dark brown) + $4H^+$(aq) + $2S^{2-}$(aq) → MnS(s) (cream yellow) + S(s) + $2H_2O$

Ni^{2+}(aq) (green) + $6NH_3$(aq) → $Ni(NH_3)_6^{2+}$(aq) (purple/blue)
$Ni(NH_3)_6^{2+}$(aq) (purple/blue) + $2OH^-$(aq) → $Ni(OH)_2$(s) (light green) + $6NH_3$(aq)

Zn^{2+}(aq) + $4NH_3$(aq) → $Zn(NH_3)_4^{2+}$(aq)
$Zn(NH_3)_4^{2+}$(aq) + $4OH^-$(aq) → $Zn(OH)_4^{2-}$(aq) + $4NH_3$(aq)
$Zn(OH)_4^{2-}$(aq) + S^{2-}(aq) → ZnS(s) (white) + $4OH^-$(aq)

Assignment 66 – $Ba^{2+}/Cu^{2+}/Fe^{2+}/Hg_2^{2+}/Ni^{2+}/Pb^{2+}/Sr^{2+}$

Difficulty level: 7

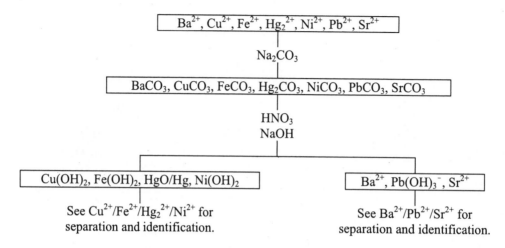

These cations are similar in that they all form carbonate precipitates. Copper (II), iron (II), and nickel (II) form hydroxide precipitates in base. Mercury (I) disproportionates in basic solution to form mercuric oxide (HgO) and mercury (Hg). Lead (II) also forms a hydroxide precipitate, but it dissolves in excess base.

Reactions:

$2H^+(aq) + CO_3^{2-}(aq) \rightarrow H_2O + CO_2(g)$

$Ba^{2+}(aq) + CO_3^{2-}(aq) \rightarrow BaCO_3(s)$ (white)

$Cu^{2+}(aq)$ (light blue) $+ CO_3^{2-}(aq) \rightarrow CuCO_3(s)$ (pale blue)
$Cu^{2+}(aq)$ (light blue) $+ 2OH^-(aq) \rightarrow Cu(OH)_2(s)$ (blue)

$Fe^{2+}(aq) + CO_3^{2-}(aq) \rightarrow FeCO_3(s)$ (algae green)
$Fe^{2+}(aq) + 2OH^-(aq) \rightarrow Fe(OH)_2(s)$ (pea green)

$Hg_2^{2+}(aq) + CO_3^{2-}(aq) \rightarrow Hg_2CO_3(s)$ (algae green)
$2Hg_2^{2+}(aq) + 2OH^-(aq) \rightarrow HgO/Hg(s)$ (black) $+ H_2O$

$Ni^{2+}(aq)$ (green) $+ CO_3^{2-}(aq) \rightarrow NiCO_3(s)$ (light green)
$Ni^{2+}(aq)$ (green) $+ 2OH^-(aq) \rightarrow Ni(OH)_2(s)$ (light green)

$Pb^{2+}(aq) + CO_3^{2-}(aq) \rightarrow PbCO_3(s)$ (white)
$Pb^{2+}(aq) + 3OH^-aq) \rightarrow Pb(OH)_3^-(aq)$

$Sr^{2+}(aq) + CO_3^{2-}(aq) \rightarrow SrCO_3(s)$ (white)

Assignment 67 – $Co^{2+}/Cu^{2+}/Fe^{2+}/Mg^{2+}/Mn^{2+}/Ni^{2+}/Ti^{4+}$

Difficulty level: 7

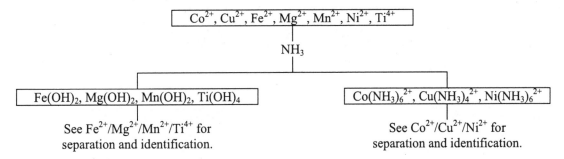

All seven cations form hydroxide precipitates in basic solution, but cobalt (II), copper (II), and nickel (II) form ammonia complexes that dissolve their hydroxide precipitates.

Reactions:

$Co^{2+}(aq)$ (pink) $+ 6NH_3 \rightarrow Co(NH_3)_6^{2+}(aq)$ (yellow/brown)

$Cu^{2+}(aq)$ (light blue) $+ 4NH_3 \rightarrow Co(NH_3)_4^{2+}(aq)$ (dark blue)

$Fe^{2+}(aq) + 2NH_3(aq) + 2H_2O \rightarrow Fe(OH)_2(s)$ (algae green) $+ 2NH_4^+(aq)$

$Mg^{2+}(aq) + 2NH_3(aq) + 2H_2O \rightarrow Mg(OH)_2(s)$ (white gel) $+ 2NH_4^+(aq)$

$Mn^{2+}(aq) + 2NH_3(aq) + 2H_2O \rightarrow Mn(OH)_2(s)$ (brown/orange) $+ 2NH_4^+(aq)$

$Ni^{2+}(aq)$ (green) $+ 6NH_3(aq) \rightarrow Ni(NH_3)_6^{2+}(aq)$ (purple/blue)

$Ti^{4+}(aq) + 4NH_3(aq) + 4H_2O \rightarrow Ti(OH)_2(s)$ (brown/orange) $+ 4NH_4^+(aq)$

Assignment 68 – $Ba^{2+}/Bi^{3+}/Co^{2+}/Cr^{3+}/Cu^{2+}/Fe^{3+}/Hg^{2+}/K^+/Na^+/$ Sr^{2+}/V^{4+}

Difficulty level: 7

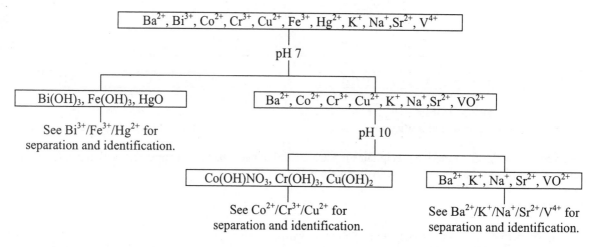

These cations can be split into three main groups according to their solubility at different pHs. Bismuth (III), iron(III), and mercury (II) are acidic and readily form hydroxide precipitates in water. Cobalt (II), chromium (III), and copper (II) only form hydroxide precipitates in basic solution. Barium (II), potassium (I), sodium (I), strontium (II), and vanadium (IV) cations do not form hydroxide precipitates, even in very basic conditions.

Reactions:

$Bi^{3+}(aq) + 3H_2O \rightarrow Bi(OH)_3(s)$ (white) $+ 3H^+(aq)$

$Co^{2+}(aq)$ (pink) $+ NO_3^-$ (aq) $+ OH^-(aq)$ (pH 10) $\rightarrow Co(OH)NO_3(s)$ (aqua blue)

$Cr^{3+}(aq)$ (purple) $+ 3OH^-(aq)$ (pH 10) $\rightarrow Cr(OH)_3(s)$ (gray)

$Cu^{2+}(aq)$ (light blue) $+ 2OH^-(aq) \rightarrow Cu(OH)_2(s)$ (blue)

$Fe^{3+}(aq) + 3H_2O \rightarrow Fe(OH)_3(s)$ (red/orange) $+ 3H^+(aq)$

$Hg^{2+}(aq) + H_2O \rightarrow HgO(s)$ (yellow) $+ 2H^+(aq)$

Assignment 69 – Ba²⁺/Ca²⁺/Co²⁺/Cu²⁺/Fe²⁺/Mn²⁺/Ni²⁺/V⁴⁺

Difficulty level: 8

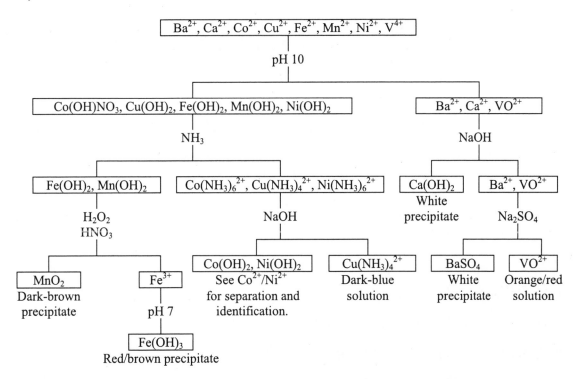

Cobalt, copper, iron, manganese, and nickel are all located next to each other in the periodic table. They all form hydroxide precipitates at pH 10, but only cobalt (II), copper (II), and nickel (II) form complexes with ammonia. In excess base, cobalt (II) and nickel (II) once again form hydroxide precipitates, but copper stays dissolved in the ammonia complex. Cobalt and nickel behave very similarly, and manganese and iron also behave very similarly, as can be predicted by their juxtapositions in the periodic table. However, both sets of cations can be separated because of differences in solubility after oxidation. Barium (II), calcium (II), and vanadium (IV) are three of the few cations that do not form hydroxide precipitates at pH 10. Calcium (II) does form a hydroxide precipitate, but only in very basic solution. Sulfate precipitates out barium (II). The bright-orange/red vanadium solution distinguishes the vanadium cation.

Reactions:

$Ba^{2+}(aq) + SO_4{}^{2-}(aq) \rightarrow BaSO_4(s)$ (white)

$Ca^{2+}(aq) + 2OH^-(aq) \rightarrow Ca(OH)_2(s)$ (white)

$Co^{2+}(aq) + NO_3{}^-(aq) + OH^-(aq)$ (pH 10)
$\qquad\qquad \rightarrow Co(OH)NO_3(s)$ (aqua blue)
$Co(OH)NO_3(s)$ (aqua blue) $+ 6NH_3(aq)$
$\quad \rightarrow Co(NH_3)_6{}^{2+}(aq)$ (yell/brn) $+ NO_3{}^-(aq) + OH^-(aq)$
$Co(NH_3)_6{}^{2+}(aq)$ (yellow/brown) $+ 2OH^-(aq)$
$\qquad\qquad \rightarrow Co(OH)_2(s)$ (pink/tan) $+ 6NH_3(aq)$

$Cu^{2+}(aq)$ (light blue) $+ 2OH^-(aq) \rightarrow Cu(OH)_2(s)$ (blue)
$Cu(OH)_2(s)$ (blue) $+ 4NH_3(aq)$
$\qquad\qquad \rightarrow Cu(NH_3)_4{}^{2+}(aq)$ (dark blue) $+ 2OH^-(aq)$

$Fe^{2+}(aq) + 2OH^-(aq) \rightarrow Fe(OH)_2(s)$ (pea green)
$2Fe(OH)_2(s)$ (pea green) $+ H_2O_2(aq) + OH^-(aq)$
$\qquad\qquad \rightarrow 2Fe(OH)_3(s)$ (red/orange) $+ OH^-(aq)$
$Fe(OH)_3(s)$ (red/brown) $+ 3H^+(aq) \rightarrow Fe^{3+}(aq) + 3H_2O$

$Mn^{2+}(aq) + 2OH^-(aq) \rightarrow Mn(OH)_2(s)$ (brown/orange)
$Mn(OH)_2(s)$ (brown/orange) $+ H_2O_2(aq) + OH^-(aq)$
$\qquad\qquad \rightarrow MnO_2(s)$ (dark brown) $+ 2H_2O + OH^-(aq)$

$Ni^{2+}(aq)$ (green) $+ 2OH^-(aq) \rightarrow Ni(OH)_2(s)$ (light green)
$Ni(OH)_2(s)$ (light green) $+ 6NH_3(aq)$ (pH 10)
$\qquad\qquad \rightarrow Ni(NH_3)_6{}^{2+}(aq)$ (purple/blue) $+ 2OH^-(aq)$
$Ni(NH_3)_6{}^{2+}(aq)$ (purple/blue) $+ 2OH^-(aq)$
$\qquad\qquad \rightarrow Ni(OH)_2(s)$ (light green) $+ 6NH_3(aq)$

305

Assignment 70 – $Cd^{2+}/Co^{2+}/Cr^{3+}/Cu^{2+}/Mg^{2+}/Mn^{2+}/Ni^{2+}/Zn^{2+}$

Difficulty level: 8

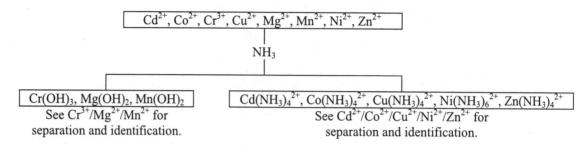

All eight cations form hydroxide precipitates at pH 10, but cadmium (II), cobalt (II), copper (II), nickel (II), and zinc (II) favor the ammonia complex when ammonia is present.

Reactions:

$Cd^{2+}(aq) + 4NH_3(aq) \rightarrow Cd(NH_3)_4^{2+}(aq)$

$Co^{2+}(aq) \text{ (pink)} + 4NH_3(aq) \rightarrow Co(NH_3)_4^{2+}(aq) \text{ (yellow/brown)}$

$Cr^{3+}(aq) \text{ (purple)} + 3NH_3(aq) + 3H_2O \rightarrow Cr(OH)_3(s) \text{ (gray)} + 3NH_4^+(aq)$

$Cu^{2+}(aq) \text{ (light blue)} + 4NH_3(aq) \rightarrow Cu(NH_3)_4^{2+}(aq) \text{ (dark blue)}$

$Mg^{2+}(aq) + 2NH_3(aq) + 2H_2O \rightarrow Mg(OH)_2(s) \text{ (white gel)} + 2NH_4^+(aq)$

$Mn^{2+}(aq) + 2NH_3(aq) + 2H_2O \rightarrow Mn(OH)_2(s) \text{ (brown/orange)} + 2NH_4^+(aq)$

$Ni^{2+}(aq) \text{ (green)} + 6NH_3(aq) \rightarrow Ni(NH_3)_6^{2+}(aq) \text{ (purple/blue)}$

$Zn^{2+}(aq) + 4NH_3(aq) \rightarrow Zn(NH_3)_4^{2+}(aq)$

Assignment 71 – Al³⁺/Ba²⁺/Bi³⁺/Cd²⁺/Cr³⁺/Cu²⁺/Hg²⁺/K⁺/Na⁺/ NH₄⁺/Pb²⁺/Sb³⁺/Sn⁴⁺/Sr²⁺/V⁴⁺/Zn²⁺

Difficulty level: 8

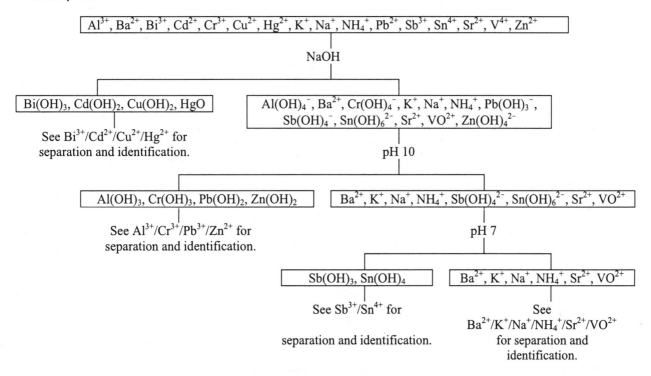

These cations can be split into four main groups according to their solubility at different pHs. Bismuth (III), cadmium (II), copper (II), and mercury (II) precipitate in basic conditions. Aluminum (III), chromium (III), lead (II), and zinc (II) also precipitate in basic solution, but these hydroxides dissolve in excess base since they are amphoteric. Antimony (III) and tin (IV) are also amphoteric, but their hydroxides dissolve more readily in basic solutions. Barium (II), potassium (I), sodium (I), ammonium, strontium (II), and vanadium (IV) cations do not form hydroxide precipitates at any pH.

Reactions:

$Al^{3+}(aq) + 4OH^-(aq) \rightarrow Al(OH)_4^-(aq)$
$Al(OH)_4^-(aq) + H^+(aq)$ (pH 10)
　　　　$\rightarrow Al(OH)_3(s)$ (white) $+ H_2O$
$Bi^{3+}(aq) + 3OH^-(aq) \rightarrow Bi(OH)_3(s)$ (white)
$Cd^{2+}(aq) + 2OH^-(aq) \rightarrow Cd(OH)_2(s)$ (white)
$Cr^{3+}(aq) + 4OH^-(aq) \rightarrow Cr(OH)_4^-(aq)$ (green)
$Cr(OH)_4^-(aq)$ (green) $+ H^+(aq)$ (pH 10)
　　　　$\rightarrow Cr(OH)_3(s)$ (gray) $+ H_2O$
$Cu^{2+}(aq)$ (light blue) $+ 2OH^-(aq) \rightarrow Cu(OH)_2(s)$
(blue)
$Hg^{2+}(aq) + 2OH^-(aq) \rightarrow HgO(s)$ (yellow) $+ H_2O$
$Pb^{2+}(aq) + 3OH^-(aq) \rightarrow Pb(OH)_3^-(aq)$

$Pb(OH)_3^-(aq) + H^+(aq)$ (pH 10) $\rightarrow Pb(OH)_2(s)$
(white)
$Sb^{3+}(aq) + 4OH^-(aq) \rightarrow Sb(OH)_4^-(aq)$
$Sb(OH)_4^-(aq) + H^+(aq)$ (pH 7)
　　　　$\rightarrow Sb(OH)_3(s)$ (white) $+ H_2O$
$Sn^{4+}(aq) + 6OH^-(aq) \rightarrow Sn(OH)_6^{2-}(aq)$

$Sn(OH)_6^{2-}(aq) + 2H^+(aq)$ (pH 7)
　　　　$\rightarrow Sn(OH)_4(s)$ (white gel) $+ 2H_2O$
$Zn^{2+}(aq) + 4OH^-(aq) \rightarrow Zn(OH)_4^{2-}(aq)$
$Zn(OH)_4^{2-}(aq) + 2H^+(aq)$ (pH 10)
　　　　$\rightarrow Zn(OH)_2(s)$ (white gel) $+ 2H_2O$

Assignment 72 – $Ag^+/Al^{3+}/Co^{2+}/Cr^{3+}/Cu^{2+}/Hg_2^{2+}/Ni^{2+}/Pb^{2+}/$ $Sb^{3+}/Sn^{4+}/Zn^{2+}$

Difficulty level: 8

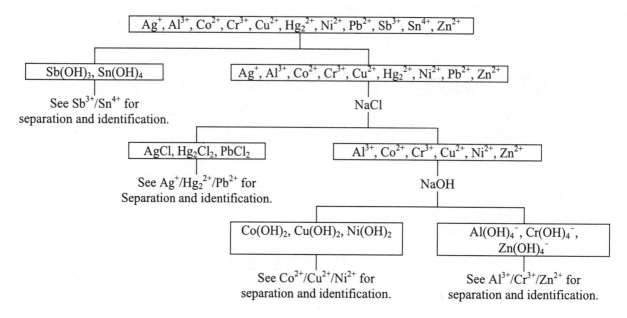

Antimony (III) and tin (IV) are acidic and form hydroxides in water. Adding chloride is a simple way to separate out silver (I), mercury (I), and lead (II). The remaining cations all form hydroxide precipitates in basic solution, but aluminum (III), chromium (III), and zinc (II) are amphoteric and will dissolve in excess base.

Reactions:

$Ag^+(aq) + Cl^-(aq) \rightarrow AgCl(s)$ (white)

$Al^{3+}(aq) + 4OH^-(aq) \rightarrow Al(OH)_4^-(aq)$

$Co^{2+}(aq)$ (pink) $+ NaOH \rightarrow Co(OH)_2(s)$ (tan)

$Cr^{3+}(aq)$ (purple) $+ 4OH^-(aq) \rightarrow Cr(OH)_4^-(aq)$ (green)

$Cu^{2+}(aq)$ (light blue) $+ 2OH^-(aq) \rightarrow Cu(OH)_2(s)$ (blue)

$Hg_2^{2+}(aq) + 2Cl^-(aq) \rightarrow Hg_2Cl_2(s)$ (white)

$Ni^{2+}(aq)$ (green) $+ 2OH^-(aq) \rightarrow Ni(OH)_2(s)$ (light green)

$Pb^{2+}(aq) + 2Cl^-(aq) \rightarrow PbCl_2(s)$ (white)

$Sb^{3+}(aq) + 3H_2O \rightarrow Sb(OH)_3(s)$ (white) $+ 3H^+(aq)$

$Sn^{4+}(aq) + 4H_2O \rightarrow Sn(OH)_4(s)$ (white gel) $+ 4H^+(aq)$

$Zn^{2+}(aq) + 4OH^-(aq) \rightarrow Zn(OH)_4^-(aq)$

308

Assignment 73 – Ag$^+$/Bi^{3+}/Cd^{2+}/Co^{2+}/Cu^{2+}/Fe^{3+}/Hg^{2+}/Hg$_2$$^{2+}$/ Mn^{2+}/Ni^{2+}/Pb^{2+}/Sb^{3+}/Sn^{4+}/Zn^{2+} (The Sulfides)

Difficulty level: 9

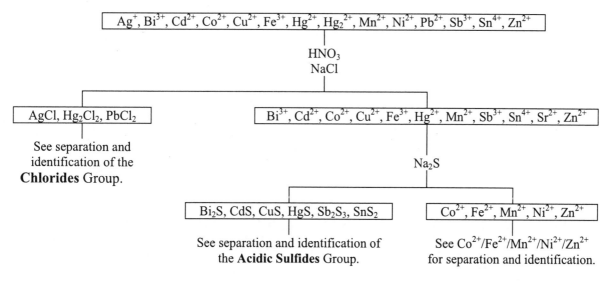

These are all cations that form sulfide precipitates. Adding chloride is a simple way to separate out silver (I), mercury (I), and lead (II) since these are the only cations that form chloride precipitates. The other cations can be divided into two groups according to their sulfide solubilties. In acidic solution, there is not as much free sulfide since it associates with hydrogen to form hydrogen sulfide ($2H^+ + S^{2-} \rightarrow H_2S$). Thus, the more insoluble sulfides precipitate in acidic solution, but the more soluble sulfides only precipitate in basic sulfide.

Reactions:

$Ag^+(aq) + Cl^-(aq) \rightarrow AgCl(s)$ (white)

$2Bi^{3+}(aq) + 3S^{2-}(aq) \rightarrow Bi_2S_3(s)$ (dark brown)

$Cd^{2+}(aq) + S^{2-}(aq) \rightarrow CdS(s)$ (orange)

$Cu^{2+}(aq)$ (light blue) $+ S^{2-}(aq) \rightarrow CuS(s)$ (dark brown)

$Hg^{2+}(aq) + S^{2-}(aq) \rightarrow HgS(s)$ (black)

$Hg_2^{2+}(aq) + 2Cl^-(aq) \rightarrow Hg_2Cl_2(s)$ (white)

$Pb^{2+}(aq) + 2Cl^-(aq) \rightarrow PbCl_2(s)$ (white)

$2Sb^{3+}(aq) + 3S^{2-}(aq) + H^+(aq) \rightarrow Sb_2S_3(s)$ (orange) $+ H^+(aq)$

$Sn^{4+}(aq) + 2S^{2-}(aq) + H^+(aq) \rightarrow SnS_2(s)$ (yellow) $+ H^+(aq)$

Additional Reactions

Although *Virtual ChemLab: Inorganic* is primarily focused on inorganic qualitative analysis, many possible reactions are not used in the qualitative analysis schemes. Among these reactions are oxidation-reduction reactions and reactions involving the formation of precipitates containing two cations. Thus, instructors can use *Virtual ChemLab: Inorganic* in the classroom to demonstrate these reactions while teaching the chemical principles behind them.

Oxidation-Reduction Reactions

Oxidation-reduction reactions are reactions in which one substance is oxidized and the other substance is reduced. One of the previous reactions found in the assignments is an example:

$$2Fe^{3+}(aq) + 3S^{2-}(aq) \rightarrow 2FeS(s) \text{ (black)} + S(s)$$

(Remember that in oxidation-reduction reactions, both charge and mass must be balanced.) In this example, one sulfide ion is oxidized and iron (III) is reduced. In this case, the sulfide ion is the reducing agent and iron (III) is the oxidizing reagent. Hydrogen peroxide is another reagent involved in oxidation-reduction reactions. However, hydrogen peroxide can act as either a reducing agent or an oxidizing reagent:

$$Mn^{2+}(aq) + 2OH^-(aq) + H_2O_2(aq) \rightarrow MnO_2(s) \text{ (dark brown)} + 2H_2O$$

$$MnO_2(s) \text{ (dark brown)} + 2H^+(aq) + H_2O_2(aq) \rightarrow Mn^{2+}(aq) + 2H_2O + O_2(g)$$

In this case, hydrogen peroxide acts as an oxidizing agent in basic solution; the oxygen is reduced (from the -1 oxidation state to –2) and manganese (II) is oxidized. However, in acidic solution, hydrogen peroxide acts as a reducing reagent; the oxygen is oxidized (from the -1 oxidation state to 0) and manganese (IV) is reduced.

Not only do the available cations undergo oxidation-reduction reactions with the reagents, but the cations themselves can interact to carry out oxidation-reduction reactions. One main example is silver (I) and iron (II):

$$Ag^+(aq) + Fe^{2+}(aq) \rightarrow Ag/Ag_2O(s) \text{ (brown)} + Fe^{3+}(aq) \text{ (yellow)}$$

In this reaction, iron (II) is oxidized and silver (I) is reduced to silver metal. Notice that not all of the silver is reduced, but a combination of silver metal and silver (I) oxide is produced. (The reaction is not completely balanced.) The following cation/cation oxidation-reduction reactions occur in basic solution:

$$2Hg_2^{2+}(aq) + Sb(OH)_3(s) \text{ (white)} + 3OH^-(aq) \rightarrow 2Hg(s) \text{ (gray)} + Sb(OH)_6^-(aq)$$

$$Hg^{2+}(aq) + 2VO^{2+}(blue) + OH^-(aq) + 2H_2O \rightarrow Hg(s) \text{ (gray)} + 2V^{5+}(aq) + 5OH^-(aq)$$

In these last two reactions, the mercury cations (the mercurous ion in the first reaction and the mercuric ion in the second reaction) are reduced to mercury metal and the other cations are oxidized.

311

Cation/Cation Precipitates

Cations can also interact with each other to form precipitates. This occurs when a cation precipitates with a polyatomic anion that contains another cation. A polyatomic anion is a negatively charged molecule composed of more than one atom. Sodium hydroxide and hydrogen peroxide oxidize both chromium (III) and vanadium (IV) to chromium (VI) and vanadium (V) respectively. Chromium (VI) forms CrO_4^{2-} (chromate), a polyatomic anion. Vanadium (V) can exist as the polyatomic anion VO_3^{-}. Both CrO_4^{2-} and VO_3^{-} form precipitates with several of the other cations.

$BaCrO_4$ – $Ba^{2+} + Cr^{3+} + NaOH + H_2O_2$:

$Ba^{2+}(aq) + Cr^{3+}(aq)$ (purple) $+ 4OH^-(aq) \rightarrow Ba^{2+}(aq) + Cr(OH)_4^-(aq)$ (green)

$2Ba^{2+}(aq) + 2Cr(OH)_4^-(aq)$ (green) $+ 3H_2O_2(aq) + 2OH^-(aq) \rightarrow 2BaCrO_4^{2-}(s)$ (cream/yellow) $+ 8H_2O$

$CuCrO_4$ – $Cu^{2+} + Cr^{3+} + NaOH + H_2O_2$ then pH 7:

$Cu^{2+}(aq)$ (blue) $+ 2Cr^{3+}(aq)$ (purple) $+ 10OH^-(aq) + 3H_2O_2(aq) \rightarrow$
$$Cu(OH)_2(s) \text{ (green)} + 2CrO_4^{2-}(aq) \text{ (yellow)} + 8H_2O$$

$Cu(OH)_2(s)$ (green) $+ CrO_4^{2-}(aq)$ (yellow) $+ 2H^+(aq)$ (pH 7) $\rightarrow CuCrO_4(s)$ (red/orange) $+ 2H_2O$

$Ba(VO_3)_2$ – $Ba^{2+} + V^{4+} + NaOH + H_2O_2$:

$Ba^{2+}(aq) + 2VO^{2+}(aq)$ (green) $+ H_2O_2$ (aq) $+ 6OH^-(aq) \rightarrow Ba(VO_3)_2(s)$ (white) $+ 4H_2O$

$Cu(VO_3)_2$ – $Cu^{2+} + V^{4+} + NaOH + H_2O_2$:

$Cu^{2+}(aq)$ (blue) $+ 2VO^{2+}(aq)$ (green) $+ H_2O_2$ (aq) $+ 6OH^-(aq) \rightarrow Cu(VO_3)_2(s)$ (pea green) $+ 4H_2O$

Answers for Inorganic Qualitative Analysis Unknowns

Unknown	Cation	Unknown	Cation	Unknown	Cation
1	Na^+	43	Ba^{2+}, Ca^{2+}	85	Zn^{2+}
2	K^+	44	Sr^{2+}	86	Sb^{3+}
3	Na^+, K^+	45	Ba^{2+}, Mg^{2+}	87	Sn^{4+}
4	Water	46	Ca^{2+}	88	Al^{3+}
5	Water	47	Sr^{2+}, Ca^{2+}	89	Ag^+, Mg^{2+}, Cu^{2+}
6	Na^+	48	Mg^{2+}	90	Ag^+, Mg^{2+}, Cr^{3+}
7	K^+	49	Sr^{2+}, Mg^{2+}	91	Ag^+, Mg^{2+}, Co^{2+}
8	Na^+, K^+	50	Water	92	Ag^+, Ca^{2+}, Cu^{2+}
9	Pb^{2+}	51	Ca^{2+}, Mg^{2+}	93	Ag^+, Ca^{2+}, Cr^{3+}
10	Hg_2^{2+}	52	Ba^{2+}, Sr^{2+}, Ca^{2+}, Mg^{2+}	94	Ag^+, Ca^{2+}, Co^{2+}
11	$Ag+$	53	Sr^{2+}, Ca^{2+}, Mg^{2+}	95	Ag^+, Sr^{2+}, Cu^{2+}
12	Water	54	Ba^{2+}, Ca^{2+}, Mg^{2+}	96	Ag^+, Sr^{2+}, Cr^{3+}
13	Ag^+, Hg_2^{2+}, Pb^{2+}	55	Ba^{2+}, Sr^{2+}, Mg^{2+}	97	Ag^+, Sr^{2+}, Co^{2+}
14	Hg_2^{2+}, Pb^{2+}	56	Ba^{2+}, Sr^{2+}, Ca^{2+}	98	Ag^+, Ba^{2+}, Cu^{2+}
15	Ag^+, Pb^{2+}	57	Co^{2+}, Cu^{2+}	99	Ag^+, Ba^{2+}, Cr^{3+}
16	Ag^+, Hg_2^{2+}	58	Co^{2+}, Ni^{2+}	100	Ag^+, Ba^{2+}, Co^{2+}
17	Water	59	Cu^{2+}, Ni^{2+}	101	Hg_2^{2+}, Ba^{2+}, Co^{2+}
18	Ag^+, Hg_2^{2+}, Pb^{2+}	60	Co^{2+}, Cu^{2+}, Ni^{2+}	102	Hg_2^{2+}, Ba^{2+}, Cr^{3+}
19	Ag^+, Hg_2	61	Water	103	Hg_2^{2+}, Ba^{2+}, Cu^{2+}
20	Ag^+, Pb^{2+}	62	Ni^{2+}	104	Hg_2^{2+}, Sr^{2+}, Co^{2+}
21	Hg_2^{2+}, Pb^{2+}	63	Cu^{2+}	105	Hg_2^{2+}, Sr^{2+}, Cr^{3+}
22	Ag^+	64	Co^{2+}	106	Hg_2^{2+}, Sr^{2+}, Cu^{2+}
23	Pb^{2+}	65	Water	107	Hg_2^{2+}, Ca^{2+}, Co^{2+}
24	Hg_2^{2+}	66	Co^{2+}	108	Hg_2^{2+}, Ca^{2+}, Cr^{3+}
25	Co^{2+}, Cr^{3+}	67	Cu^{2+}	109	Hg_2^{2+}, Ca^{2+}, Cu^{2+}
26	Co^{2+}, Cu^{2+}	68	Ni^{2+}	110	Hg_2^{2+}, Mg^{2+}, Co^{2+}
27	Cr^{3+}, Cu^{2+}	69	Co^{2+}, Cu^{2+}, Ni^{2+}	111	Hg_2^{2+}, Mg^{2+}, Cr^{3+}
28	Water	70	Cu^{2+}, Ni^{2+}	112	Hg_2^{2+}, Mg^{2+}, Cu^{2+}
29	Co^{2+}, Cr^{3+}, Cu^{2+}	71	Co^{2+}, Ni^{2+}	113	Pb^{2+}, Mg^{2+}, Cu^{2+}
30	Cr^{3+}	72	Co^{2+}, Cu^{2+}	114	Pb^{2+}, Mg^{2+}, Cr^{3+}
31	Cu^{2+}	73	Al^{3+}, Sb^{3+}	115	Pb^{2+}, Mg^{2+}, Co^{2+}
32	Co^{2+}	74	Al^{3+}, Sn^{4+}	116	Pb^{2+}, Ca^{2+}, Cu^{2+}
33	Co^{2+}, Cr^{3+}, Cu^{2+}	75	Al^{3+}, Zn^{2+}	117	Pb^{2+}, Ca^{2+}, Cr^{3+}
34	Water	76	Sb^{3+}, Sn^{4+}	118	Pb^{2+}, Ca^{2+}, Co^{2+}
35	Co^{2+}	77	Sb^{3+}, Zn^{2+}	119	Pb^{2+}, Sr^{2+}, Cu^{2+}
36	Cu^{2+}	78	Sn^{4+}, Zn^{2+}	120	Pb^{2+}, Sr^{2+}, Cr^{3+}
37	Cr^{3+}	79	Water	121	Pb^{2+}, Sr^{2+}, Co^{2+}
38	Cr^{3+}, Cu^{2+}	80	Al^{3+}, Sb^{3+}, Sn^{4+}	122	Pb^{2+}, Ba^{2+}, Cu^{2+}
39	Co^{2+}, Cr^{3+}	81	Al^{3+}, Sb^{3+}, Zn^{2+}	123	Pb^{2+}, Ba^{2+}, Cr^{3+}
40	Co^{2+}, Cu^{2+}	82	Al^{3+}, Sn^{4+}, Zn^{2+}	124	Pb^{2+}, Ba^{2+}, Co^{2+}
41	Ba^{2+}, Sr^{2+}	83	Sb^{3+}, Sn^{4+}, Zn^{2+}		
42	Ba^{2+}	84	Al^{3+}, Sb^{3+}, Sn^{4+}, Zn^{2+}		